THE MAKERS OF CHRISTENDOM

General Editor: CHRISTOPHER DAWSON

THE LIFE OF ST. LOUIS

THE MAKERS OF CHRISTENDOM

General Editor: CHRISTOPHER DAWSON

The Life of St. Louis

BY

JOHN OF JOINVILLE

TRANSLATED BY

RENÉ HAGUE

FROM THE TEXT EDITED BY

NATALIS DE WAILLY

SHEED AND WARD

NEW YORK · 1955

CONTENTS

INTRODUCTION

JOHN OF JOINVILLE was a man whose generous spirit was easily moved to admiration; particularly was he moved when he saw a man of high rank sacrificing all that was dear and devoting even his life to what was to him the greatest of all causes: the armed fight against the enemies of the faith and the protection or rescue of the "humble folk of Our Lord", the poor nameless pilgrims who aided Christendom only by their suffering. When his King was canonised, there was but one thing that clouded John's joy—that Louis had not been enrolled among the martyrs. From a great family in Champagne, the house of Brienne, allied by marriage[1] to the family of Joinville, came at least two heroes to whom John extended an admiration something akin to that which he felt for Louis: John of Brienne, twelfth King of Jerusalem, whose disaster on the banks of the Nile in 1219 anticipated that of Louis' expedition thirty years later, and the "great Count Walter", on whom, murdered in prison at Cairo after the defeat at Gaza in 1244, Joinville looked as a martyr.

The connection between the two families, to both of which the pilgrimage of the Cross was a dear tradition, goes back to the first ancestor of John who is known to us.[2] Some time early in the eleventh century, before the Crusade was preached, there was a follower of Engelbert of Brienne, named Stephen. He married one of his leader's daughters, and built the "new castle" on the hill overlooking the town of Joinville.[3] It is interesting when

[1] By the marriage of Felicity of Brienne to our Joinville's great-grandfather Geoffrey.

[2] For John of Joinville's family see H. F. Delaborde, *Jean de Joinville et les Seigneurs de Joinville, suivi d'un catalogue de leurs actes*, 1894, in which is included a genealogical table. Du Cange also prints one, but it does not always agree with Delaborde, whose statements are supported by the deeds he catalogues. What I have written here I owe chiefly to Delaborde and to Gaston Paris in the *Histoire Littéraire de la France*, vol. xxxii.

[3] There is a small, abridged and modernised, but well annotated edition of extracts from Joinville, by L.F. Flutre (1942), which contains a useful little map of the environs of Joinville.

we remember that five generations later his descendant, John, in his *Life of St. Louis*, speaks of St. Louis' arguments with the clergy, and of his own troubles in connection with the Abbey of St. Urbain, that Stephen, too, was so high-handed in his demands on the local Abbey of Montiérender that King Robert the Pious ordered him to be excommunicated. Nor were these two the only Lords of Joinville who had similar disputes. Stephen's son, Geoffrey I, who succeeded his father in the lordship, was also threatened with excommunication by Pope Leo IX. His son, Geoffrey II, appears to have died childless, and it is with his nephew, Geoffrey III, who was Lord of Joinville after his father Roger, that the crusading tradition of the family is started.[1] This Geoffrey—"old Geoffrey" as he called himself to distinguish himself from his son, "young Geoffrey" ("Geoffrey le Valet")—was with the great Count Henry of Champagne in Palestine, where his conduct earned him the position, which was made hereditary in his family, of Seneschal of Champagne.[2] His son, Geoffrey IV, fought and died at Acre, where, after the fall of the city, he was buried; and it was this Geoffrey's son—Geoffrey V, Geoffrey "Trouillart" or "Trullard"[3]—who, in the eyes of our John, his nephew, was the hero of the family, and in whom appears something that reminds us of his nephew's character. He was twice overseas: first, with his father at Acre. King Richard of England was so impressed by his courage that he allowed him to quarter his arms with the Plantagenet lion.[4] It was this shield that John brought proudly and piously back from Palestine and hung in his chapel of Saint Lawrence at Joinville, where it remained until 1544, when it was stolen by Charles V's ruffians. After his

[1] A later tradition tried to connect the Joinville family with Godfrey of Bouillon; according to this, Stephen would have been a cousin of the great Duke. But Delaborde says that the story is not found before 1549, in Wassebourg's *Antiquités de la Gaule Belgique*.

[2] The family maintained that the position was hereditary since the time of Geoffrey III; but their claim was not formally recognised till the time of John's father, Simon. (See Delaborde, p. 285, no. 189.)

[3] For " Trouillart " see note to the *Epitaph*, p. 298.

[4] See the *Epitaph*: King Richard did not arrive at Acre till June 1191, and Geoffrey Trouillart was back in Joinville by the end of 1190. He must, therefore, have been honoured by Richard for helping him in France against Philip Augustus. The " lion " in the difference was not the royal " leopards " we know, but the old Plantagenet lion.

father's death he returned to Champagne to settle his affairs. A little more than ten years later he takes the Cross again, at the tourney of Écry which gives a start to the Fourth Crusade,[1] and when the leader of the Crusade, the Count of Champagne, dies, he is one of the party of lords, which includes the historian Geoffrey of Villehardouin, Marshal of Champagne, which offers the leadership in turn to the Duke of Burgundy, the Count of Bar, and finally to the Marquis Boniface of Montferrat. Villehardouin sheds some hypocritical tears for those who refused the bait of Constantinople and took the road to Syria. Among these was Geoffrey. There is something of a pious sneer in Villehardouin's tone when he says that those who left the main body achieved little. It was little enough, indeed, but it cost Geoffrey his life, for in Syria he died, late in 1203, or early in 1204, at Krak, the huge castle of the Knights Hospitallers. I must confess that I like to share his nephew's admiration, and that it pleases me that Delaborde quotes Geoffrey's contemporary Guyot de Provins:

> *Queus estoit Joffrois de Joinvile ?*
> *Meillors chevaliers par Saint Gille*
> *N'avoit de lui de ça lou Far.*[2]

He was unmarried, and the lordship of Joinville passed to his brother Simon, the father of our historian John. Simon also served overseas. He was with King John[3] at the taking of Damietta in November 1219, though he was home again a couple of months later, in January 1220; so that when John tells us that St. Louis' men were astounded that a city which their fathers had besieged for so long should fall to them so easily, his remark has behind it the memory of a familiar story. John was the first child born of

---

[1] Villehardouin, c. 2.
[2] " And what a man was Geoffrey de Joinville! No better knight, by Saint Giles, was there this side the Strait " (*i.e.* of Messina). Guyot's editor, however, (Orr, *La Bible de Guiot de Provins*, Manchester, 1917), points out that he may refer to one of the other crusading Geoffreys.
[3] John of Brienne had been suggested by Philip Augustus as a suitable husband for Mary, daughter of Isabella of Jerusalem and Conrad of Montferrat. He was an older man than Simon—past sixty when he married nineteen-year-old Mary—but a friend of his; the " Minstrel of Rheims " (§139 of De Wailly's edition) speaks of John's pleasure when he heard of the King's choice and how he shared it with his friends, including " le seigneur de Joinvile ", *i.e.* Simon.

his father's second wife, Beatrix; Delaborde fixes his birth as being after June 1224 and before May 1225. We know little of his youth except that he must have served as a squire at the Court of his overlord, Count Thibaut IV of Champagne, poet and Crusader. He tells us himself that in 1241 he accompanied his master and carved for him at the great feast given at Saumur by St. Louis. He tells us, too, that he took no part in the campaign of Taillebourg in 1242—he was not yet knighted—but in 1245 he and his brother learnt something of fighting under the Count of Chalon (see §277). About 1239 he was married to Alix of Grand-pré. The marriage was not, presumably, consummated for several years; the date of the birth of his first son, Geoffrey, is not known, but he tells us that his second son, John, was born in 1248, just when he was on the eve of leaving with St. Louis on the crusading pilgrimage. He had taken the Cross at the same time as St. Louis, in 1244. It is the next six years of his life that are best known to us, from the account he gives of his experiences in Egypt and Palestine.

In 1254 he was back in France for good. He was now a man of considerable importance, a close friend of the King, and a high officer in the County of Champagne.[1] He was not infrequently at Court (he mentions several occasions) and he tells us (§665) of at least one important mission with which he was entrusted. But when St. Louis asked him to accompany him on his expedition to Tunis he not only refused but speaks very strongly of the folly and even wickedness of those who did not attempt to dissuade the King from his fruitless and unhappy journey.

Joinville was a very old man, ninety-two, when he died in 1317, on the eve of Christmas. He had lived under six Kings of France,

[1] The Seneschal was in charge of arrangements for important functions at Court and was of necessity an authority on etiquette. I believe that on only three occasions does Joinville fail to give a knight his title, *mes sires* (monseigneur), and in each instance it is his friend Oliver of Termes. Antoine Thomas's *Francesco da Barberino et la littérature provençale en Italie* (1883) has a couple of stories about Joinville in his old age. Barberino was concerned by a question of table manners: when two persons of equal rank are seated side by side and there is no squire to cut the meat ("*écuyer tranchant*"), which of the two should do so? Meeting Joinville at Poissy, and being told that there was no greater authority on such matters, he asked him. "The one who has the knife on his right," was Joinville's answer, and it is for that reason that good servants are taught to lay the knife at the right hand.

from Louis VIII to Philip V. He was buried in his own chapel of St. Lawrence, but his grave was desecrated in 1793, and of castle and chapel nothing is left. A very touching document survives (see p. 238)—a letter he wrote in 1315 to Louis X, in which he says that "plus tost que je pourray, ma gent seront apparilié pour aleir ou il vous plaira"—in the MS. you can see that his secretary had first written "je et ma gent", but the first two words are struck out.

Not the least debt we owe to the poor pilgrims ("le peuple menu Nostre Signour") whose bones were scattered in the Balkan forests, in Asia Minor, in Syria, in Egypt, is the fresh youth of French prose.[1] The earliest chronicles of the Crusade, and the letters written home by Crusaders, were in Latin; the desire, however, for news of the pilgrims in a form that could be read by all created a demand for translations of the Latin chronicles and for original accounts in the vernacular—for books such as the "romant" (i.e. a book in French), to which Joinville refers at the end of his own book. William of Tyre's history, for example, was translated, and it was from a vernacular continuation of this translation that Joinville took the story of King Richard's being used as a bogey man to silence the Saracen children when they cried.[2] His own book is sometimes spoken of as though it contained the memories of an old man, writing down his version of a story that had happened many years ago, and he has been both admired for the excellence of his memory and excused, when his memory failed him, on the ground that he is writing many years after the event. It is true that when he first wrote eighteen years (from 1254 to 1272) had elapsed since his return from overseas; but he was only twenty-three years old when he left home, and twenty-nine when he returned. He was even younger when he wrote the *Credo*. The date of this he fixes for us in §777—he wrote it at Acre after the King's brothers had left and before the King went to fortify Caesarea, i.e. between August 1250 and April 1251. It is apparent, however, from §820 that what we now have is a second edition, which was written in 1287.[3] There is

[1] " le χλωρόν des Grecs "—Sainte-Beuve, writing of Joinville.
[2] Mas-Latrie's edition of the *Chronique d'Ernoul*, 1871, p. 282.
[3] See De Wailly, 491.

nothing to show that much alteration was made in this later edition, as was done with the larger book. Joinville was interested in the physical production of books—in the *Credo* he attaches as much importance to the pictures as he does to the text, or even more; and when he wishes to describe St. Louis' foundations in France it is the metaphor of the illuminator which he uses—"Ainsi comme li escrivains qui a fait son livre, qui l'enlumine d'or et d'azur, enlumina lidiz roys son royaume de belles abbaies que il y fist".

It is different, however, with the book he wrote after his return. But, first, a word about the title. Joinville gives no definite title at the head of his book. He refers to it, however, first (§2) as "un livre des saintes paroles et des bon faiz nostre roy saint Looys", and later (§19) as "la vie nostre saint roy Looys". It is, perhaps, because as a life it is manifestly incomplete that the title "The History of St. Louis" or even "The Memoirs of John of Joinville" has been preferred to the author's own description. When you complete your first reading of it one thing cannot fail to strike you, that the book falls into three parts, and that the longest part is sandwiched between two shorter parts of a very different character. The middle section, indeed, appears to contain the memoirs of John of Joinville when he was overseas (though with special reference to St. Louis). At the beginning and end there appear to have been tacked on shorter sections which are concerned with the virtues of St. Louis. We have a good deal of evidence concerning the date at which the book, or the edition of it which we have, was written.[1] Joinville tells us that he made the book at the instance of Queen Jeanne of Navarre, who died on April 2nd, 1305, and that he was unable to finish it in her lifetime. From 35, we learn that John II, Duke of Brittany (the first to bear the title of Duke), was alive when he was writing, and John II died in November 1305. Finally, the last words of the book (though they do not apply to more than the particular copy in which they were first written) give us the date October 1309.

§555, however, mentions Hugh III, Duke of Burgundy (at Acre with King Richard), and speaks of him as being the grand-

[1] See Gaston Paris in *Histoire Littéraire de la France*, vol. xxxii, pp. 291 ff.

father of the Duke "recently dead",[1] and this
to Hugh IV, who died in 1272. It appears lik
Queen Jeanne asked Joinville to write the book
des saintes paroles" he already had by him
written in 1272, of his companionship with St. L
be suggested that this will appear more probab
considers some feats of memory (the yellow stripes o
tunic in §407, the accuracy of most of the dates, Sa
the King's order in §389 to light the binnacle lamp) th   would be
astonishing in an octogenarian, unless he had kept very full notes,
but would be no more than remarkable in a man of forty-seven
writing eighteen years after the event. To this consideration might
be added the differences in style and certainty of execution between
what can be roughly described as the hagiographical and autobiographical sections, though we should remember that the
difference in subject matter may possibly account for what we
might attribute to a difference in time of composition. Joinville's
six years overseas had obviously made a deep and lasting impression on him—and no doubt on his conversation—but he had
little aptitude for the writing of history (in his historical digressions
the facts are inclined to be muddled), and there is a distinct change
of tone whenever, in the autobiographical section, he has occasion
to speak of anything that was outside his personal experience.
There is one further slight point that is worth considering, though
it may be no more than a coincidence: the suggested date (1272)
of a first edition of Joinville's memoirs of his years overseas with
St. Louis is only two years from the date of the Saint's death,
which was followed by a tremendous outburst of popular devotion.
Of the sixty-five miracles recorded in Guillaume de Saint Pathus's
Les Miracles de St. Louis, fourteen are dated 1271.[2]

[1] "L'aioul cesti duc qui est mors nouvellement." But see De Wailly's argument
(p. 480) on the rendering of "nouvellement" and the identification of "cesti
duc" with Robert, who died in March 1306.

[2] See, however, Alfred Foulet in the *Romanic Review*, 1941, pp. 233–43.
Foulet argues that Gaston Paris's view—of two "editions"—is untenable.
From a comparison of Joinville's testimony in the life by William of St. Pathus
(and of other details which are common to that life and to Joinville) with Join-
ville's life, he concludes that "Joinville's deposition during the canonisation
inquest of 1282, considered in conjunction with the 1287 redaction of the
Credo, should be viewed as the initial step in the composition of the *Vie de S.
Louis*". The date apart, the real point which Foulet makes is the unity of the

...ville has often been written of as though the chief interest ...ich his book has to offer was the story of his adventures and the attractive picture it gives us of its author. But it is worth remembering that his avowed intention was to give a picture of St. Louis, and with this in mind it is interesting to see how that picture would have been affected had he confined himself to the overseas section of his book—roughly from chapters xxiv to cxxxiv inclusive. In the earlier part of the book we should not be troubled by missing the historical chapters xv–xxiv (though we should sacrifice the great feast at Saumur and the story of Queen Blanche's kissing the German boy on the forehead, because his mother, St. Elizabeth of Hungary, must have kissed it so often); the rather tedious sermon about God's threats in chapter vii will go; but much that is of great value would be lost (some of the most trifling and incidental stories are the ones that are the most illuminating): St. Louis' remark about clothes (38) and his injunction to speak up at table; Joinville's preferring " thirty mortal sins " to leprosy; the argument between the Jew and the knight and St. Louis' rough-and-ready remedy for unbelief; the oak tree at Vincennes, dear to French tradition; the story of the broken seal.

This last in particular has a double interest, for it illustrates two points: that Joinville is at his best when he was present at what he describes, and that the supreme kingly virtue which he wishes to emphasise is that of " loyalty "—loyalty in the sense of his word *l!aultei*, a complete disregard of self-interest when faced with a question—even a political question—of right and wrong. Towards the end of the book, again, it is only Joinville's personal experiences that are of real interest; two of them are his dreams, and in one of these dreams (ch. cxlviii) the King, standing outside the chapel at Joinville, smiling and saying that he is not thinking

Vie; as did Bédier, whom he quotes approvingly: " le sénéchal a écrit l'histoire du roi Louis, l'histoire de saint Louis, et l'histoire de Jean de Joinville, et ces trois histoires forment un chef d'oeuvre complet, mais d'une seule venue, où tout est concerté pour que son a⊤i revive tout entier." (That men of the stature of Bédier and Paris should disagree on the point of the artistic unity of the work is a comfort to one who hesitates to disagree with either.) The most that Foulet will grant is that before Joinville had made his deposition " he had doubtless narrated his memoirs of the King, but it must have been in piecemeal fashion, without plan or perspective ".

of leaving just yet, not only has that sharpness and clarity which sometimes impress the mind so vividly in dreams, but speaks with the tone of intimacy and kindness which Joinville had the art of conveying in words.

When we come, again, to consider the central and much the longest section of the book there is one thing to note and one thing to bear in mind. We should bear in mind that, however enthralled Joinville was by the excitement and hardships and adventures of a campaign overseas and his taste of an Egyptian prisoner-of-war camp, he had constantly in his mind the character of his hero, and it is from love for Louis and a desire to describe his virtues that he writes. As, moreover, he wishes his book to provide examples which St. Louis' heirs may take to heart, a number of things are included as digressions simply because they illustrate a virtue which Joinville wishes his readers to imitate: the generosity of Count Henry of Champagne and of John the Armenian, for example; the long digression in praise of Count Walter of Brienne, the story of Amaury de Montfort and the unbelievers, the debate between the monks and the Jews; many such matters are introduced for the same reason.

It is noteworthy that Joinville is at his best when his own experience coincides with an opportunity to speak of Louis' courage, or charity, or humour; of his hasty temper, too; his "difficultness"; and even his harshness to or lack of consideration for his brave wife; his crossness to the unfortunate servant Ponce, who was late in bringing his horse; his extreme and even unreasonable severity, as experienced by the unhappy young men who made the journey from Lampedusa to Hyères towed in a boat behind the ship, as a punishment for delaying the fleet by guzzling fruit in the orchards on the island; even, a less dignified fault, that petulance which we hide from the world but do not, unhappily, scruple to display to those who are near to us—as when Louis complains (ch. lxxix) that his brother Robert would have been more assiduous in visiting him than was Alfonse: Louis is so much the mainspring of his work that it might well be argued that Joinville would not have written at all—even the *Credo* bears marks of Louis' tutorship; its very subject, faith, is at the root of

Louis' teaching—had it not been the King who led the expedition to Egypt.

If one were able to question Joinville and ask him what sort of a character he had attempted to depict he might well have answered: the character of a *preudome*. That most difficult word sums up all the range of virtues that lie between personal courage and piety —discretion, determination, charity, prudence, justice—the quality of possessing just that particular virtue which is applicable to a given situation or emergency—courage, as when Walter of Châtillon, guarding the village street in the last march of the harassed French, rises in his stirrups and calls " ou sont mi preudome? "; piety (even among the infidels), as when the old man who visited Joinville and his companions in prison is described as a " preudome de sa loi ". Joinville quotes an interesting remark of Philip Augustus, St. Louis' grandfather, about the difference between a *preux homme*, a man who was no more than physically brave, and a *preudome*, whose powers " li vient dou don Dieu ".

Sainte-Beuve, whose essay on Joinville is full of understanding and sympathy, draws a contrast between the thirteenth-century notion of the *preudome* and the debased and more worldly standard we find in Froissart, and hints that Joinville fell a little short of the religious ideal of chivalry, as though he were halfway between St. Louis and Froissart. Although he readily applied the word to men of religion, it is true that he uses it freely for men of whom St. Louis would only have used the term *preux*, and that the military virtues and the virtues proper to a man in a high and responsible position were those which he recognised the most readily. " Par chevalerie ", he tells us in the *Credo* (and the context makes it plain that he means more " fighting " or " soldiering " than what we mean by " chivalry "), " par chevalerie covient conquerre lou regne des ciex".

Nevertheless, the *preudome* represented to Joinville the summit of human virtue; it was he whom he naturally and without reflection admired. But when Queen Jeanne asked him to write of St. Louis' virtues and he looked again at his book he may have felt that he should make an attempt to write at least something of the more conventional details of hagiography—the details of prayers and devotions and fastings, of devotion to the Church and the religious Orders, of monastic foundations. Fortunately, he had little fluency in such composition, and though he praises the King for his frugality at table, for example, it is not difficult to see that he finds his hospitality and the fine manner in which he entertained his guests more attractive to describe. Joinville is the frankest and most honest of writers and, though he was also a most pious man, he does not mind admitting that for his own part there is a standard of sanctity at which he has no intention of aiming.

St. Louis was two things to Joinville; a very dear friend and master whose memory was to be cherished, and a saint to whom he had a great devotion. But the friendship was based on many years' comradeship and hardships shared, and it was to the description of that comradeship that his talents were naturally adapted. Not realising that in describing the comrade he was at the same time giving us the truest and most interesting picture of the saint, he might be surprised to find that, to a modern reader, his attempts to treat particularly of his friend's sanctity do little to increase the reader's knowledge. We might, in fact, go further and say that much of the impression we get of St. Louis is obtained indirectly; it is obtained, that is, through the extremely vivid picture we have of the sort of man who admired him, and of the effect that admiration produced in Joinville's own conduct and ideas.

At the root of *léaultei* is truth, and Joinville is the most truthful of men. Little remains of the enquiries that were made as a prelude to St. Louis' canonisation,[1] and what Joinville tells us of them is doubly characteristic of him: he insists on Louis' love of truth (truth even to Saracens, and even " when a matter of ten

[1] They are published, by H. F. Delaborde, in *Mémoires de la Société de l'Histoire de Paris et de l'Ile de France*, xxii, 1896, pp. 1–71. The Life of St. Louis by William of St. Pathus (Queen Margaret's confessor) appears, however, to be a translation of a Latin digest of the evidence (also edited by Delaborde, 1899). Partly, I suppose, because it is based on the memories of different sorts of people, of different stations in life, from Counts to serving men, it is less conventional in tone, and enlivened by more real detail than the " official " lives of Geoffrey of Beaulieu (St. Louis' confessor), and William of Chartres (his chaplain). Gibbon sarcastically notes, " Read, if you can, the life and miracles of St.Louis, by the confessor of Queen Margaret "—advice that is better given as a serious compliment to two most interesting compilations.

thousand pounds was at stake ") and at the same time he stresses the importance of his own evidence. There are biographies in which the character of the writer emerges even more clearly and attractively than that of the subject. In A. J. A. Symons' *The Quest for Corvo*, for example, the revelation of Symons' own character has a greater and more lasting attraction than his quest. This is not completely true of Joinville, because in his book both author and subject arouse our charity, but in his case there is the added interest that the virtues we see in the author were derived from, or at all events fostered by, the subject. Perhaps the most celebrated and certainly one of the most touching passages in the book provides an example not only of Joinville's devotion to truth but also of the way in which Louis and Joinville are so fused in the book that the most striking stories about Joinville are often the most revealing stories about the King; it is after the conference at Acre, where the question of returning to France has been discussed, and Joinville thinks that he is going to be left alone in Palestine. He tells us that as he put his arms through the little barred window he thought that, whatever happened, he would not go back on his word—he would not go home while there were still humble folk in Egyptian prisons—and there is no doubt but that he would, indeed, have taken service under one of the overseas barons.[1]

[1] It happens that this passage is the only one where Joinville's exact truthfulness has been suspected—his statement that he and William of Beaumont were the only two from France who voted for staying in Palestine appears to conflict with the King's own statement that the greater part of the barons were in favour of his staying, with which agrees the continuation of John Sarrasin's letter in the Rothelin. But Delaborde's suggestion in *Romania* (xxiii, p. 148) that the decision to stay was reached between the second and third of the three councils, when it was known that the Egyptians were not respecting their agreement with Louis, accounts for the discrepancy. Later, however, Foulet has shown (*Modern Language Notes*, 1934, 464–8) that there is no real contradiction between Louis and Joinville, who are the only first-hand authorities. Louis' letter reads as follows: " Quorum major pars concorditer asserebat, quod si nos recedere contingeret his diebus, praedictam terram dimitteremus omnino in abmissionis articulo constitutam . . . His igitur consideratis attente, praedictae terrae sanctae compatientes miseris et pressuris, qui ad ejus subsidium veneremus, ac captivorum nostrorum captivitatibus et doloribus condolentes, licet nobis dissuaderetur a multis morari in partibus transmarinis, maluimus tamen adhuc differre passagium." The Count of Jaffa was present at the conference of which Joinville speaks, and was naturally in favour of the King's staying in Palestine. When, accordingly, the King writes of the " major pars " as being in favour of this stay, he must refer to the Syrian barons, who would outnumber the French—the " multi " who wished him to return to France immediately.

An even more striking instance, considering the freedom of modern speech (for we may say with Joinville that " a peinne puet l'on parler que on ne die 'que dyables y ait part' ! "), is the occasion where Joinville dismissed a knight who, when they were pitching camp (§567), had struck another. In dismissing him, Joinville had said, " God help me, you shall stay in my company no longer "; and though the knight was repentant and Joinville was begged to have him back, he took his oath so seriously that he said that he could not reinstate him unless the Legate dispensed him from the oath—which, unfortunately, the Legate was unwilling to do.

One result of his love of truth is that we find no deliberate exaggeration or distortion in the facts he records, and he is careful to distinguish between what he saw and heard himself and what he knows (the journey to Tunis, for example) only by hearsay. This is not to say that there are not a few errors—minor errors in dates and names—where his memory is at fault, nor that there are not times where his concentration on his own experiences sets the facts somewhat out of focus. Thus in the account of the battle of Mansura on Shrove Tuesday his own private engagement at the little bridge he held (which is mentioned by no other writer) is given as much importance as the main battle. It is easy, however, to make allowance for such differences in emphasis, and it is to this personal preoccupation that we owe a host of vivid details which bring colour and depth to the black and white of historical writing.

At the same time Joinville is distinguished by his unwillingness to colour his story by the inclusion of idle and scandalous gossip. There are but few occasions on which he writes hardly of any man, and never does he do so without cause. (It would not, I think, be fair to hold against him his remark that when the envoys of Frederick II arrived in Palestine with letters to the Sultan and instructions to do what they could to hasten the release of the

---

It is interesting that the poem printed in *Romania*, xxii, 1893, p. 544 (it is quoted, except for the first stanza, in Dr. Evans' introduction), uses the same argument as Joinville—that the King still had the clergy's money and that it would be shameful to leave any poor men in the hands of the infidels—but such arguments might have occurred to many at Acre in 1250, and no one can be sure that Joinville was the author. Gaston Paris was inclined to believe that he was. Not so Bédier, who also prints the poem in his *Chansons de Croisade*, 1909.

prisoners, many said that it was as well that they had come too late or they might secretly have hindered the release—for the anti-imperial Syrians may well have been so spiteful, and Joinville does not associate himself with the story.) About the battle of Mansura he felt very strongly, but he will not give the names of those he thought most worthy of censure, for they were dead when he wrote. John of Beaumont, again, was a man who was particularly offensive to Joinville—loud-mouthed and disobliging—but he no more than records his ill manners: he does not, as does the " Minstrel of Rheims " (who is little more than a gossip-monger), repeat the story that Beaumont was held responsible for the failure to keep the Nile open to traffic and for the consequent lack of provisions in the camp.[1] About the greatest mistake of all— Robert of Artois' foolish dash to Mansura—Joinville is just but not uncharitable. To the author of the *Eracles* it is an opportunity for the introduction of details possibly true but certainly discreditable; Matthew Paris seizes his chance to show his spite against the French.

It sometimes happens that we may have spent a long time in reading about a past event and have found difficulty in making the dead tale come to life in the imagination, when a chance remark will suddenly set the characters in motion like a film. We can read of the Crusaders starving in besieged Antioch during the First Crusade, but when William of Tyre tells us that food was so scarce that noble ladies stayed indoors and silently starved to death rather than face the shame of openly begging, and that the proudest knights were brought to spying out who had food for dinner that day and quietly walking in and sitting down uninvited, then even those who have not known poverty or hunger recognise what hunger was in the city. There are books which are first known to us by some such piercing remark, a quotation from a poem, a passage from an historian, but when we come to read the whole book we are disappointed to find that what all the world knows is pretty well the only thing worth knowing. It is here that the joy in Joinville is so constant. Every chapter has something which either gives the reader another delighted thrill

---

[1] *Récits d'un Ménestrel de Reims*, edited by De Wailly, 1876, §388.

of recognition or tells a little more of the endearing character of the author.

Many of our generation have sat in a tent in the North African sun and reached out to take a drink from the canvas water bottle or earthenware *gargoulette* hanging on the tent rope, as Joinville hung it; many have heard Mass in a stores tent, at one end a temporary altar, at the other piles of kit, tins of dehydrated potatoes, as Joinville heard it in a tent, with the corpse of his friend lying on a bier, and his jaunty comrades chatting in the background.[1] The C.O. of the neighbouring unit, with his taste for practical jokes, is known to us as the Count d'Eu was known; and many have queued, as Joinville did, at the entrance to the prisoner-of-war cage. You may read other historians, again—Matthew Paris, Jean Sarrasin, Makrisi's chronicle—and though you know that Louis' army was encumbered by women and children, it is not till Joinville tells us how he took the little ten-year-old boy Bartholomew by the hand, when they were captured, and kept hold of him so that he should not be taken and sold as a slave, and later, when they got back to Acre, had some dinner fetched for him, that you can visualise the children as little boys and girls with names we know.

Of the political history of St. Louis' reign, of his consolidation of the Capetian supremacy (the continuation of the work of his grandfather and of his mother), Joinville tells us little in detail; it lay outside the scope of his book. But his account of St. Louis' years in Syria shows us how he gave a new though short-lived vigour to the conception of a unified French state in that country. It is apparent from Joinville that his authority was unquestioned and that he was in effect, though not in name, the King of French Syria.[2] More generally, he succeeded admirably in describing how St. Louis' personal virtue, withstanding all those attacks of expediency and policy which bring corruption upon great power,

---

[1] Another similar and perhaps even more familiar reminiscence occurs from William of Tyre (ii, p. 332, in Paulin Paris's edition, 1879, of the old French translation), where King Amaury I was besieging Damietta: the rain was so heavy and continuous that they dug little trenches round their tents: " il covenoit à chascun entor sa tente faire fosse por recevoir la pluie, qu'ele n' entrast dedenz leur liz."

[2] See Grousset, iii, p. 509, and De Wailly's notes *Sur le pouvoir royal* (pp. 454–9).

was rewarded by a prestige that has never been enjoyed by another monarch.

THE TEXT OF JOINVILLE[1]

There are but three MSS.; the earliest in date (of the fourteenth century—perhaps, Foulet suggests, as early as 1320) is the Brussels MS. (A), brought back to France by Maurice of Saxony; the Lucca MS. (L), which was found at about the same time; and a MS. (B), which was first used by De Wailly and had been in the possession of M. Brissart-Binet. The two last belong to the sixteenth century. They have been " modernised ", and in the modernisation the sense of the original has often been distorted. It is agreed that they have a common source, intermediate between them and the original, which is not shared by A. The chief value of B is that it fills in some gaps in L.

Printed editions. The first editor was Antoine de Rieux, whose edition was printed at Poitiers in 1547.[2] It was his boast that he had polished and given grace to the rude language of the original, which he found among some documents that had belonged to King René of Sicily, and he so fulfilled his boast that few editors have earned more obloquy. The MS. which he used has never been found, but it was undoubtedly already much corrupted, for many passages are complete nonsense and long sections bear no relation at all to our book. It must have been related to the MS. (also lost) used in 1617 by the next editor, Claude Ménard, who conscientiously printed the MS. as he had it; and it was Ménard's text that Du Cange printed (lacking any MS.) in his magnificent edition, enriched by his notes and lengthy dissertations, of 1668.

It was the discovery of two MSS. in the eighteenth century— the Brussels and Lucca MSS.—which made possible the first

---

[1] See De Wailly, pp. xi–xxx; Gaston Paris in the *Histoire Littéraire de la France*, xxxii, and *Romania*, 1874 (in which he reviews De Wailly's edition and De Wailly answers his remarks); and Alfred Foulet, *Modern Language Quarterly*, 1945. Marius Sepet (*Revue des Questions historiques*, 1872, pp. 220–31) answers Père Cros, S.J., who maintained that the text of St. Louis' *Établissements* given in the MSS. of Joinville had been tampered with in order to minimise St. Louis' respect for the Church; in the course of his refutation of Père Cros, Sepet describes the origin and value of the MSS. more clearly than De Wailly.
[2] It is by error that a copy of the 1561 Poitiers edition is given in the British Museum catalogue as possibly having been printed in 1535.

printed edition, that of 1761, which could hope to approach Joinville's original dictation. Three editors in turn were engaged in the work—Melot and Sallier, who both died before it was finished, and Capperonnier, who completed it. The book is a folio of great beauty, more elegant than Du Cange's; the text follows the Brussels MS., variants—though not all the variants—from L being printed at the foot of the page.

The edition (Daunou and Naudet's) in the twentieth volume of the *Recueil des Historiens des Gaules et de la France* (1840), admirable for its notes, is on the same lines, though B is at times corrected from L. Further corrections from L were included in Michel's edition of 1859, the text of which is reprinted in his edition of 1881.

It is to De Wailly, however, that we owe what has generally been accepted as the standard edition. His full edition, accompanied by notes and a translation into modern French, appeared in 1874.[1] De Wailly had the advantage of being able to use the MS. referred to above as B; in addition he was at pains to work the text back to the spelling current in Champagne at the time Joinville wrote. He believed that he had brought the reader as close as was humanly possible to the original text, and this belief has been commonly accepted, though it should be tempered by a reading of Gaston Paris's review in *Romania*, iii (1874), and (to obtain a very different view of the relation of the MSS. to Joinville's original) of Corrard's remarks in the *Revue Archéologique* of 1867. Corrard believed that the MSS. we have had already suffered the same sort of alterations as those which had been suffered by the lost MSS. of De Rieux and Ménard—repetitions, interpolations, glosses, etc.—and although most readers would agree that De Wailly gave a satisfactory answer to his arguments, enough remains to make it difficult to be quite as optimistic as De Wailly. Gaston Paris hints at another matter which deserves consideration: admitting that De Rieux' and Ménard's MSS. were corrupt, but remembering that a bad MS. may at times retain something which is lost in a better one, to what extent can we, arguing back from the printed text to the

[1] It is this edition of De Wailly's that has been followed in this translation; references to Joinville in the introduction and notes are to the paragraphs in his edition, the numbering of which has been followed in the translation.

MS., use what we conclude must have been the reading of the latter to correct our own MSS.? Two examples: in §354 the words " au col " in the first sentence are from Ménard's text (i.e. the Saracens came to the galley with Danish axes on their shoulders), and few, I believe, would say that De Wailly was wrong in admitting them, even though they are absent from our MSS. A further example, from §328, raises a more complicated question. Many, I believe, would agree that in the text of the MSS. the reason for the Legate's displeasure is by no means clear, and that if the reason was that he believed it to be foolish of Joinville to endanger his health by fasting, Joinville would have expressed himself more fully; and, moreover, that to explain the oddness of the sentence by Joinville's conversational style is to attribute to him altogether too great a degree of informality in his writing. The fuller version of the sentence (quoted in the note to this passage) found in De Rieux and Ménard is, to my mind, not only much clearer but also much more likely to have been written by Joinville. The complication arises from a conflict between a natural desire not to imitate De Rieux and try to improve upon Joinville, and the contrary desire to take an opportunity to remove from the MS. text, with justification, a carelessness and obscurity that were not present in the original. For my part, I think that the view of Joinville as a man who in his writing, or dictating, gaily rambled on with a charming but heedless inconsequence, has been exaggerated, and that both Ménard and De Rieux[1] call for more attention.

Translations. The first translation into English was that of Thomas Johnes (1748–1816) of Hafordychtryd, Cardiganshire, who printed his translation in 1807 at his own press (" at the Hafod Press by James Henderson "). He was also a translator of Sainte Palaye's Life of Froissart, of Froissart's Chronicle, of the Travels of Bertrand de la Brocquière to Palestine, and of the Chronicle of

---

[1] De Rieux included a number of passages omitted by Ménard—the capture of Bagdad, for example (ch. cxiv), the fossilised fish (§602), the harshness of Queen Blanche to Margaret (ch. cxix), etc. May we, too, grant him one phrase that savours more of the original than of his own refinement? Joinville compares the legs of those who suffered from " camp fever " to an old boot (" une vieille heuse "); De Rieux adds " stuffed away for ages behind a cupboard " (" vieilles bottes qui avoient esté cachées long temps derriere ung coffre").

Monstrelet. Unfortunately, although Capperonnier's edition was available to him (and he translated from it the extracts he included from Makrisi), he preferred to translate Du Cange's, on the ground that that of 1761 " would not be intelligible for three-fourths of its readers, who, unless perfectly well versed in the old French language, would be fatigued and disgusted with it ". This translation was reprinted by Bohn in 1848 in a volume of *Chronicles of the Crusade*, which included also Richard of Devizes, and "Geoffrey of Vinsauf's" *Itinerarium Regis Ricardi*. James Hutton's translation of 1868 is abridged; so, too, is Ethel Wedgwood's of 1906, in which there is also some rearrangement of the contents. The translation by Sir Frank Marzials in Everyman's Library (*Memoirs of the Crusades*—it contains also his translation of Villehardouin) was first published in 1911. What he has to say in the introduction about translation is interesting, but I cannot agree that he was right in concluding that one should use " turns of speech, and a vocabulary, that are either archaic or suggest archaism". The translation by Dr. Joan Evans (1939) is more archaic in style and more consistently so. There is a typographic neatness and care in a modern, or modernised, French version by Henri Longnon (1928), which well become the quality of the work.

THE LIFE OF ST. LOUIS

I

DEDICATION AND PROLOGUE

1. To his good Lord Louis,*[1] son of the King of France, by the grace of God, King of Navarre, Count Palatine of Champagne and Brie, John, Lord of Joinville, his seneschal in Champagne, sends greeting, love and honour, and his ready service.

2. I must tell you, my dear Lord, that my Lady the Queen, your mother, who was a dear friend to me—God grant her His kind mercy—was most earnest in asking me to have a book written of the holy sayings and good deeds of our King Saint Louis. I gave her my promise to do so, and now by the help of God the book is finished, and is in two parts; the first part tells how he ordered himself at all times by the will of God and of the Church, and for the well-being of his Kingdom; the second part of the book treats of the great things he did as a knight and a soldier.

3. As it is written, my Lord, " Do first what belongs to God, and He will direct you in all your other works", I have first had written what concerns the three things of which I have spoken— the good of men's souls, the good of their bodies, and the governing of the people.

4. What I have written besides this, I have written to do additional honour to that true saint; for it is through them that a man can best see that from the beginning of his reign to the end of his life no layman of our time spent his whole life in so saintly a manner. I was not with him when he died, but Count Peter of Alençon,* his son, who was my dear friend, was there, and he told me of the fine end he made; you may read of this in the last part of my book.

5. I cannot but think that it was an injustice to him not to include him in the roll of the martyrs, when you consider the great hardships he suffered as a pilgrim and Crusader during the six years

---

[1] The asterisks in the text refer to the Notes, pp. 255–300.

that I served with him; in particular because it was even to the Cross that he followed Our Lord—for if God died on the Cross, so did St. Louis; for when he died at Tunis it was the Cross of the Crusade that he bore.

6. My second book will tell you of his great deeds of knighthood and of his high courage. These were such that four times I saw him risk death that he might save his people from harm. Of this you may read later.

II

ST. LOUIS' DEVOTION TO HIS PEOPLE

7. The first occasion on which he risked death was when we arrived off Damietta. All his Council advised him, I heard, to stay in his ship until he saw how his knights fared in landing.

8. This advice they gave him because if he landed with the knights and his people were killed and he with them the whole enterprise would be lost; but if he stayed on board his ship he could himself undertake a new expedition to take Egypt. But he would not listen to any of them; he leapt fully armed into the water, his shield round his neck, his spear in his hand, and he was among the first to land.

9. The second occasion on which he risked death was this: when he was leaving Mansura for Damietta* his Council urged him, so I was told, to go to Damietta by galley. And this advice they gave him, it was said, because if things were to fall out badly for his people he might still be able himself to free them from captivity.

10. There was another special reason: the poor condition of his body. He was suffering from several diseases; he had a double tertian fever and a severe dysentery,* and the "camp fever", which attacked his mouth and legs. Even so, he would not listen to anyone. He said that he would never abandon his people, but would meet whatever end was to be theirs. That evening his dysentery made it necessary for him to have the ends of his drawers cut away, and he fainted several times from the camp fever; of this, too, you may read later.

11. The third occasion on which he ran the risk of death was when he stayed for four years in the Holy Land, after his brothers had left. We were then in great danger of death, for while the King was stationed at Acre he had hardly one man of arms in his command for every thirty that the people of Acre had when the town was captured.*

12. The only reason I know for the Turks' failing to come and take us in the town was God's love for the King. He put fear into the hearts of our enemies that they might be afraid to come and attack us. Such is the meaning of the words, " If you fear God, all things that see you will hold you in fear." Again, it was against the advice of his Council that he stayed in Acre, as you may read later. He risked his own life for the safety of the people of the Holy Land, who would have been lost had he not remained.

13. The fourth occasion on which he risked his life was when we were coming back from overseas and were off the island of Cyprus. Our ship struck with such force that the bottom carried away three fathoms of the keel on which it was built.

14. The King then sent for fourteen of the master mariners, some from our own ship and some from other ships that were in company with him, and asked them what was best for him to do. They all advised him—and this you may read of later—to move into another ship; they could not see how his ship could stand the force of the waves, for the bolts which held the timbers were all strained. As an example of the danger which the ship was running, they pointed out to the King that when we were on our journey overseas a vessel in similar case had been lost; I saw myself, at the Count of Joigny's, the woman and child who were the only survivors.

15. This was the King's answer: " Sirs, I can see that if I leave this ship she will be abandoned, and I can also see that there are more than eight hundred persons in her. Every man's life is as dear to him as mine is to me, and no one accordingly will dare to stay in the ship; they will all stay in Cyprus. For that reason I shall not, please God, endanger the many lives that she carries. I shall stay in the ship to save my people."

16. So he stayed, and God, in whose help he trusted, preserved us for ten weeks from the dangers of the sea; thus we came safely to port, as you may read later. But Oliver of Termes, a man who had borne himself well and fought with vigour overseas, left the King and stayed in Cyprus; it was eighteen months before we saw him again. So you may see how the King protected over eight hundred lives that were on board.

17. In the last part of this book we shall speak of his end, and tell you how he died in sanctity.

18. My Lord the King of Navarre, I must tell you that I made a promise to my Lady the Queen, your mother (God grant her His kind mercy), to write this book. I have done as I promised; and as I can see no one who has so good a right to it as you who are her heir, I am sending it to you; and I hope that you and your brothers and all those to whom it is read may take its good example to heart and put it into practice, so that God may smile upon you.

BOOK ONE

III

THE VIRTUES OF ST. LOUIS

19. In the name of Almighty God, I, John, Lord of Joinville, seneschal of Champagne, am dictating the life of our holy King Louis; what I saw and what I heard during the six years that I was with him in the pilgrimage overseas and after we had come home. But before I tell you of the great things that he did and of his virtue as a knight, I shall tell you what I saw and heard of his holy sayings and good teaching, so that they may be found set out in their order for the edification of those who hear them.

20. St. Louis loved God with his whole heart and it was on Him that he modelled his actions. This could be seen in that, as God died for the love of His people, so did the King more than once

put his own body in danger of death for the love he bore his people; and this although, had he wished it, he might well have been excused. Of this I will tell you more later.

21. The great love that he had for his people was shown by what he said, when he lay very sick at Fontainebleau, to his eldest son, my Lord Louis.* " Dear son," he said, " I pray you to win the love of the people of your Kingdom. In truth, I would rather that a Scotsman* came from Scotland and governed them, so long as his rule was good and fair, than that you should be seen by the world to govern it ill." The holy King so loved truth that not even to the Saracens would he break his word when he had once made an agreement with them, as I shall tell you later.*

22. In eating he was so temperate that never once in my life did I hear him order any dish for his table, as many rich men do. He was content to eat what his cook prepared for him and what was set before him. In his speech he was restrained. Never in my life did I hear him speak ill of any man, nor name the devil— whose name is much heard in the Kingdom now, a thing which I think can hardly be pleasing to God.

23. He mixed his wine with water, measuring the water according to the amount that he saw the wine could stand. Once in Cyprus he asked me why I put no water in my wine. I told him that the doctors were responsible for this; they told me that I had a large head* and a cold stomach and that it was impossible for me to get drunk. The King told me that they were deluding me, for if I did not learn to water my wine in my youth and tried to do so when I was old, I should be attacked by gout and diseases of the stomach, so that I should never enjoy my health; and if I drank my wine neat when I was an old man I should be drunk every evening; and it was a mighty ugly thing for a good man* to get drunk.

24. He asked me whether I wished to be respected in this world and enjoy Paradise after my death. When I answered that I did, " Take care, then," he said, " not consciously to do or say any- thing which, if all the world were to know it, you could not acknowledge and say ' Yes, that was what I did or that was what I said '." He told me also to beware of contradicting what anyone said in my presence, or of giving him the lie, so long as my silence

did not involve me in any sin or harm; for it is hard words that are behind the quarrels in which countless men have been killed.

25. He would say that a man should so dress and arm himself that the serious men* of this world should not say that he went too far nor young folk that he did not go far enough. I reminded the father of our present King of this when we were speaking of the embroidered surcoats that are made nowadays, and I told him that in my travels overseas I never saw embroidered tunics, whether they were the King's or another's. He told me that he had such tunics embroidered with his arms* that had cost him eight hundred pounds *parisis*. I answered that he would have put the money to better use if he had given it away for the love of God and had had his robes made of good satin* worked with his coat of arms, as his father did.

IV

St. Louis' Horror of Sin

26. Once the King called me and said to me, " I hesitate to speak to you of what touches God, for I know the subtlety of your mind; as I wish to ask you a question, I have fetched the two friars you see here." The question was this. " Tell me, Seneschal," he asked, " what sort of a thing is God? " " Sir," I answered, " God is something so good that there cannot be any better." " Indeed," he said, " an excellent answer; for the very words in which you answered are written in this book I hold in my hand."

27. " But now," he went on, " I have another question: which would you prefer—to be a leper, or to have committed a mortal sin? " I could never tell him a lie, and I answered that I would rather commit thirty mortal sins than become a leper. After the friars had gone he called me by myself and made me sit at his feet and said, " How was it that you gave me that answer yesterday? " When I told him that I was still of the same mind, he said to me, " That is a wild and foolish way of speaking: you should know that there is no leprosy so ugly as being in mortal sin;

for the soul that is in mortal sin is in the likeness of the devil, and that is why no leprosy can be more revolting.

28. " We know well enough that when a man dies he is cured of the leprosy of his body; but when a man who has committed a mortal sin is dying he cannot know for certain that in his lifetime his repentance has been sufficient to win God's pardon: so it is that he must be very afraid that this leprosy will stay with him as long as God is in Paradise. Hence I beg you," he said, " with all my strength, to set your heart, for the love of God and for my love, to choosing rather that any evil should befall your body, either from leprosy or from any other sickness, than that mortal sin should enter into your soul."

29. He asked me whether I washed the feet of the poor on Maundy Thursday. " God forbid, sir! " I answered. " No, I will not wash the feet of those brutes!" " In truth," he said, " that was a poor answer; you should not despise what God did as a lesson to us. I pray you, then, first for God's sake and then for my sake, to make it your habit to wash them."

V

HIS LOVE FOR GOOD MEN

30. So great was his love for every sort of people who believed in God and loved Him that he gave the constableship of France to my Lord Giles le Brun,* although he did not come from the Kingdom of France, because he was widely known—and rightly, I believe—for his love of God and his faith in Him.

31. Master Robert of Sorbon* was well known as being a man of great worth and uprightness, and for this the King would have him eat at his table. It happened one day that he was eating next to me, and we were speaking quietly to one another; the King reproved us and said, " Speak louder, for your companions think that you may be speaking ill of them. If you are speaking at table of something which should give us pleasure, then speak up; but if not, then be silent."

32. Once, when the King was in a gay mood, he said to me, " Come, Seneschal, give me the reasons why a *preudome* is better than a pious man."* Then there began an argument between me and Master Robert. When we had been disputing for a long time, the King gave his finding. " Master Robert," he said, " I would dearly love to have the name of being a *preudome*, so long as I deserved it, and you would be welcome to the rest. For a *preudome* is so grand and good a thing that even to pronounce the word fills the mouth pleasantly."

33. He said, on the other hand, that it was an evil thing to take what belonged to another, for the restoration of what one has taken was so irksome that just to say " restore ", the r's in it rasped your throat;* they stand for the devil's rakes; for the devil continually drags back to himself those who wish to restore the property of others. And this he does with great subtlety, for he entices great usurers and great robbers into giving to charity what they should restore to their victims.

34. He told me to tell King Thibaut,* from him, to be careful when building the convent of the Friars Preachers at Provins not to embarrass his soul by the great sum of money he was devoting to it. " For prudent men should treat their property while they are still alive as executors should; good executors, that is, first put right any injustice of which the dead man has been guilty and restore what belongs to others. They give in alms only what is left of his estate."

VI

OF ROBERT OF SORBON, AND OF CLOTHING

35. One Whit Sunday the holy King was at Corbeil, where there were eighty knights assembled. After dinner the King went down into the churchyard below the chapel, and in the doorway was talking to the Count of Brittany, the father of the present Duke* (God keep him). Master Robert of Sorbon came to find me there, took me by the skirt of my gown and led me up to the King, all

the other knights following us. " Master Robert," I asked him, " what do you want with me? " " I want to ask you a question," he answered. " If the King were sitting in this yard, and you were to go and sit above him on his bench, would you be greatly to blame? " I agreed that I should.

36. " Then," said he, " you are equally to blame for what you are doing now: you are more finely dressed than the King; for you are dressed in ermine and fine green cloth, and the King is not." " Saving your grace, Master Robert," I answered, " I am in no way to be blamed for wearing green and ermine. It was my father and my mother who left me this gown. It is you who are in the wrong; you are the son of working folk,* and you have given up the clothes your father and mother wore and are dressed in finer woollen cloth* than the King." Then I took hold of the skirt of his surcoat and of the King's and said, " See, now, if I am not right." But the King argued in Master Robert's defence with the greatest vigour.

37. Later, my Lord the King called my Lord Philip, his son and father of our present King, and King Thibaut; he sat down by the door of his oratory, and, placing his hand on the ground he said, " Sit down here, close by me, so that we may not be overheard." " Indeed, sir," they answered, " we should not be so bold as to sit so close to you." He said to me also, " Come, Seneschal, sit down here." I did so, and I sat so close to him that my gown was touching his. Then he made them sit down, too, after me, and said to them, " Indeed, you have been very wrong; for you are my sons, and yet you have not immediately done all that I asked you. You must see to it that such a thing never happens again with you." And they assured him that it would not.

38. Then he told me that his purpose in calling us was to admit to me that he had been wrong in supporting Master Robert against me. " But," he said, " I saw that he was so abashed that he badly needed my help. Nevertheless, you must not take too much to heart anything I may have said in his defence. As the Seneschal said, your dress should be neat and good, so that your wives may love you the more and your people think the more of you. For the sage tells us that our dress and our arms should be such that

the serious men of this world cannot say that they are extravagant nor the young people that they are too mean."

VII

Danger at Sea, and of God's Warnings

39. Let me tell you now of a lesson he taught me at sea, when we were on our way home from overseas. It happened that the force of a wind which they call " Garban "*—not one of the four master winds—caused our ship to strike, off the island of Cyprus. The sailors were so terrified by the blow our ship received that they were tearing their clothes and the hair of their beards. The King leapt out of bed barefoot—it was at night—and, dressed only in his tunic, nothing more, he stretched himself out on the deck in the form of a cross before the body of Our Lord,* like a man who thought his death was imminent. The day after this had happened the King called me by myself and said to me:

40. " Seneschal, God has just shown us a glimpse of the greatness of His power. For one of these little winds, so small that we hardly have a name for it, came near to drowning the King of France, his children, his wife, and his people. Now Saint Anselm tells us that these are Our Lord's warnings, as though God wished to say, ' I might well have killed you then had I been so minded.' ' Lord God,' says the saint, ' why do You warn us? For it is not for Your own profit or advantage that You send us Your warnings; had You lost us You would be none the poorer, and had You kept us You would be none the richer. Your warning, then, is not for Your profit but for our benefit, if only we can turn it to good use.' "

41. We should apply the warning that God has given us in such a way that if we feel that there is anything in our hearts, anything in our being, which is displeasing to God we should be quick to be rid of it; and if we think there is anything that will give Him pleasure we must hasten to set our hands to it. If we do this, Our Lord will give us more blessings both in this world and in the next than we can imagine. But if we do not do this, He will treat us

as a good master should treat his bad servant; if the bad servant
will not mend his ways after a warning, the master punishes him
with death or with other greater afflictions that are worse than
death.

42. Our present King, then, should be careful, for he has survived
danger* as great as that we were in, or greater. Let him mend his
evil ways, that God's hand may not strike cruelly on him or on his
possessions.

VIII

OF TRUE FAITH

43. As I shall tell you later, the holy King did all that lay in his
power, whenever he spoke to me, to instil in me a firm faith in the
Christian religion which God has given us. He said that our belief
in the articles of faith should be so firm that neither for death nor
for any hurt that might come to our persons should we be willing
to transgress them in any way either by word or by deed. He said,
too, that the Enemy is so subtle that when folk are dying he works
with all his might to make them die with some doubt of the articles
of our faith; for he sees that he cannot rob a man of the good works
he has done and, what is more, that the man is lost to him if he
dies in the true faith.

44. That is why we should be on our guard and watch against the
trap; and when the Enemy sends such a temptation, we should
say to him, " Be off! You shall not tempt me from my firm belief
in all the articles of faith; even though you were to have all my
limbs cut off, yet will I live and die in this mind." The man who
does this beats the enemy with his own weapon, with the sword
with which he was trying to kill him.

45. He used to say that faith and belief were things to which we
should give full credence, even when our certainty rested only on
hearsay. On this point he asked me a question: What was my
father's name? I told him, " Simon ". He then asked me how I
knew. I answered that I thought I could be certain of it and
believe it, since my mother had been my witness. " Then," he

said, " you should believe no less firmly in all the articles of faith, of which the apostles are your witness, as you hear sung every Sunday in the *Credo*."

IX

The Bishop of Paris Consoles a Theologian

46. He told me that Bishop William* of Paris had told him that a great master of divinity had come to him and asked to speak to him. "Tell me what it is you want," said the Bishop. The master was on the point of telling him, when he burst into tears. " Master," said the Bishop, " do not lose heart; no man's sin can be greater than God's forgiveness." " But, my Lord, I must tell you," said the master, " that I cannot hold my tears; for I fear that I have lost my faith. I cannot force my heart to believe in the Sacrament of the altar as Holy Church teaches; and yet I know that this is one of the temptations of the Enemy."

47. "Tell me, Master," said the Bishop, "when the Enemy sends you this temptation does it give you pleasure? " " Far from it," said the master; " nothing could distress me more." " Tell me again," said the Bishop, " would you, for gold or silver, utter with your own mouth anything which denied the Sacrament of the altar or the other holy sacraments of the Church?" " Not for anything in the world, I assure you, would I do such a thing," said the master. " I would rather have all my limbs torn from my body than utter such words."

48. " Now let me tell you something more," said the Bishop. " You know that the King of France is at war with the King of England; and you know that the castle which lies on their very frontiers is that of La Rochelle in Poitou. Let me ask you a question, then. Had the King put you in charge of the defence of La Rochelle, which is right on the troubled border, and me in charge of the castle of Montlhéry, which is in the peaceful country in the heart of France, to which of us should the King be the more grateful when the war was over—to you who had successfully held La Rochelle, or to me who had held Montlhéry? " " In God's

name, my Lord," said the master, " to me, who had held La Rochelle for him."

49. " Master," said the Bishop, " what I am telling you is that my heart is like the castle of Montlhéry, for I have no temptation nor doubts about the Sacrament of the altar. That is why I can tell you that if God is grateful to me for my firm and untroubled faith, he is four times as grateful to you for holding your heart for him in this woeful struggle, and for your devotion to him in refusing to surrender it for any worldly treasure or for any mischief that might be done to your body. I tell you, then, be comforted—for this is a matter in which your state is more pleasing to Our Lord than mine." When the master heard this he knelt to the Bishop and his mind was set at rest.

X

THE COUNT OF MONTFORT'S FAITH: OF DEBATING WITH UNBELIEVERS

50. The holy King told me that some men from Albi came once to the Count of Montfort,* who was at that time holding the country of the Albigensians* for the King, and asked him to come and see the body of Our Lord which had turned into flesh and blood in the priest's hands. " Do you," he answered, " who are unbelievers, go and see this sight, for I believe firmly in all that Holy Church teaches us of the Sacrament of the altar. And do you know," he added, " what my reward will be for having in this mortal life believed exactly in the teaching of Holy Church? I shall have in heaven a finer crown than the angels. They see Him face to face, and that is why they cannot but believe in Him."

51. The King told me also that there was once a great debate at the monastery of Cluny between clerks and Jews. There was a knight present who had been charitably fed at the monastery by the Abbot for the love of God. He asked the Abbot to allow him to be the first to speak, and rather unwillingly his request was granted. He stood up, then, and, leaning on his crutch, he asked

them to bring the most learned of the clerks and the greatest master of the Jews. This they did; and he asked but one question, which he put so: " Master," said the knight, " I want to know whether you believe that the Virgin Mary, who bore God in her womb and in her arms, gave birth a virgin, and whether she is indeed the Mother of God."

52. The Jew answered that he believed no such thing. Then the knight told him that it was indeed the act of a fool to enter her church and her house when he neither believed in her nor loved her. " And I can assure you," he added, " that you shall pay for your folly." He raised his crutch and struck the Jew on the side of the head, felling him to the ground. The Jews all fled, taking with them their wounded master; and that was the end of the debate.

53. Then the Abbot came up to the knight and told him that he had been most foolish; the knight answered that the Abbot had been a great deal more foolish to arrange the debate, for before it was finished there would have been a great many good Christians who would have gone away with their faith impaired, having been deceived by the Jews' arguments. " I agree myself," said the King, " that no one who is not a very learned clerk should argue with them. A layman, as soon as he hears the Christian faith maligned, should defend it only by the sword, with a good thrust in the belly, as far as the sword will go."

XI

DAILY LIFE OF ST. LOUIS: A GREYFRIAR PREACHES OF JUSTICE

54. He so arranged the business of governing his country that every day he heard the hours of the Office sung, and a Requiem Mass without chant, and then a sung Mass of the day or the feast, if there was one. Every day after dinner he rested on his bed, and when he had slept and rested he said the Office of the Dead privately in his room with one of his chaplains, before hearing Vespers. In the evening he heard Compline.

55. A Greyfriar came to him at the castle of Hyères, which was where we disembarked. To point a lesson to the King, he said in his sermon that he had read both the Bible and the books which speak of infidel princes; he had never found, he said, either in Christian or infidel countries, that any Kingdom had been lost or had changed its ruler except through some offence against justice. " The King," he said, " is going to France. Let him take care to give his people true and prompt justice, that Our Lord may allow him to hold his Kingdom in peace all the days of his life."

56. It is said that the good man who gave this advice to the King is buried at Marseilles and that God has worked many fine miracles in that city through his intercession. For all the appeals that the King could make to him, he would not stay with him longer than one day.

XII

St. Louis' Justice

57. The King never forgot this lesson, but governed his country in accordance with the laws and the will of God, as I shall tell you later. He so arranged his business that my Lord of Nesle* and the good Count of Soissons* and we others of his household were able, after we had heard our Mass, to listen to the pleas that were brought to the gate of the palace—what are now called the " requests ".

58. When he came back from church he would send for us, sit down on the foot of his bed and make us all sit around him. Then he would ask us whether there were any pleas which could not be settled without reference to him. We would give him the names of the parties, whom he would send for and ask, " Why will you not accept what our people offer? "* They would reply, " Because, sire, they are offering too little "; and he would say, " You would do well to accept what they are ready to offer." In this way the Saint would do his best to direct them to what was fair and reasonable.

59. Often in the summer he went after Mass to the wood of Vincennes and sat down with his back against an oak tree, and

made us sit all around him. Everyone who had an affair to settle could come and speak to him without the interference of any usher or other official. The King would speak himself and ask, " Is there any one here who has a case to settle? " All those who had would then stand up and he would say, " Quiet, all of you, and your cases shall be dealt with in turn." Then he would call my Lord Peter of Fontaines and my Lord Geoffrey of Villette* and say to one of them, " Now give me your judgment in this case."

60. When those who spoke for him or for the other party said anything which he saw needed correction he corrected it himself. Once in the summer I saw him as he went to the gardens in Paris to give judgment for his people. He wore a tunic of natural wool, a sleeveless surcoat of cotton, and a black satin* cloak round his shoulders; he wore no cap, but his hair was well combed, and on his head he wore a hat of white peacocks' feathers.* He had carpets spread so that we could sit about him, and all who had business with him would stand around. Then he settled their claims as I have just told you he used to do in the wood of Vincennes.

XIII

St. Louis and the Claims of the Clergy

61. Another occasion on which I saw him was at Paris. It was when a message came to him from all the French prelates that they wished to speak with him. The King went to the palace to hear what they had to say; Bishop Guy of Auxerre was there, the son of my Lord William of Mello. As spokesman for the whole hierarchy, he addressed the King as follows: " Sir, the lords here present, archbishops and bishops, have bidden me warn you that in your hands Christendom, of which you should be the guardian, is being destroyed." When the King heard this accusation, he crossed himself, and asked how that might be.

62. " Sir," he answered, " it is because men have now so little regard for excommunication that they are prepared to die without obtaining absolution, and refuse to give the Church the satisfaction

she demands. These lords accordingly require you, for the love of God and in execution of your duty, to give an order to your provosts and bailiffs that all who have been under sentence of excommunication for a year and a day must be forced by seizure of their goods to obtain absolution."

63. The King's answer was that he would gladly give such orders in all cases where certain proof of guilt were given to him. The Bishop said that they could by no means consent to this condition, since they refused to acknowledge the King's jurisdiction in their cases. The King told him that he would not change his mind, for it would be unreasonable and an offence against God to force people to seek absolution when it was the clergy who were wronging them.

64. " I can give you an example of this," he added, " in the Count of Brittany. For seven years, while he was excommunicated, he fought the prelates of Brittany at law; and finally he won from the Pope a judgment against them all. Had I in the first year forced the Count of Brittany to obtain absolution I should have sinned towards God and towards him." The prelates had to be satisfied with this; and afterwards I never heard of such a claim being put forward again.

XIV

St. Louis and the Spirit of Justice

65. When the King made peace* with the King of England, he did so against the wish of his Council. They said to him, " Sir, we think that you are throwing away the territory which you are ceding to the King of England; he has no rights over it, for his father forfeited it by judgment." The King's answer was that while he well knew that the King of England had no right to it, there was yet a good reason why he should give it to him. " We have married sisters,* and our children are first cousins. It is fitting, therefore, that there should be peace between us. Moreover from the peace I am making with the King of England I derive

the great honour of having him as my vassal, which he was not
before.*"

66. The King's respect for the spirit of the law may be seen in
the case of my Lord Renaud of Trie. He brought the Saint a document which said that the King had given the county of Dammartin
in Gouelle to the heirs of the then lately deceased Countess of
Boulogne. The seal* of the letter was broken, so that all that
remained was the lower half of the legs in the King's figure and
the stool on which his feet rested. The King showed it to all of us
who were in Council with him and asked us to help him to come
to a decision.

67. We were unanimous that he was under no obligation to give
effect to the document. The King then asked John Sarrasin,* his
chamberlain, to give him another letter which he had asked him to
fetch. When he had it in his hand he said to us, " My Lords, this is
the seal which I used before I went overseas; you can see quite
clearly from this seal that the broken impression fits the complete
seal. I cannot, then, in good conscience withhold the said county."
Then he called my Lord Renaud of Trie and told him that he
made the county over to him.

BOOK TWO

XV

His Birth and Coronation

68. We have now, in the name of Almighty God, written down
some part of the good sayings and teachings of our holy King,
Louis, that those who hear them may find them set out consecu-
tively; thus they may derive more profit from them than they
would have had they been confused with the story of his deeds,
which story we shall now begin, in the name of God and of St.
Louis.

69. He was born, he told me, on the feast of St. Mark* the

Evangelist, after Easter. In many places on that day the cross is carried in procession; and in France these are known as the " black crosses ".* This, then, was in a way a foretelling of the great number of folk who died in the two Crusades: in the Crusade of Egypt, that is, and in the other in which, at Carthage, he himself died; whence there was in this world great mourning, and in Paradise there is a great joy, for those who in these two pilgrimages died as true Crusaders.

70. He was crowned on the first Sunday of Advent.* The Introit of the Mass for that Sunday runs *Ad te levavi animam meam*, etc., which is to say, "To You, God, my dear Lord, I shall lift up my soul, and in You is my trust." From childhood to death he had great trust in God; when he was on his deathbed his last words were a cry to God and His saints, and in particular to my Lord St. James and my Lady St. Genevieve.

XVI

GOD PROTECTS HIM IN THE EARLY TROUBLES OF HIS REIGN

71. God, in whom he had such trust, watched over him continually from his childhood till the end of his life. In his childhood, in particular, He watched over him, when his need was greatest, as I shall tell you later. His soul God watched over by the teachings of his mother,* who taught him to believe in God and to love Him, and chose for him the company only of men of religion. Child though he was, she made him hear all the hours of the Office and listen to the sermons on feast days. He used to recall that his mother had sometimes told him that she would rather he died than that he committed a mortal sin.

72. In his youth he had great need of God's help, for his mother had come from Spain and had neither friends nor relations in all the Kingdom of France. When the French barons saw that the King was a child and his mother a foreigner, they made his uncle, the Count of Boulogne,* their leader and accepted him as their sovereign. After his coronation some of the barons demanded

from the Queen the surrender of large territories, and when she refused they all assembled at Corbeil.

73. The holy King told me that neither he nor his mother, who were then at Montlhéry, dared to return to Paris, until the citizens of Paris came out in arms to fetch them. He told me also that all the way from Montlhéry to Paris the road was full of armed and unarmed men, all praying God to send him a long and happy life and defend him and keep him from his enemies. And as you may read later, God heard their prayer.

74. At the conference which the barons held at Corbeil, those who were present decided, it was said, that the good Count Peter of Brittany* should rebel against the King; they agreed also that they would in person answer the summons which the King would issue against the Count, but that they would each bring with them only two knights. Their object was to see whether the Count could get the better of the Queen—a foreigner, as you have already heard—and there are many who say that he would have done so, and put down the King and Queen, had not God, who never failed him, helped the King in his need.

75. And the way in which God helped him was this: Count Thibaut of Champagne,* who later became King of Navarre, answered the King's summons with three hundred knights; and the reinforcements he brought obliged the Count of Brittany to throw himself on the King's mercy and, it is said, to hand over to the King, as a condition of the peace, the counties of Anjou and the Perche.

XVII

KING RICHARD OF ENGLAND, AND QUEEN ALIX OF CYPRUS

76. I must now make a digression in order to refresh your memory of some events of which you will read later. Let us recall, then, that the good Count Henry the Generous* had two children by the Countess Mary,* who was a sister both of the King of France and of King Richard of England. The elder was called Henry, the younger Thibaut. This Henry, the elder, was a Crusader in the

pilgrimage to the Holy Land, when King Philip and King Richard besieged and took Acre.

77. Immediately after the fall of Acre⋆ King Philip returned to France, for which he was greatly blamed. King Richard remained in the Holy Land, where he so distinguished himself by his prowess that the Saracens were greatly in awe of him. Thus it is told in the chronicle of the Holy Land⋆ that when the Saracen children were crying the women would call out to silence them, " Quiet, King Richard is coming for you! " And when the horses of the Saracens or Bedouins shied at a bush, they used to say to them, " Do you take it for King Richard? "

78. This King Richard succeeded in his plan of giving in marriage to Henry of Champagne, who had also stayed with him, the Queen of Jerusalem,⋆ who was the direct heiress to the Kingdom. By this Queen Henry had two daughters: the first was the Queen of Cyprus; and the younger married my Lord Erard of Brienne, from which a great house is sprung, well known in France and Champagne. I have no occasion now to speak of the wife of my Lord Erard of Brienne, but I must speak of the Queen of Cyprus, who is concerned in my story, and I shall explain how that is so.

XVIII

The Barons Attack the Count of Champagne

79. After the King had put down Count Peter of Brittany,⋆ all the barons of France were so angered against Count Thibaut of Champagne that they decided to send for the Queen of Cyprus, who was the daughter of the elder son of the Count of Champagne, in order to dispossess Count Thibaut, whose father was the second son.

80. Some of them, however, intervened to reconcile Count Peter and Count Thibaut, and the matter was arranged on the understanding that Count Thibaut promised to marry Count Peter's daughter. The day was fixed on which Count Thibaut should marry the lady, and she was to be brought for the wedding to a

Premonstratensian monastery near Château-Thierry called, I think, Val-Secret. The French barons, who were nearly all related to Count Peter, charged themselves with this mission. They took the lady to Val-Secret for the wedding, and sent for the Count of Champagne, who was then at Château-Thierry.

81. But while he was on his way to marry her, my Lord Geoffrey of la Chapelle came to him with a letter of credence from the King and said to him, " My lord Count of Champagne, the King has learnt that you have agreed with Count Peter of Brittany to take his daughter in marriage; the King accordingly sends you word that, unless you wish to lose all that you hold in the Kingdom of France, you shall not do so; for you know that the Count of Brittany has done more harm to the King than any living man." The Count of Champagne took the advice of his companions and returned to Château-Thierry.

82. When Count Peter and the barons of France who were waiting at Val-Secret heard this they were all wild with anger and mortification at his withdrawal. Immediately they sent for the Queen of Cyprus. As soon as she arrived they made an agreement to summon all the armed force they could raise and invade Brie and Champagne from the French side, while the Duke of Burgundy, whose wife was the daughter of Robert of Dreux, was to enter Champagne from Burgundy; and they fixed a day for assembling before the city of Troyes, which they were to seize if possible.

83. The Duke raised as many men as he could; the barons did the same. Burning and destroying, they marched in from one side, while the Duke of Burgundy invaded from his, and from another direction the King of France came to give battle to them. The Count of Champagne was so hard pressed that he burnt his towns himself before the barons arrived, to prevent them from finding them provisioned. Among other towns which he burnt were Épernay, Vertus and Sézanne.

XIX

THE DISPUTE IS SETTLED

84. When the people of Troyes saw that there was no hope of assistance from their Count they sent for help to Simon, Lord of Joinville, father of the present Lord of Joinville. At nightfall, as soon as the news came, he summoned all his men at arms and set out for Troyes, which he reached before dawn.* Foiled in their plan to take the city, the barons retired baffled from Troyes and camped in the meadows of Isle, where the Duke of Burgundy was already stationed.

85. Knowing that they were there, the King of France marched straightway to give them battle. The barons sent to him and asked him to withdraw his person from the quarrel, while they attacked the Count of Champagne, the Duke of Lorraine, and the rest of the King's people, although they had three hundred knights less than the Count and the Duke. The King's answer was that he would not have them giving battle to his people without his being with them in person. They sent a message back to him that if he so wished it they would gladly arrange for the Queen of Cyprus to make peace, but he answered that he would agree to no peace, nor would he allow the Count of Champagne to do so, until they had quitted the County of Champagne.

86. They withdrew accordingly, and, leaving Isle, where they had established themselves, they camped below Jully, while the King lay at Isle, from which he had driven them. When they found that the King had followed them there they moved to Chaorce; even there they were afraid to await the King, and moved to Laignes, which belonged to the Count of Nevers, who was of their party. Thus the King reconciled the Count of Champagne and the Queen of Cyprus; by the terms of peace the Count made over to the Queen land to the annual value of about two thousand pounds, and a sum of forty thousand pounds, which the King paid on his behalf.

87. In return for this forty thousand pounds the Count of Champagne sold to the King the following fiefs: the Counties of

Blois, Chartres, Sancerre and the Viscounty of Châteaudun. There were some who said that these fiefs were only pledged to the King, but once overseas I asked our King, St. Louis, about this, and it is not true.

88. The land which Count Thibaut gave to the Queen of Cyprus is now held by the present Count of Brienne and the Count of Joigny: for the Count of Brienne's grandmother was a daughter of the Queen of Cyprus, and wife of the great Count Walter of Brienne.*

XX

COUNT HENRY THE GENEROUS

89. To show you the origin of the fiefs which the Lord of Champagne sold to the King, I must explain that the great Count Thibaut, who is buried at Lagny, had three sons; the first was called Henry, the second Thibaut, and the third Stephen. Henry was Count of Champagne and Brie, and was called " Henry the Generous "—a name he well deserved, for he was generous both to God and to this world. To God, as you may see from the Church of Saint Stephen at Troyes and other fine churches which he founded in Champagne; and to men of this world, as appeared in the affair of Artaud of Nogent and on many other occasions of which I would gladly tell you did I not fear to interrupt my story.

90. There was no burgher in the world whom the Count trusted more than Artaud of Nogent. He was so rich that he could afford to build the castle of Nogent l'Artaud. It happened one Pentecost Day that Count Henry was on his way down from the palace at Troyes to hear Mass at St. Stephen's. At the foot of the steps he was confronted by a poor knight, who knelt to him and said, " Sir, I beg you for God's sake to give me from what you have sufficient to marry my two daughters whom you see here."

91. Artaud, who was walking behind him, said to the poor knight, " Sir Knight, it is not courteous in you to ask this of my Lord, for he has given away so much that he has no more to give." The generous Count turned to Artaud and said, " Sir Villain, you

are wrong in saying that I have nothing more to give; I have you. Take him, Sir Knight; I give him to you; and, furthermore, I shall be your warrant for him." The knight was in no way embarrassed, but took Artaud by the cloak and told him that he would not release him until he had paid a ransom; and before he was freed Artaud paid up to the tune of five hundred pounds.

92. Count Henry's younger brother was called Thibaut, and was Count of Blois. The third brother was Stephen, Count of Sancerre. All that they inherited, including their two counties and their dependant fiefs, these two brothers held from Count Henry; afterwards they held them from Count Henry's heirs, who had the County of Champagne, until King Thibaut sold them, as you have heard, to the King of France.

XXI

The Great Court at Saumur

93. To return to our story. After this affair the King held a full court at Saumur in Anjou. I was present and I can witness that the arrangement was the finest I ever saw. The Count of Poitiers,* whom the King had newly knighted on the feast of St. John, ate at his table by his side. Below the Count sat Count John of Dreux, whom he had also just knighted, and below him the Count de la Marche; below him the good Count Peter of Brittany.* Facing the King's table, and opposite the Count of Dreux, was my Lord the King of Navarre in a tunic and cloak of satin,* with a fine belt, clasp and golden cap. And I carved for him.

94. Facing the King, his brother, the Count of Artois, served him with meat, and the good Count John of Soissons carved with the knife. As a guard for the King's table were my Lord Humbert of Beaujeu, later Constable of France, my Lord Enguerrand of Coucy, and my Lord Archambaud of Bourbon. Behind these three barons were at least thirty of their knights, in velvet tunics, as their attendant guards; and behind them was a great number of men-at-arms, wearing the arms of the Count of Poitiers

embroidered on satin. The King wore a tunic of dark blue satin, a surcoat and cloak of scarlet velvet lined with ermine, and a cotton cap, which did not suit him at all well, for he was then a young man.

95. The King held this feast in the palace of Saumur, which, it was said, Henry,* the great King of England, had built for holding his high festivals. The building is designed in the style of the White Monks' cloisters, but I think there is none that can even approach it in size, and for this reason: the King's table was along one side of the cloister, and he was surrounded by knights and men-at-arms who took up a great deal of space; but there was also another table at which twenty bishops and archbishops ate; and after the bishops and archbishops was a table next to theirs, at the far end of the cloister from the King's, for his mother, Queen Blanche.

96. Waiting upon the Queen were the Count of Boulogne,* who afterwards became King of Portugal, the good Count Hugh of Saint Pol, and an eighteen-year-old German who was said to be the son of Saint Elizabeth of Thuringia,* for which reason Queen Blanche, out of devotion, I heard, kissed his forehead, because she thought his mother must have kissed him there so often.

97. On the other side, at the end of the cloister, were the kitchens, cellars, bakeries and butteries, and from that end the King and Queen were served with meat and wine and bread. In all the other wings and in the central courtyard such a concourse of knights sat at table that I could not possibly count them. Many folk said that they had never seen so many surcoats or other garments of cloth of gold and silk at one feast, and that there were at least three thousand knights present.

XXII

THE BATTLE OF TAILLEBOURG IN 1242

98. After this feast, the King brought the Count of Poitiers to Poitiers to take formal possession of his fiefs. When he arrived there he would have been glad to be back in Paris, for he found

that the Count of la Marche, who had eaten at his table on St. John's day, had assembled at Lusignan, near Poitiers, as large an armed force as he could raise. The King stayed for nearly a fortnight at Poitiers; it was too dangerous for him to leave until he had reached an agreement with the Count of la Marche, though how he did so I do not know.

99. Several times I saw the Count arrive at Poitiers from Lusignan to confer with the King, and he would always bring with him his wife the Queen of England,* the mother of the English King. It was commonly said that it was a bad peace* that the King and the Count of Poitiers had made with the Count of la Marche.

100. It was not long after the King's return* from Poitiers that the King of England arrived in Gascony to make war on him. St. Louis rode out against him with as many of his people as he could assemble. The King of England and the Count of la Marche went to give battle opposite the castle known as Taillebourg, on a difficult river called the Charente, which can be crossed only by a very narrow stone bridge.

101. As soon as the King reached Taillebourg, and the two armies were in sight of one another, our people, who had the castle on their side of the river, forced their way across with great difficulty and danger in boats and pontoons, and attacked the English. That was the beginning of a sharp fight. When the King saw what was happening he took his share of the danger with the others; for when he crossed over to the English side, for one man that he had with him, the English had a good twenty. By the grace of God, however, when the English saw the King cross they broke and shut themselves up in the city of Saintes. Some of our people entered the city in the mêlée with them and were captured.

102. These prisoners of ours at Saintes reported that they heard a sharp quarrel break out between the King of England and the Count of la Marche; the King accused the Count of having promised when he sent for him that he would find considerable support in France; and that same evening he left Saintes for Gascony.

XXIII

SUBMISSION OF THE COUNT OF LA MARCHE

103. The Count of la Marche had no alternative but to come and throw himself on the King's mercy, with his wife and children. As one of the conditions of peace, the King obtained a large part of the Count's territory: how much, I do not know, for at that time I had never yet worn the mailed coat of knighthood, and I was not present; but I heard that in addition to the land which the King gained the Count made over to him ten thousand pounds* *parisis*, which were due to him from the King's treasury, and a similar amount yearly.

104. While we were at Poitiers I saw a knight whose name was my Lord Geoffrey of Rancon. It was said that the Count of la Marche had done him a grave injury, and Lord Geoffrey had sworn on the gospels that he would not have his hair cut short like a knight but would wear it long like a woman, with a parting, until the day when he should see vengeance taken on the Count of la Marche either at his own hands or another's. When my Lord Geoffrey saw the Count with his wife and children kneeling before the King and imploring his mercy, he called for a stool, had his parting combed out and his hair cut short in the presence of the King, the Count of la Marche and all the company.

105. In this campaign against the King of England and the barons (I have heard from those who came back from it) the King made rich grants. But neither for these, nor for the expenses of this campaign or his others at home or abroad, did he ever make a levy from his barons or knights or men or from his good towns of which they could complain: and small wonder, for he acted on the advice of the good mother who was by his side; what he did was by her advice and that of the tried counsellors who were still with him from the time of his father and grandfather.

XXIV

ST. LOUIS TAKES THE CROSS, WITH HIS BROTHERS AND OTHER
NOBLES, INCLUDING THE AUTHOR

106. After the events* of which I have just spoken it was the will of God that the King should be overtaken at Paris by a grievous sickness. He was brought so low, it was said, that one of the ladies who were nursing him said he was dead and wished to cover his face with the sheet. Another lady, who was on the other side of the bed, would not allow her, and said that his soul was still in his body.

107. While the King was listening to their argument, Our Lord worked in him and soon sent him back his health. He had lost the power of speech, but as soon as he was again fit to speak he asked for the Cross to be given to him, which was done. When the Queen, his mother, heard that he could speak again she was overjoyed. But when she heard that he had taken the Cross, as he told her, too, himself, she was as miserable as if she had seen him dead.

108. After he had taken the Cross all his three brothers did the same—Robert, Count of Artois,* Alfonse, Count of Poitiers, and Charles, Count of Anjou,* who was afterwards King of Sicily. Hugh, Duke of Burgundy, also took the Cross, and William, Count of Flanders, brother of the Count Guy of Flanders who died recently,* the good Hugh Count of Saint Pol, and my Lord Walter, his nephew, who bore himself well overseas and would have done great things had he lived.

109. With them were the Count of la Marche and his son, my Lord Hugh le Brun, the Count of Sarrebrück, and his brother, my Lord Gobert of Apremont: it was in company with the Count of Sarrebrück that I, John of Joinville, crossed the seas in a ship which, being cousins, we hired together. We were twenty knights; he led one ten, and I the other.

XXV

Preparations for the Crusade

110. At Easter, in the year of grace 1248, I sent for my own men and those who held of me, to come to Joinville; and there on the eve of Easter, when all whom I had sent for had come, was born of my first wife, the sister of the Count of Grandpré, my son John, Lord of Ancerville. All that week we were feasting and dancing; my brother, the Lord of Vaucouleurs and the other great men who were there each gave a dinner in turn, on the Monday, Tuesday, Wednesday and Thursday.*

111. On the Friday I said to them, " My Lords, I am going overseas, and I do not know whether I shall return. Come forward, then. If I have wronged you in any way, I will put it right, as has been my custom, for all of you in turn who have any claim on me or on my people." In making my settlement I was guided by the general feeling of all who held from me; and that I might not influence them, I withdrew from the discussion and agreed without question to all their decisions.

112. As I did not wish to take with me any money that might not rightly be mine, I went to Metz in Lorraine to pledge a great part of my estate. You must understand that on the day I left home to go to the Holy Land I did not have a thousand pounds' income from my property, for my lady my mother was still alive; but this did not stop me from going with nine knights under me, and myself one of three knights-bannerets.* I tell you this, because had I not had the help of God, who never failed me, I could not have held out for so long a time as the six years which I spent in the Holy Land.

113. As I was preparing to leave, John, Lord of Apremont* and Count of Sarrebrück in his wife's right, sent to me and told me that he had settled his affairs in readiness to go overseas at the head of ten knights. He asked me if I would be willing to share with him the hire of a ship. I agreed, and his people and mine hired one at Marseilles.

XXVI

PROWESS OF A CLERK

114. The King summoned all his barons to Paris; there he had them take an oath that they would be faithful and loyal to his children should anything happen to him in his journey. He asked me also to do so, but I would not take the oath, because I was not the King's man.*

115. On my way to Paris I saw three dead men in a cart. A clerk had killed them, and I was told that the bodies were being taken to the King. When I heard this I sent one of my squires after them to find out how it had come about. The squire I sent told me that when the King came out of his chapel he went to the porch to see the bodies and asked the Provost of Paris how it had happened.

116. The Provost told him that the dead men were three of his sergeants from the Châtelet, who used to frequent deserted streets in order to rob folk. " They found," he told the King, " this clerk whom you see and stripped him of all his clothes. The clerk went off to his lodging in his shirt, fetched his crossbow and had a boy bring him his cutlass. When he saw the sergeants he called out to them and said it was over with them now. He drew his bow and fired, and struck one of them through the heart; the other two ran away, but the clerk took the cutlass which the boy was holding and chased them in the moonlight, which was clear and bright.

117. " One of them tried to get through a hedge into a garden, but the clerk," said the Provost, " struck him with the cutlass and cut right through his leg so that it is hanging only by the boot, as you may see. He then went after the other man, who tried to escape into a house where he was not known, in which the inmates were still awake. The clerk struck him on the crown of his head with such force that he split his skull to the teeth, as you may also see. Then, sir, he showed the neighbours in the street what he had done and came to surrender himself to your justice. I have brought him, sir, so that you may do what you will with him, and here he is."

118. " Sir Clerk," said the King, " your prowess has cost you the

priesthood; but by reason of that prowess I engage you in my service at my charges, and you shall come overseas with me. And I tell you this so that my officials may know that I will not shield them in any of their misdeeds." When the crowd which had assembled heard the King's words, they called out to Our Lord and prayed God to send the King a long and happy life and to bring him back to them in joy and health.

XXVII

The Author Leaves His Home

119. I went home after this, and the Count of Sarrebrück and I agreed to send on our equipment in carts to Auxonne, there to be put on the river Sâone and sent by the Sâone and Rhône to Arles. 120. The day I left Joinville I sent for the Abbot of Cheminon, who had the name of being the worthiest man in the Order of White Monks. Once at Clairvaux on a feast of Our Lady, when St. Louis was present, I heard this said of him by a monk who pointed him out to me and asked me whether I knew him. " Why do you ask me? " I said, and he answered, " Because I think he is the finest man in the whole Order of White Monks."
121. " Let me tell you, too," he said, " a story that was told me by a good man who slept in the same dormitory as the Abbot of Cheminon. The Abbot felt so hot that he had bared his chest, and this good man who was sleeping in the same dormitory saw the Mother of God go to the Abbot's bed and draw his gown over his chest so that the draught might not do him any harm."
122. The Abbot of Cheminon gave me my scrip and pilgrim's staff; and then I left Joinville, barefooted and in my shirt, never to enter the castle again until my return; and thus I went to Blé-court and Saint Urbain* and to visit other relics of the saints in the neighbourhood. On my road to Blécourt and Saint Urbain I would not look back towards Joinville for fear lest my heart should weaken at the thought of the lovely castle I was leaving and of my two children.

123. I and my companions dined at Fontaine-l'Archevêque opposite Donjeux, and there Abbot Adam of Saint Urbain (God grant him His mercy) gave a great store of fine jewels to me and the nine knights I had with me. Thence we went to Auxonne; and from Auxonne we went down the Sâone to Lyons with the equipment we had loaded into boats. The great war-horses were led beside the boats.

124. At Lyons we embarked on the Rhône to go to Arles-le-Blanc; and by the Rhône we saw a castle called Roche de Glun which the King had had razed because Roger, the lord of the castle, was accused of robbing pilgrims and merchants.

XXVIII

They Set Sail, and Sight a Marvellous Mountain

125. In the month of August we embarked in our ships at the Rock of Marseilles. On the day we embarked, the entry port of the ship was opened and all the horses we had to take overseas were taken on board. Then the door was closed and well tamped, in the same way as you bung a cask, for when the ship is at sea the whole door is under water.

126. When the horses had been embarked, our Master Mariner called to his sailors, who were in the prow of the ship, " Is all fast? " " Aye, aye, sir," they answered; " the clerks and priests may come forward." As soon as they had done so, he called out to them, " In the name of God, strike up a song! " They all sang in unison *Veni, Creator Spiritus*; the master called to the sailors, " In the name of God, make sail." And so they set the sails.

127. Soon the wind filled the sails and had taken us out of sight of land, so that we could see nothing but sky and water; and every day the wind took us farther from the homes in which we were born. How foolhardy, then, the man is who dares to run so grave a risk when he has in his possession what belongs to another, or is in mortal sin. For when you go to sleep at night you do not know

whether you may find yourself in the morning at the bottom of the sea.

128. An awesome marvel befell us at sea; we sighted a mountain*, off the Barbary Coast, which was quite round. It was about the time of Vespers when we sighted it, and all that night we sailed on and thought that we must have made over fifty leagues; but in the morning we found ourselves still off this same mountain; and this happened two or three times. The sailors were greatly perturbed when they saw it and told us that our ships were in great danger, as we were off the country of the Saracens of Barbary.

129. Then a good priest, who was known as the Dean of Maurupt, told us that in his parish, whenever he had had trouble from drought or too much rain—in any trouble, indeed—he had held three processions on three Saturdays, and immediately God and His Mother had rid them of the trouble. It was then a Saturday. We made the first procession round the two masts of the ship. For my part, I had myself carried round, as I was very sick. That was the last we saw of the mountain, and on the third Saturday we arrived at Cyprus.

XXIX

ARRIVAL AT CYPRUS: THE TARTAR ENVOYS

130. The King was already there when we arrived, and we found that a great store of provisions was ready for him—wine and money and corn. There was such a supply of wine that in the middle of the fields by the seashore his men had built great piles of barrels of wine which they had been buying for two years before his arrival; they had put them one on top of the other, so that when you looked at them from the front you would have thought that they were great wooden barns.

131. The wheat and barley were also heaped out in the fields. At first sight you thought they were hills; the rain had been beating on the grain for a long time and had made it sprout on the outside, so that all you could see was green grass. But when they were ready to ship it to Egypt they tore off the outside crust of grass,

and inside the wheat and barley were as fresh as if they had been newly threshed.

132. The King would have been glad to press on to Egypt without delay—so I have heard him say when we were in Syria—had not his barons advised him to wait for those of his people who had not yet arrived.

133. While the King was waiting in Cyprus, the great King of the Tartars* sent his ambassadors to him with friendly and gracious messages. Among other things, he sent word that he was prepared to help him to win the Holy Land and free Jerusalem from the hands of the Saracens.

134. The King received the ambassadors very graciously and sent back his own; it was two years before they returned to him. He sent the King of the Tartars by his ambassadors a tent made in the form of a chapel, which was very costly, being made entirely of fine cloth of scarlet. To see if he could attract them to our faith, the King had pictures embroidered in the chapel of the Annunciation of Our Lady and all the other articles of faith. He sent these by two Friars Preachers,* who knew the Saracen tongue, so that they could explain it to them and teach them what they should believe.

135. The two friars returned to the King at the time when his two brothers went back to France. They found that he had gone from Acre, where his brothers had left him, to Caesarea; he was strengthening the place and had neither peace nor truce with the Saracens. As for the reception of the King of France's ambassadors, I shall tell you later just what they themselves told the King. Their report to him was full of wonderful stories which I cannot tell you now; I must not interrupt the subject I have begun. To proceed, then.

136. Although my land brought me in less than a thousand pounds a year, when I went overseas I engaged at my own charges nine knights, two of them knights bannerets, with myself as the tenth in command. When I arrived in Cyprus and had paid for the ship, all I had left was two hundred and forty pounds *tournois*. Some of my knights accordingly told me that unless I could raise some money they would leave me. But God, who never failed me,

provided for me in this way: The King was then at Nicosia; he sent for me and engaged me at his own charges and placed eight hundred pounds in my coffers; I then had more money than I needed.

XXX

THE EMPRESS OF CONSTANTINOPLE

137. While we were waiting at Cyprus the Empress of Constantinople* sent me a message that she had landed at Paphos, a city in Cyprus, and asked me and my Lord Erard of Brienne to fetch her. When we arrived we found that a strong wind had broken the anchor cables of her vessel and driven it to Acre. All that was left of her baggage was the cloak she was wearing and a surcoat she wore at dinner.* We brought her to Limassol, where the King and Queen and all the barons of France and of the army received her with great honour.

138. The next day I sent her some cloth for making a dress, with some ermine, some woollen material and satin for lining it. The good knight, my Lord Philip of Nanteuil, who was in the King's household, met my squire on his way to the Empress. When the good man saw what I had done he went to the King and said that I had put great shame on him and the other barons in sending these clothes to the Empress before they realised that she needed them.

139. The purpose of the Empress's visit was to ask the King's help for her husband, who had stayed at Constantinople; and she did her work so well that she took with her more than a hundred letters in duplicate from me and from other friends she had in Cyprus. In these letters we were bound by oath, should the King, after his return from overseas, or the Legate, decide to send three hundred knights to Constantinople, to fulfil our undertaking and make the journey.

140. In fulfilment of my oath, when we were actually leaving on our way home I told the King in the presence of the Count of Eu, whose letter I have, that if he wished to send the three hundred

knights I was ready to keep my word and go. The King answered
that he had not the means to do so, for his treasury was so ill
supplied that he had drained it to the dregs. After our arrival in
Egypt the Empress went to France. She took with her her brother,
my Lord John of Acre, whom she married to the Countess of
Montfort.

XXXI

THE TARTARS DEFEAT THE SULTAN OF ICONIUM: THE SULTAN OF BABYLON IS POISONED

141. At the time when we arrived in Cyprus the Sultan of Iconium
was the richest of all the infidel kings. He had done a marvellous
thing: he had had a great part of his gold melted down and poured
into earthenware jars in which they store the wine overseas, and
which hold a good three or four measures of wine; then he had the
pots smashed. The masses of gold were displayed in the middle of
one of his castles so that anyone entering the castle could see and
touch them; there were six or seven of them.

142. His great wealth was displayed in a pavilion which the King
of Armenia sent to the King of France; it was worth at least
five hundred pounds and the King of Armenia told him that he
had been given it by a *ferrais* of the Sultan of Iconium. The *ferrais*
is the man who looks after the Sultan's pavilions and keeps his
houses clean.

143. In order to free himself from the suzerainty of the Sultan of
Iconium, the King of Armenia* approached the King of the Tartars and acknowledged his suzerainty in return for his assistance;
thus he was able to bring sufficient force to attack the Sultan of
Iconium. It was a long fight, and the Tartars killed so many of the
Sultan's men that he was heard of no more. In Cyprus there was
much talk of the great battle that was going to be fought, and some
of our men-at-arms crossed to Armenia to take part in it and
make some money; but not one of them came back.

144. The Sultan of Babylon* expected that the King would attack
Egypt in the spring; he planned accordingly first to overthrow

his mortal enemy, the Sultan of Homs, and besieged him in the city of Homs. The Sultan of Homs did not know how he could get the better of the Sultan of Babylon, for he realised that unless his enemy's life was cut short he would overthrow him. He accordingly bribed the Sultan of Babylon's *ferrais* to poison him.

145. The poison was administered in this way: the *ferrais* knew that every day after dinner the Sultan was in the habit of playing chess, sitting on the mats at the foot of his bed. He placed the poison in the mat on which he knew the Sultan sat every day. It happened, then, that the Sultan, who was barefooted, turned and put his weight on an open wound which he had on his leg. Immediately the poison entered into the flesh and paralysed all that side of his body; whenever the action of the poison reached his heart he would be for two days without being able to drink, or eat, or speak. His people left the Sultan of Homs in peace and brought their master back to Egypt.

XXXII

The Crusaders Leave Cyprus and Arrive off Damietta

146. At the beginning of March, by the King's order, the King, the barons, and the other pilgrims ordered the ships to be loaded again with wine and food, ready to sail when he should give the word. On the Friday before Pentecost* the King saw that everything was in order, and he and the Queen embarked. He told his barons to follow him in their ships and to set a straight course for Egypt. On the Saturday he sailed, and all the other ships with him. It was a beautiful sight; as far as your eye could see, the whole sea seemed to be covered with towels, by the canvas of ships' sails, whose number, large and small, was given as eighteen hundred vessels.

147. The King anchored off a hill called the Point of Limassol, with all the other ships around him. On Whitsunday he landed; but after we had heard Mass a violent and gusty wind from Egypt rose with such force that of the two thousand eight hundred knights the King was leading to Egypt there were only seven

hundred left with him; the rest were scattered and driven to Acre or other distant places and were unable to rejoin him for a long time.

148. On the Monday after Pentecost the wind had fallen. The King and those of us who, by God's grace, had not been separated from him set sail again and met the Prince of the Morea and the Duke of Burgundy, who had been staying in the Morea. On the Thursday after Pentecost, the King arrived off Damietta. There we found all the Sultan's forces on the seashore: fine people to look upon, for the Sultan's arms are gold and the sun shone on the golden blazonry. The noise they made with their trumpets and Saracen horns was terrifying to hear.

149. The King summoned his barons to receive their advice about what he should do. Many thought that he should wait until the rest of his people had returned, for he had hardly a third part of his force left with him. But he would not listen to them. The reason he gave was that to do so would put heart into his enemies; more, there is no safe anchorage off Damietta where he could wait for his people without the risk of a strong wind driving the fleet away from their objective, as had happened to the others on Whitsunday.

XXXIII

THE LANDING

150. It was accordingly agreed that the King should land on the Friday before Trinity Sunday* and give battle to the Saracens unless they declined it. The King told my Lord John of Beaumont* to lend a galley to my Lord Erard of Brienne and me, to land us and our knights, since the big ships were unable to reach the shore.

151. By the grace of God, when I got back to my ship, I found a small ship which my Lady of Beirut,* a cousin of the Count of Montbéliard and of mine, had given me, in which were eight of my horses. When the Friday came I and my Lord Erard armed ourselves and went to the King to ask for the galley: whereupon my Lord John of Beaumont answered that we were not to have it.

152. When our people saw that there was to be no galley for us they let themselves drop pell-mell from the ship into our longboat, so much so that the longboat looked like sinking. When the sailors saw that it was gradually going under, they hurriedly deserted it for the ship, leaving my knights in the boat. I asked the master how many people too many there were in it; he told me twenty men-at-arms; I asked him whether, if I relieved him of that number, he could land us safely. "Yes," he answered; and I lightened it so that in three journeys he took them to the ship in which were my horses.

153. While I was getting these people across, a knight of my Lord Erard of Brienne, called Plonquet, tried to jump from the ship into the longboat; but the boat moved off and he fell into the sea and was drowned.

154. When I got back to my ship I put into my dinghy a squire that I had knighted, called my Lord Hugh of Vaucouleurs, and two squires, both excellent soldiers; one was called my Lord Villain of Versey, and the other my Lord William of Dammartin; these two hated one another bitterly, and as they had had one another by the hair in the Morea it was impossible for anyone to make them compose their quarrel. But I made them forgive their ill-will and kiss one another, by swearing to them on the gospels that we should not land while they were still nursing their anger.

155. As we set off for the shore we came alongside the longboat of the King's flagship, which was carrying the King. His people began to shout to me (we were moving faster than they) to land by the ensign of St. Denis which was in another boat preceding the King. I paid no attention to them, but landed opposite a large body of Turks, at least six thousand of them, mounted.

156. As soon as they saw that we had landed, they spurred towards us. As we saw them approach, we fixed the points of our shields* into the sand and the shafts of our lances with the points towards the enemy; and when they saw that they were nicely set to pierce them through the belly they turned tail and fled.

XXXIV

THE COUNT OF JAFFA'S FINE GALLEY

157. A good knight who had just landed, my Lord Baldwin of Rheims, sent me a message by his squire asking me to wait for him. I answered that I should be glad to, for one should certainly wait for so good a man in such a case; and for this he was grateful to me all his life. With him a thousand mounted men* joined us; and so you may see that though when I landed I had with me neither squire nor knight nor soldier that I had brought from home, yet God never left me without help.

158. The Count of Jaffa* landed on our left. He was a cousin of the Count of Montbéliard, and of the house of Joinville. He made the finest landing of all; for his whole ship was painted within and without* with his coat of arms, which is *or*, a cross *patee gules*. He had three hundred oarsmen in his galley, every one with a shield of his arms, and for every shield there was a pennon embroidered with his arms in gold.

159. As they came along, the rowers driving it on with their oars, the galley seemed to fly; and what with the beating of the pennons in the wind, and the ship's trumpets and drums and Saracen horns, the noise was like lightning crashing from the heavens. As soon as they had run the galley as far up on the sand as they could, he and his knights leapt out in their fine arms and equipment and drew up beside us.

160. I forgot to tell you that as soon as the Count of Jaffa landed he had his tents and pavilions put up; and when the Saracens saw this, they immediately rallied opposite us and came spurring back as though they meant to charge us. But when they saw that we stood firm they were quick to retire.

161. The galley which carried the ensign of St. Denis landed a good crossbow shot to our left. As they landed, a Saracen charged into their ranks, either because he could not hold his horse in or because he thought the others must be following him: he was cut to pieces.

XXXV

THE TOWN FALLS

162. When the King heard that the ensign of St. Denis was ashore he strode across the galley, refusing even for the Legate* who was with him to lag behind the standard, and leapt into the water, which came up to his armpits. His shield round his neck, his helmet on his head, lance in hand, he joined his men on the beach. When he had landed and could see the Saracens he asked what people they were. He was told that they were Saracens. He couched his lance under his arm and put his shield before him, and would have flung himself upon them had not his wiser companions held him back.

163. Three times the Saracens sent the Sultan a message by carrier pigeons* to say that the King had landed; but he was suffering from an attack of his disease, and they had no answer from him. When they heard nothing, they thought that the Sultan must be dead and abandoned Damietta. The King sent on a knight to see what had happened. He came back and told the King he had been into the Sultan's palace and the news was true. Then the King sent for the Legate and all the prelates in the army, and a high *Te Deum Laudamus* was sung. The King and all of us mounted and we went to camp outside Damietta.

164. The Turks were most unwise to abandon the city without cutting the bridge of boats, which would have greatly hampered us. But when they left they did a great deal of damage to us by setting fire to the market, where all the goods and merchandise were stored. It was as bad as though tomorrow someone—which God forbid—were to set fire to the Petit-Pont in Paris.

165. But now we must admit that Almighty God was most gracious to us in saving us from death and danger when we landed, for we had to come in on foot and attack a mounted enemy. Our Lord was again gracious to us in giving us Damietta, which we could not have taken except by starvation, as we may realise when we remember that it was only so that King John took it in our father's times.*

XXXVI

ILL BEHAVIOUR OF THE CRUSADERS

166. Our Lord can speak of us as he spoke of the children of Israel when he said, " Et pro nichilo habuerunt terram desiderabilem." And what does He then say? He says that they have been unmindful of God who saved them. And later I shall tell you how we, too, were unmindful of Him.

167. First, however, to return to the King. He sent for his barons, clergy and lay, and asked them to give him the assistance of their advice in dividing what had been captured in the town. The first to speak was the Patriarch,* who said, " Sir, I think that you should keep the wheat and barley and rice and all the food, so that you may provision the town; and that an order should be published throughout the camp that all other goods must be brought to the Legate's lodging, under pain of excommunication." All the rest of the barons agreed with him, but in the event the value of all the goods brought to the Legate's lodging did not amount to more than six thousand pounds.

168. When this had been done, the King and his barons sent for the good knight, my Lord John of Valery, and said to him, " My Lord of Valery," said the King, " we have agreed that the Legate shall pay over to you the six thousand pounds to divide as you think best." " Sir," said the good knight, " I thank you for the great honour you do me, but I cannot, please God, accept that honour and the charge you offer me, for by so doing I should run counter to the good custom of the Holy Land. When a city is taken from the enemy it is customary for the King to keep one-third of what is found in the city and for the pilgrims to have two-thirds.

169. " When King John took Damietta he respected the custom, and our elders say that the Kings of Jerusalem before him also respected it. If you are willing to hand over to me two-thirds of the wheat, barley, rice, and other victals, I shall be pleased to undertake their division among the pilgrims." The King

decided against doing so, and there the matter rested, with the result that many were dissatisfied by his neglect of the good old custom.

170. The King's people should have kept the inhabitants in hand by fair treatment; but, so I heard, they let them the shops in which to sell their goods at as high a rent as possible. This was noised abroad, and many of the merchants gave up coming to the camp. The barons should have husbanded their resources for the right time and place; but they indulged themselves in giving great dinners with extravagant dishes.

171. The common folk took up with loose women, for which, when we came back from captivity, the King dismissed many of them. I asked him why he had done so, and he told me that, to his own certain knowledge, and at a time when the army had never been in such distress, those whom he had dismissed had kept their brothels hardly a stone's throw from his tent.

XXXVII

Attacks on the Camp: Walter of Autrèche is Killed

172. I must return to my story, however, and tell you how, shortly after our capture of Damietta, all the Sultan's cavalry took up a position facing the camp and blockaded it from the landward side. The King and all the knights armed themselves. When I was fully armed I went to speak to the King and found him sitting on a chair, and some of the good knights of his own division with him, all in full armour. I asked him to allow me and my people to make a sortie from the camp and prevent the Saracens from attacking our tents. When my Lord John of Beaumont heard my request he shouted after me and ordered me, from the King, not to leave my tent until the King gave me the word.

173. I have already spoken of the good knights who were with the King; there were eight of them, all good men, who had won the prize for arms, both at home and overseas, and such we considered in the front rank of knighthood. The names of these knights of the

King's company were: my Lord Geoffrey of Sargines,* my Lord Matthew of Marly, my Lord Philip of Nanteuil, my Lord Humbert of Beaujeu, Constable of France. This last was not present; he and the commander of the crossbowmen and most of the King's men-at-arms were outside the camp to protect it from Turkish damage.

174. It was that day that my Lord Walter of Autrèche armed himself at all points in his tent and, mounting his horse, with his shield round his neck and his helmet on his head, ordered the flaps of the tent to be lifted and spurred his horse towards the Turks. As he rode alone out of his tent, all his people raised a loud cry of "Châtillon!" But it happened that before he reached the Turks he fell and the horse galloped over his body. The horse, whose housing bore his arms, went over to the enemy; for the greater part of the Saracens were mounted on mares, which attracted it to their ranks.

175. Those who saw what happened told us that four Turks attacked Lord Walter as he lay on the ground, and as they passed by him they gave him great blows with their maces. The Constable of France, with some of the King's men-at-arms, rescued him, and they carried him back to his tent in their arms. When he was brought in he was speechless; some of the doctors and surgeons in the camp came to him, and as he did not seem to be in danger of death they bled him in both arms.

176. Very late that evening my Lord Aubert of Narcy told me that we ought to go and see him, because we had not yet done so and he was a very brave man and had a fine name. As we went into his tent, his chamberlain met us and asked us to walk gently so as not to wake his master. We found him lying on some rugs of ermine; we went quietly up to him and saw that he was dead. When the King was told, he answered that he was glad that he had not a thousand such men, for they would want to act without his orders as this man had done.

XXXVIII

THE COUNT OF POITIERS ARRIVES

177. Every night the Saracen rank and file stole into the camp and murdered our people if they found them asleep. They killed, for example, the Lord of Courtenay's sentry and left his body lying on a table after cutting off his head and taking it with them. This they did because the Sultan paid a golden besant for every Christian head.

178. The reason why we were harassed in this way was that each night the divisions took their turn to supply a mounted camp guard. When the Saracens wanted to enter the camp they waited until the noise of the guard and the horses had gone by; then they made their way into the camp behind the horses, and came out before it was light. The King accordingly ordered the divisions who were in the habit of doing their guard on horseback to do so on foot; thus the whole camp was secured by the guard, who were stationed at intervals that allowed each man to touch his neighbour.

179. After this, the King decided not to leave Damietta until the arrival of his brother, the Count of Poitiers, who was bringing the *arrière-ban** of France. To prevent the Saracen cavalry from charging the camp, he had it closed in by deep ditches. Every night these ditches, and the entrances to the camp, were guarded by crossbowmen and men-at-arms.

180. When the feast of St. Remy* had gone by and there was no news of the Count of Poitiers (which greatly disturbed the King and all the army, who were afraid that some disaster had overtaken him), I reminded the Legate that when we were at sea the Dean of Maurupt had made us hold three processions, on three Saturdays, and that before the third Saturday we landed in Cyprus. The Legate agreed with me and announced that there would be three processions in the camp, on three Saturdays.

181. The first procession started from the Legate's lodging and went to the Church of Notre Dame in the town. This church had been converted from the Saracen mosque, and the Legate had

dedicated it in honour of the Mother of God. On the first two Saturdays the Legate preached in the presence of the King and the men of most note in the army, to whom he gave a plenary indulgence.

182. Before the third Saturday came round the Count of Poitiers arrived; and it was as well that he had not done so earlier, for in that fortnight there was so violent a storm at sea off Damietta that more than two hundred and forty vessels, large and small, were battered to pieces and foundered, with all who were in them lost and drowned. Had the Count of Poitiers arrived earlier he and all his people would have been overwhelmed.

183. On his arrival the King summoned all the barons of the army to decide which road to take, to Alexandria or to Babylon. The good Count Peter of Brittany and the greater part of the barons were agreed that the King should go and besiege Alexandria, because that town had a good harbour where the ships that supplied the army could unload. The Count of Artois was opposed to this and said that there was only one place on which the army should march—Babylon—for it was the capital of the whole Kingdom of Egypt. He said that if your first aim is to kill the snake you must crush its head. The King disregarded all the other suggestions of his barons and followed his brother's plan.

XXXIX

ON THE MARCH TO BABYLON

184. At the beginning of Advent he set out with his army, as the Count of Artois had advised, for Babylon. Quite close to Damietta, we came on a stream which breaks off from the main river. It was decided that the army should halt for a day and dam the stream so that we could cross over. This was done quite easily. We made our dam close up against the river so that the water was turned back into the main stream without difficulty. As we were crossing, the Sultan sent five hundred of the best mounted horsemen in his army to harass the royal army and delay our march.

185. On St. Nicholas' day* the King gave the order to make ready to ride on, with the warning that no one was to be so rash as to charge the Saracens who had appeared. But when the army moved off on its march and the Turks saw that they were not going to be attacked and learnt from their spies of the King's prohibition, they grew bolder and attacked the Templars, who were in the van. One of the Turks bore to the ground a knight of the Temple, right under the hooves of the horse of Brother Renaud of Vichiers, who was at that time the Marshal of the Temple.

186. When he saw this he cried out to his brothers, " At them, in God's name! I can stand no more of this! " He spurred forward, and the whole army followed him. Our horses were fresh, while the enemy's were already tired. Thus it was, as I heard, that not one of them escaped; they were all killed—some of them, who took to the river, being drowned.

XL

Of The Nile

187. But I must first, in order to explain some matters which bear on my story, tell you of the river which flows through Egypt and of the Earthly Paradise. This river is different from all other rivers. Whereas the others are fed by smaller rivers and streams as they continue their downward course, this river has no tributaries. What happens, on the contrary, is that it reaches Egypt by only one channel, and then divides itself into seven branches which spread through the whole country.

188. When the feast of St. Remy is past these seven rivers flood the country and cover the low-lying ground. When the floods subside each peasant goes and ploughs his own ground with a wheel-less plough. With this they turn into the soil wheat, barley, cumin, and rice, and it produces crops that could not be bettered. No one knows whence the flood comes; it must be simply by the will of God. Without it, nothing could be raised in Egypt, for there is no rain and the heat of the sun would burn everything

up. The river is always muddy; when the inhabitants wish to drink it they draw it in the evening and crush three or four almonds or beans in it, and the next morning you could not drink better water.*

189. Before the river reaches Egypt there are people whose practice it is to set nets in it in the evening. When the morning comes they find in them the produce which is imported into this country, ginger, that is, and rhubarb, wood of aloes and cinnamon. These spices are said to come from the Earthly Paradise; they fall from the trees in Paradise, just as dry branches are brought down by the wind in our woods at home. This dry wood which falls into the river is sold by merchants in our own country. The river water has this property, that when we hung it on our tent ropes in the white earthenware pots they make in Egypt it used to become as cool in the heat of the day as fresh spring water.

190. The inhabitants said that the Sultan of Babylon had often tried to find the source of the river; he sent men who carried a supply of a sort of bread they call biscuit (from being twice baked), on which they lived until they came back to the Sultan. They reported that they had explored the river and had reached a high mass of precipitous rocks which it was impossible to climb. The source of the river was in this cliff. There seemed to be a great profusion of trees on the mountain above, and they said that they had found marvellous wild animals of different kinds, lions and snakes and elephants, which came and watched them from upon the river bank while they ascended the stream.

191. But to return to my original subject: I should add that when the river arrives in Egypt it sends out its branches, as I said before. One branch runs to Damietta, another to Alexandria, a third to Taunis, and a fourth to Rexi.* The King of France advanced with his army as far as the Rexi branch and camped between the Damietta and Rexi branches. All the Sultan's forces were camped on the far bank of the Rexi, facing us, to prevent us from crossing. This was an easy task for them, as it was impossible to cross the river to their side except by swimming.

XLI

Attempts to Cross the River: The Sultan Dies

192. The King decided to have a causeway made across the river to cross to the Saracen side. To protect those who were working on it he had two towers made; these are called " cat-castles " for there are two fortified towers in front of the " cats " and two house-like buildings behind the towers to protect the men on watch from the fire of the Saracens' engines, of which they had sixteen ready for action.

193. When we arrived the King had eighteen engines made, with Jocelyn of Cornaut as master-engineer. Our engines bombarded theirs, and theirs returned our fire; but I never heard that ours did much damage. The King's brothers took the daylight watch by the cats and we other knights the night watch. We had now reached the week before Christmas.

194. It was not until the cats were ready that work was started on the causeway, since the King did not wish the men who were carrying the earth to be hit by the Saracens, who could aim and fire on them across the river. In making this causeway the King and all the barons of the army were short-sighted. They had already dammed one of the arms of the river, as I have told you. That was an easy matter, because they were able to build the dam at the point where the branch left the main stream. It was this that made them think that they could dam the Rexi branch, at a point which was already half a league below its separation from the river.

195. To hinder the completion of the King's causeway the Saracens dug deep holes in the bank on their side. As the water reached these holes it poured in and made a new great gap to cross. As a result, they undid in one day the work that had taken us three weeks, by digging out on their side as much as we had filled in on ours.

196. The Sultan had died from the disease he contracted before the city of Homs,* and in his place they had appointed as general a

Saracen called Scecedin, the son of the sheik. It was said that the Emperor Frederick had knighted him. Scecedin sent a part of his army to attack us from the Damietta side; this they did, crossing at a town called Sormesac on the Rexi river.* On Christmas Day I and my knights were dining with my Lord Peter of Avallon. While we were at dinner the enemy galloped up to our camp and killed several poor folk who had gone into the fields on foot. We went to arm ourselves.

197. We returned too late to find our host, my Lord Peter, who had left the camp in pursuit of the Saracens. We spurred after him and rescued him from the enemy, who had thrown him to the ground, and brought him and his brother, the Lord of the Val, back to the camp. The Templars, who had come up as soon as the alarm was given, guarded the rear with steadiness and bravery. The Turks harassed us until we reached the camp. After this the King ordered that our camp should be enclosed by ditches on the Damietta side, from the Damietta river across to the Rexi.

XLII

The Camp is Attacked, and the Saracens Worsted

198. The Turkish general, Scecedin, whom I mentioned before, was the most esteemed of all the pagans. He bore on his banner the arms of the Emperor,* who had made him knight. His banner was barred: on one bar were the Emperor's arms, on the next those of the Sultan of Aleppo, and on the third the arms of the Sultan of Babylon.

199. His name, Scecedin, the son of the sheik, may be rendered " the old one, the son of the old one ". This name counted for much with the pagans, for of all people they pay most honour to the old, when men may see that God has kept them from the tongue of evil until their old age. This bold Turk Scecedin, so the King's spies reported, boasted that on the feast of St. Sebastian* he would dine in the King's pavilions.

200. Knowing this, the King divided the work among his forces;

his brother, the Count of Artois, was to guard the cats and the engines; he himself and the Count of Anjou, who was afterwards King of Sicily, took the duty of guarding the camp on the side of Babylon; while the Count of Poitiers and we of Champagne were appointed to guard the Damietta side. The Turkish prince then sent his forces over to the island* on which we were encamped and which lies between the Damietta and Rexi streams. He drew up his division in a line from one stream across to the other.

201. The King of Sicily attacked and worsted them. Many were drowned in one or other of the streams, but there was still a large number whom we dared not attack, since the fire of the Saracen engines swept the ground between the two rivers. In this attack which the King of Sicily threw against the Turks Count Guy of Forez cut his way through the Turkish ranks on horseback; he and his knights attacked a division of Saracen men-at-arms, who flung him to the ground. His leg was broken, and two of his knights carried him back in their arms. The King of Sicily was with difficulty rescued from the danger into which he had run, and this day's work won him a great name.

202. The Turks attacked the Count of Poitiers and us. We charged them and pursued them for a long time; they lost a number of men, but we came back without loss.

XLIII

GREEK FIRE

203. One night when we were on guard at the cat-castle they brought up an engine called a petrary; this was the first time they had done this, and they loaded the sling with Greek fire.* When the good knight my Lord Walter of Ecurey, who was with me, saw it he said:

204. " My Lords, this is the worst danger we have yet had to face, for if they set fire to our cats and we stand fast we shall be burnt and lost: and if we leave the post we have been given to guard we shall be shamed. No one, then, but God alone can save us

in this peril. My advice is, whenever they launch the fire, get down on hands and knees and pray to Our Lord to preserve us from this danger."

205. As soon as they sent over the first shot, we went on hands and knees as he showed us. The first shot went between our two cats and fell on the dam in front of us which the men had been making to block the stream. Our firemen were ready to put out the blaze, and as the Saracens were prevented from firing directly at them by the wings of the two shelters which the King had had built, they aimed up in the air so that their shots fell right down on them.

206. This is what Greek fire was like: it came straight at you, as big as a vinegar barrel, with a tail of fire behind it as long as a long spear. It made such a noise as it came that it seemed like the thunder of heaven; it looked like a dragon flying through the air. It gave so intense a light that in the camp you could see as clearly as by daylight in the great mass of flame which illuminated everything. Three times that night they bombarded us with Greek fire, and four times they fired it from the revolving cross-bow.*

207. Whenever our holy King heard that they were sending over Greek fire he would rise from his bed and hold up his hands to Our Lord, weeping, and saying, "Dear Lord God, hold my people safe." I do in truth believe that his prayers were of great help to us in our need. In the evening, when the Greek fire had been falling, he would send one of his chamberlains to know how we stood and whether the fire had done us any damage.

208. Once when they were thus bombarding us the fire fell on the river bank, close beside the cat which the men of my Lord of Courtenay were guarding. Up, then, came a knight they called the Albigensian and said to me, "Sir, unless you can give us some help, we shall all be burnt, for the Saracens have put over so many of their fire-bombs that it is like a tall hedge of fire moving on our turret." We jumped down and hurried across, and found that what he said was true. We put out the fire, but before it was extinguished the Saracens opened on us all from across the stream.

XLIV

The Cat-Castles are Burnt

209. By the day the King's brothers were on watch at the cats; they used to climb to the top of the tower and fire bolts from crossbows into their camp. The King had arranged that when the King of Sicily had the day watch at the cats, we should have the night watch. On this particular day we were due to relieve him at night. We were very uneasy in our minds, because the Saracens had given our cats a severe battering. They brought up the petrary in full daylight, a thing they had hitherto done only at night, and were throwing Greek fire at them.

210. They had brought their engines so close to the causeway which the army had made to dam the stream that no one dared approach the cats, for the engines were throwing huge stones which fell on the roadway. As a result our two cats were burnt. The King of Sicily was so beside himself that he wished to hurl himself into the flames and put them out; if he was enraged, I and my knights thanked God—had we had to go on guard that evening, we should all have been burnt.

211. When the King saw what had happened he sent for all the barons of the army and asked each of them to supply him with timber from their ships to make a new cat for the work on the dam. He explained that they must realise that there was no timber with which to make it except from the ships which had brought our baggage up the river. Each man gave what he thought he could spare, and when the cat was built the value of the timber was reckoned at ten thousand pounds or more.

212. The King decided also that the cat should not be pushed along the causeway to take the place of the other two until the day when the King of Sicily, in whose watch they had been burnt, was due to take the watch. His order was carried out. As soon as the King of Sicily came on watch he had the cat pushed right up to the spot where the other two had been burnt.

213. When the Saracens saw this they concentrated the fire of

all their sixteen engines on that part of the causeway on which the cat had been placed. When they saw that our men were chary of approaching the cat, because of the stones which were falling on the causeway along which it had been brought, they brought up the petrary, threw Greek fire at the cat, and burnt it completely. It was a great kindness that God did to me and my knights: we should have had a very dangerous watch that night, as we should also have had on the other night I mentioned.

XLV

THE BEDOUIN'S FORD: THE COUNT OF ARTOIS IS KILLED

214. When the King saw this he summoned all his barons to a council. It was agreed that it would be impossible to build a causeway to cross to the Saracen side, since our men were unable to build up more on their side than the Saracens could dig out on the other. 215. The Constable, my Lord Humbert of Beaujeu, then told the King that a Bedouin had come to him and offered to show him a good ford, on condition that he received five hundred besants. The King said that he agreed that the money should be given to him, so long as he held to his promise. The Constable spoke to the Bedouin, who said that he would not point out the ford until he had first been given the money. This condition was agreed to, and the money was handed over. 216. The King decided that the Duke of Burgundy and the chief men from overseas* who were with the army should act as a protective guard for the camp while he and his three brothers crossed the ford to which the Bedouin was to guide them. This was planned for Shrove Tuesday,* and on that day we went to the Bedouin's ford. As the day was dawning we armed ourselves at all points; when we were ready we entered the stream, our horses being obliged to swim. We were halfway across when we touched ground on which they could get a footing. On the river bank were three hundred or so Saracens, all mounted on horses. 217. I said then to my men, " My Lords, look only to the left,*

and let every man bear in that direction. The banks are wet and the horses are falling on the men and drowning them." It was indeed true that some were drowned in the crossing, among them my Lord John of Orleans, who carried a banner *vivrée*. We kept together and then turned upstream, finding a dry road; and by the mercy of God we crossed without one of us falling. As soon as we were over the Turks fled.

218. It had been arranged that the Temple should form the advance-guard and the Count of Artois have the second division behind them. But what happened was that as soon as the Count had crossed the stream he and his men flung themselves on the Turks, who fled before them. The Templars told him that he was putting a great affront on them by taking the lead when he should have followed them. They asked him to let them go first, as the King had arranged. But the Count of Artois was ashamed to answer them, for my Lord Foucaud of le Merle was holding his horse's bridle. This Foucaud of le Merle, an excellent knight, understood nothing of what the Templars were saying to the Count—he was deaf—and was calling out, "At them! At them!"*

219. When the Templars saw this they thought that they would be disgraced if they allowed the Count to precede them. They spurred their horses and dashed pell-mell after the flying Turks, right through the town of Mansura* and into the fields on the Babylon side. When they wished to turn back the Turks flung posts and beams on them in the narrow streets. There were slain the Count of Artois, the Lord of Coucy, Raoul by name, and other knights whose numbers were estimated at three hundred. The Temple, so the Master told me later, lost two hundred and eighty men-at-arms there, and all mounted.

XLVI

The Battle of Mansura, Shrove Tuesday

220. I and my knights decided to attack a body of Turks who were loading their baggage in their camp on our left, and we

charged them. While we were pursuing them through the camp I saw a Saracen mounting his horse, with one of his knights holding the bridle for him.

221. As he put his two hands on the saddle to mount I gave him my lance under the armpit and threw him down dead. When his knight saw this he left his master and his horse and struck me with his lance, as I passed, between the shoulders, and forced me down on my horse's neck. He held me so firmly that I was unable to draw the sword I carried at my belt, and was obliged to draw the one I carried attached to the harness.* When he saw that I had got my sword drawn he withdrew his lance and left me.

222. When I and my knights came out of the Saracens' camp we found about six thousand Turks, by our reckoning, who had left their tents and retired into the open. When they saw us they charged us and killed my Lord Hugh of Trichâtel,* Lord of Conflans, a banneret of my own company. I and my knights spurred to the rescue of my Lord Raoul of Wanou, also of my company, who had been unhorsed.

223. As I was coming back the Turkish lances struck me; my horse was brought to his knees by the weight of the blow and I was thrown over his ears. I got up as soon as I could, my shield round my neck and my sword in my hand, and my Lord Erard of Siverey (God give him his pardon) of my own company, came up to me and said that we should retire to a ruined house and await the arrival of the King. As we were on our way, some on foot, some mounted, a great horde of Turks fell on us. They flung me to the ground and rode over my body, sending my shield flying from my neck.

224. When they had gone by, my Lord Erard of Siverey came back to me, and brought me away, and we went on, up to the walls of the ruined house. There we were joined again by my Lord Hugh of Ecot, my Lord Frederick of Loupey, and my Lord Renaud of Menoncourt. The Turks attacked us on all sides; a party of them entered the house and thrust at us with their lances from above. My knights then asked me to hold their bridles, which I did, to prevent the horses from bolting. They put up a very strong

defence against the Turks, for which they were praised by all the good knights in the army, both those who had witnessed it and those who had only heard the story.

225. There my Lord Hugh of Ecot was wounded by three lance-thrusts in the face, my Lord Raoul, too, and my Lord Frederick of Loupey by a lance between the shoulders; the wound was so large that the blood poured out of his body as though from the bung of a cask. My Lord Erard of Siverey was struck by a sword across the face, so that his nose fell over his lip. Then my mind turned to my Lord St. James, and I prayed to him, " Dear Lord St. James, help and succour me in my need."

226. I had just finished my prayer, when my Lord Erard of Siverey said to me, " Sir, if you thought that it would be no reproach to me nor my heirs, I would go and ask the Count of Anjou, whom I can see over there in the fields, to come to your assistance. " " My Lord Erard," I answered, " I think that you would win yourself great honour by going to get us help to save our lives, for your own life is in the balance." I spoke no more than the truth, for he died of that wound. He consulted all the knights who were there, and all advised him to do as I said. When he heard this he asked me to release his horse, whose bridle I was holding with the others, and I did so.

227. He went to the Count of Anjou, and asked him to come to the help of me and my knights. A man of high rank who was with him dissuaded him, but the Count of Anjou said that he would do as my knight asked. He turned his horse to come to our assistance, and some of his men-at-arms spurred after him. When the Saracens saw them coming they withdrew from us. In front of the men-at-arms rode my Lord Peter of Auberive, sword in hand. When he saw that our opponents had withdrawn he charged a large body of Saracens who had captured my Lord Raoul of Wanou, and rescued him, severely wounded.

XLVII

MORE OF THE BATTLE

228. While I was on foot with my knights, wounded, as I have already told you, up came the King with his own division; there was a great shouting and a tremendous noise of trumpets and kettle-drums; he halted on a raised roadway. Never have I seen so fine a man in arms; he towered head and shoulders over his people, a gilded helmet on his head, and in his hand a sword of German steel.

229. When he had halted there, the good knights of his household, of whom I spoke before, with some of the brave knights of the King's division, hurled themselves into the midst of the Turks. You must know that this was a grand feat of arms; for there was no shooting of arrows nor bolts; on both sides it was a fight with mace and sword, in a mixed mass of our men and the Turks. One of my squires, who had run away, taking my banner, and come back to me, brought me a Flemish horse* of mine, which I mounted and rode right by the King's side.

230. As we stood there, the good knight, my Lord John of Valery, came to the King and told him that he advised him to bear to the right towards the river, so that we might have the assistance of the Duke of Burgundy and the force which was guarding the camp in our absence, and that his soldiers might drink, for the heat was already great.

231. The King gave orders to his sergeants to fetch the good knights who were his personal councillors, mentioning them all by name. The sergeants searched for them in the thick of the fight between our people and the Turks. The knights came back to the King and he asked their advice. They said that my Lord John of Valery was right. Then the King ordered the ensign of St. Denis and his standard-bearers to bear to the right towards the river. As the King's division moved off there was a new roar of trumpets and drums and Saracen horns.

232. He had hardly left, when he received several messages from his brother, the Count of Poitiers, the Count of Flanders, and some

of the principal men who were in their division, all asking him not to move, since they were so hard pressed by the Turks that they were unable to follow him. The King again assembled all the good knights of his Council, and they advised him to wait. After a little while my Lord John of Valery came back and reproached the King and his Council for delaying. Later, all the Council urged him to move towards the river, as my Lord of Valery had advised.

233. At that moment the Constable, my Lord Humbert of Beaujeu, arrived and told the King that his brother, the Count of Artois, was defending himself in a house at Mansura, and that he should go to his assistance. The King answered, " Lead on, Constable; I will follow you." I told the Constable that he could count me as his knight, and he thanked me heartily. So we set out for Mansura.

234. One of the King's bodyguard* then came to the Constable in a panic and told him that the King had halted and that the Turks had made their way between him and us. We turned back and saw that there was a good thousand of them between us, and we were only six. I then said to the Constable, " Sir, we cannot reach the King through all that mass. Let us go upstream and put this ditch you can see in front of you, between ourselves and the enemy. We shall thus be able to get back to the King." The Constable did as I advised. You can realise that had they noticed us we should all have been killed, but they were concerned only with the King and the other large divisions and thought, accordingly, that we were some of their own men.

XLVIII

The Author Holds a Bridge

235. As we were coming back downstream on the river bank, between the brook and the river, we saw that the King had reached the river and that the Turks were driving back the other royal divisions in a violent attack with sword and mace. They forced them all, including the King's own division, back to the

river, where they were so hard pressed that some of our men tried
to swim across to the Duke of Burgundy's side. But they were
unable to do so; the horses were tired and the day had become
extremely hot. Thus, as we came downstream, we saw the river
covered with lances and shields, with men and horses drowning
and dying.

236. We reached a little bridge over the stream, and I told the
Constable that we should stay and guard this bridge; " for if we
leave it, they will attack the King from this side, and if our men
are attacked from both sides they may well be overwhelmed."
So we held the bridge. It was said that this day we should all have
been lost had it not been for the King in person; for the Lord of
Courtenay and my Lord John of Saillenay told me that six Turks
laid hands on the King's bridle and were dragging him off prisoner.
He saved himself alone by great blows of his sword; and when his
people saw how the King defended himself they took heart, and
many gave up their attempt to cross the river and came back to
his assistance.

237. As we were guarding the bridge, straight to us from the
direction of Mansura came Count Peter of Brittany. He had been
wounded in the face by a sword cut, so that the blood was running down into his mouth. He was mounted on a strong, stocky
cob; he had thrown the reins down on the saddle-bow and was
holding the saddle with both hands, so that his men behind, who
were pressing him hard, might not force him to quicken his pace.*
It was easy to see that he thought little of them, for he was spitting
the blood out of his mouth and repeating, " God's head! Look
at them! Did you ever see such a rabble!" At the tail of his
division came the Count of Soissons and my Lord Peter of Neuville,
who was called " Caier ". They had both taken many a knock in
that day's work.

238. When they had crossed and the Turks saw that we were
holding the bridge and were not afraid to face them they ceased
their attacks. I went to the Count of Soissons, whose cousin I
had married, and said to him, " My Lord, I think that you would
do well to stay and hold this bridge, for if we abandon it the Turks
whom you can see in front of you will cross by it, and the King

will be attacked from front and rear." He asked whether, if he stayed, I would stay with him. " Of course I will," I answered. When the Constable heard us he told me not to leave until he came back, and said he would go and get us some assistance.

XLIX

Further Attacks on the Bridge

239. I stayed there mounted on my horse, and with me stayed the Count of Soissons on my right, and my Lord Peter of Neuville on my left. Then suddenly a Turk came from the direction of the King's division which was in our rear and struck my Lord Peter of Neuville from behind with a mace. The weight of the blow forced him down on the neck of his horse, and the Turk dashed over the bridge and rejoined his own men. When the Turks saw that we were not going to abandon the bridge, they crossed the stream and took up a position between it and the river, as we had done when we were on our way downstream. We moved over towards them, ready to charge them if they tried to attack the King or cross the bridge.

240. There were two of the King's men-at-arms in front of us, the one called William of Boon, the other John of Gamaches. The Turks, who were between the stream and the river, brought up a large company of foot-soldiers, who were flinging clods of earth at them but were unable to make them fall back on us. In the end they brought up another foot-soldier, who three times threw Greek fire at them. On one occasion William of Boon caught the fire-bomb on his buckler; had the fire set light to any part of his clothing he would have been burnt alive.

241. We were covered with the arrows that missed the men-at-arms. Fortunately I found a Saracen's padded jerkin,* stuffed with wadding. I turned the open side towards me and made a shield of the jerkin; it served me well, for I was wounded by the arrows in only five places, while my horse was in fifteen. One of my townsmen from Joinville, also, brought me a banner with my

arms, with a steel lance-head. Every time we saw that the men-at-arms were pressed we charged the Turks and drove them off.

242. While we were there the good Count of Soissons was joking with me and saying, " Seneschal, let these curs howl; by God's bonnet [his favourite oath] you and I shall yet talk in ladies' chambers of this day's work."

L

THE RIVER IS BRIDGED, AND THE CRUSADERS HOLD THE FIELD

243. At sunset that evening the Constable brought us the King's dismounted crossbowmen, who formed up in front of us. As soon as the Saracens saw our men set foot to the stirrup of their bows* they left us and fled. The Constable then said to me, " That was a good piece of work; now go to the King and do not leave him again until he has dismounted and gone to his tent." I had just reached the King, when my Lord John of Valery said to him, " Sir, my Lord of Châtillon begs you to give him the rearguard." The King did so with pleasure, and then moved away. As we were riding I made him take off his helmet, to get some air, and gave him my steel cap.

244. Brother Henry of Ronnay, Provost of the Hospital, who had just crossed the river, then came to the King and kissed his mailed hand and asked him whether he had any news of the Count of Artois, his brother. The King said that indeed he had news of him, for he knew for certain that his brother, the Count of Artois, was in Paradise. " Ah, sir," said the Provost, " be of good comfort; for to no King of France has come such honour as has come to you. To engage your enemy, you have swum a river; and you have beaten and driven them from the field of battle; you have captured their engines and their tents, where tonight you will sleep." The King answered that God should be worshipped for all His gifts to him, and then great tears fell from his eyes.*

245. When we arrived in the Saracen camp we found some of

their foot-soldiers were pulling at the ropes of a tent which they had taken down, while some of our rank and file were pulling on the other side. The Master of the Temple and I attacked them; they fled, and our people kept the tent.

246. During this battle there were many, showy enough in their bearing, who very shamefully withdrew and fled over the bridge of which I have been speaking; they ran in panic and we could not get one of them to stay with us; I could give the names of many, but I shall not do so, seeing that they are dead.

247. But I cannot be silent about my Lord Guy Mauvoisin, for it was with honour that he came out of Mansura. He came downstream the full length of the road which the Constable and I took upstream; and as the Turks forced back the Count of Brittany and his company, so did they my Lord Guy Mauvoisin and his. He and his won great honour from that day's work; and it is not to be wondered at that they bore themselves well, for I was told by those who were well acquainted with his dispositions that almost all his company was made up of knights who were of his own kin or his liegemen.

248. When we had worsted the Turks and driven them from their tents, and our own men had all left the Saracen camp, the Bedouins, of whom there was a very large number, had fallen upon it. They had not left one thing in the camp, but carried off everything that the Saracens had left. I have never heard it said that the Bedouins, who were subject to the Saracens, were thought the worse of for their robbery and pilfering, for it is their regular custom always to attack the weaker side.

LI

THE BEDOUINS

249. As it concerns my story, I must tell you something of what sort of people the Bedouins are. They do not believe in Mahomet, but follow the law of Ali, Mahomet's uncle.* The Old Men of the Mountain,* who maintain the Assassins, share this belief. They believe also that when a man dies for his Lord or in some good

cause his soul passes into a better and happier body than it was clothed with before; thus the Assassins pay little heed to death when they are carrying out the orders of the Old Man of the Mountain. Him, however, we can leave for the moment and speak of the Bedouins themselves.

250. They do not live in towns or cities or castles, but always lie out in the open country. In the evening they set up house for the night—or in the day time if the weather is bad—with their wives and children, in a sort of shelter made of barrel-hoops tied to poles, like the carriages in which ladies ride. Over the hoops they throw sheepskins, prepared with alum, called Damascus skins. They themselves wear big sheepskin cloaks, which cover them completely, right down to their legs and feet.

251. If it rains in the evening and the weather is wild during the night, they wrap themselves up in their cloaks, unbridle their horses and leave them to graze beside them. In the morning they spread the cloaks out in the sun and rub them with a dressing to keep them supple, and afterwards there is nothing to show that they have been soaked all night. They firmly believe that no man can die until his day comes. For this reason they will not wear armour, and when they reproach their children they say, " The curse of the Frank be on you who wears armour because he is afraid of death! " In battle they carry nothing but sword and spear.

252. Nearly all of them wear a garment like a priest's surplice. Their heads are wrapped in towels which go under the chin; this gives them a hideously ugly appearance, since their hair and beards are quite black. They live on the milk of their cattle, and hire grazing for their keep in the fields of the big landowners. It is impossible to estimate their numbers, for there are Bedouins in the Kingdoms of Egypt and Jerusalem and in all the other countries held by Saracens and unbelievers, to whom they pay a large annual tribute.

253. When I got home from overseas I saw some renegade Christians who had adopted the faith of the Bedouins. They maintained that no man could die before his appointed day. This belief of theirs is the extreme of apostasy, because it is as much as to say that God is unable to assist us. It would, indeed, be

foolish of men to serve God if we thought that He has not the power to prolong our lives and preserve us from accidents and troubles; and it is our duty to believe in Him, for all things are in His power.

LII

The Night Attack

254. To continue. That night the King and all of us came back from the dangers of the battle of which I have told you and camped on the spot from which we had driven the enemy. My people, who had stayed in our own camp when we left it, brought me a tent which the Templars had given me, and put it up for me in front of the engines we had captured from the Saracens. The King had some men-at-arms put on guard over the engines.

255. When I was in bed, where I badly needed to be, to rest the wounds that I had received during the day, I got no such repose. Before it was properly daylight there was a shout in our camp, "To arms! To arms!" I roused my chamberlain, who was sleeping at the foot of my bed, and told him to go and see what was happening. He came back terrified and cried, "Up, sir! Get up! The Saracens are on us, horse and foot. They have worsted the King's men-at-arms who were guarding the engines and have forced them back against our tent-ropes."

256. I got up and threw a padded jerkin on my back and a steel cap on my head, and shouted to my men-at-arms, "By St. Nicholas, they shall not stay here long!" Wounded as they were, my knights joined me, and we drove off the Saracen troops from the engines, throwing them back against a large body of Turkish cavalry who had advanced level with the captured engines. I sent to the King for help, for neither I nor my knights were able to put on our hauberks because of our wounds. The King sent my Lord Walter of Châtillon, who placed himself in front, between us and the Turks.

257. When the Lord of Châtillon had repulsed the Saracen foot

they fell back on a large body of Turkish cavalry; this was drawn up opposite our camp to prevent us from surprising their main army which was encamped behind them. Eight of the leaders of this body of cavalry, heavily armed, had dismounted and built up a breastwork of masonry as a protection against our crossbowmen. These eight Saracens were firing volleys into our camp, and wounded some of our men and some horses.

258. I and my knights had a discussion and decided that when it was night we would carry off the stones which sheltered them. A priest in my company (his name was my Lord John of Voisey) had his own ideas* on the matter and decided not to wait. He went out alone from our camp towards the Saracens, wearing a padded jerkin, and a steel cap on his head; he carried his spear under his arm, but with the point trailing behind him, so that the Saracens might not notice it.

259. When he was close to the Saracens, who, seeing that he was alone, paid little attention to him, he drew the spear from under his arm and rushed on them. Not one of the eight put up any defence; they all turned tail. When the mounted Saracens saw that their lords were put to flight they spurred their horses to rescue them, while half a hundred men-at-arms sallied out from our camp. The Saracen horsemen came on at the gallop, but shirked a fight with our men and swerved away.

260. This had happened two or three times, when one of our men-at-arms grasped his spear by the middle, flung it at a Turkish horseman, and caught him between the ribs; the man who was hit went off with the steel in his ribs and the shaft trailing. When the Turks saw this, they were afraid to come within range, and our men-at-arms carried off the stones. In future my priest was well known in the camp, and men pointed him out to one another, saying, " There goes my Lord of Joinville's priest, the man who routed the eight Saracens."

LIII

The Battle on Friday

261. All this happened on Ash Wednesday. The same day, a bold Saracen,* whom the enemy had made their leader in the place of Scecedin, the son of the sheik, whom they had lost in Shrove Tuesday's battle, took the coat of the Count of Artois, who had been killed in the same fight, and displayed it to the Saracen army, telling them that it was the King who had been killed and that this was his coat of arms.

262. " I show you this," he said, " because a body without a head is not to be feared, nor a people without a King. On Friday, then, we will attack them, if you agree; as, indeed, I think you must, for, since they have lost their leader, we cannot fail to take them." They all agreed to make the assault on Friday.

263. The King's spies in the Saracen camp reported this to him. He accordingly ordered all the leaders of divisions to have their men ready armed from midnight onwards, and to leave the tents for a position by the barricade; this was built of long lengths of timber, to prevent the Saracens from riding into the camp, but these were so fixed in the ground as to allow a man to get through them on foot. The King's orders were carried out.

264. Precisely at sunrise the Saracen I mentioned as having been made their leader brought up a force of four thousand mounted Turks, and stationed them in a ring round our camp, with himself in the centre, stretching from the river which comes down from Babylon to the one that flowed from our camp towards a town called Risil.* They then brought up a large body of their infantry, which formed a second circle round our camp, similar to that formed by the cavalry. In reserve, to reinforce these two bodies where necessary, they drew up the entire army of the Sultan of Babylon.

265. When they had done this, their general rode out alone on a pony to examine the dispositions of our camp; and when he saw that our divisions were stronger in one part than in another he

went back to bring up more of his own men and reinforce his line against ours. Afterwards, he sent the Bedouins, who numbered some three thousand, to cross over to the camp (lying between the two streams), which was guarded by the Duke of Burgundy. This he did in the hope that the King would send a part of his force to reinforce the Duke against the Bedouins, and would thereby weaken his main army.

LIV

Of the Same

266. He spent until midday in those arrangements. Then he had the kettledrums (nakirs, they call them) beaten, and they fell on us, horse and foot. I must tell you first of the King of Sicily (the Count of Anjou, as he then was), since he was stationed at the beginning of our line in the direction of Babylon. They opened the attack on him in the same way as a game of chess is played; first they sent the infantry against him, who threw Greek fire; then infantry and cavalry both pressed the King of Sicily so hard, who was on foot among his knights, that they were getting the better of him.

267. A message was sent to the King telling him of his brother's plight. When he heard how things were he spurred, sword in hand, through his brother's division and flung himself so far into the Turkish ranks that his horse's crupper was caught by the Greek fire. This charge of the King's relieved the King of Sicily and his men, and they drove the Turks out of their part of the camp.

268. Next to the King of Sicily's division was that of the overseas barons, led by my Lord Guy of Ibelin and his brother Baldwin. After them came the division of my Lord Walter of Châtillon, a body of good soldiers and fine knights. These two divisions resisted so vigorously that the Turks were never able to break their ranks or force them back.

269. After my Lord Walter's division was Brother William of Sonnac, the Master of the Temple, with the few brothers left

to him after Tuesday's battle. In front of his position he had built a barricade made from the Saracen engines we captured. When the Saracens launched their attack they threw Greek fire on this barricade. The fire took readily, as the Templars had included in it a great many planks of pine. The Turks, moreover, did not wait until the fire had burnt itself out, but charged the Templars through the flames.

270. In this fight Brother William, the Master of the Temple, lost an eye. He had lost the other on Shrove Tuesday; and of this wound he died—God grant him his pardon. There was an area of ground, if you can imagine it, behind the Templars, as large as a day's work for a man, which was so covered by arrows the Saracens had shot at them that not an inch of earth could be seen between the shafts.

271. After the division of the Temple was that of my Lord Guy Mauvoisin, against which the Turks had no success; they continually inundated him with Greek fire, and his men had great difficulty in putting it out.

LV

THE SARACENS ARE BEATEN OFF

272. The barricade which enclosed our camp ran down from my Lord Guy Mauvoisin's division to within a fair stone's throw from the river. From there it went in front of the encampment of Count William of Flanders, and stretched as far as the main river which runs to the sea. Opposite the barricade which ran down from my Lord Guy Mauvoisin was our division. As Count William of Flanders' force was facing the Saracens, they were afraid to approach us. God was indeed gracious to us, for I and my knights were unable to wear hauberks or shields because of the wounds we had all received on Shrove Tuesday.

273. The enemy made a sharp and vigorous attack on the Count of Flanders, with cavalry and infantry. Seeing this, I ordered our crossbowmen to fire on the cavalry. When these saw what losses we were causing them they turned tail; and when the Count's

men saw their flight they left the camp, came through the barricade, charged the Saracen infantry and worsted them. Some of the enemy were killed and some lost their bucklers. Walter of la Horgne, my Lord of Apremont's standard-bearer, there distinguished himself by his vigour.

274. After the Count of Flanders' division came that of the Count of Poitiers, the King's brother. His division was on foot, with the Count himself alone on horseback. The Turks overwhelmed this division and took the Count prisoner. When the butchers and other camp servants and the women who sold provisions heard of his capture they raised the alarm in the camp and with the help of God rescued the Count and drove the Turks out of the camp.

275. After the Count of Poitiers' division was that of my Lord Josserand of Brancion, who had accompanied the Count to Egypt, one of the best knights in the army. He had so disposed his force that all his knights were on foot, while he and his son, my Lord Henry, and the son of my Lord Josserand of Nanton were mounted. These two he kept on horseback, because they were still untried boys. Several times the Turks were getting the better of his men, but whenever he saw them being mastered he spurred and took the Turks in the rear, and they left his men to turn their attack on him.

276. Even so, this would not have saved them from falling to the Turks on the field of battle, had it not been for my Lord Henry of Cône, who was in the Duke of Burgundy's camp, a prudent knight, brave and resourceful; whenever he saw the Turks attacking my Lord of Brancion he had the King's crossbowmen fire on them across the river. In the end the Lord of Brancion came out of that distressful day with the loss of twelve knights out of twenty in his own company, in addition to other men-at-arms. He himself was so rudely handled that he could never afterwards stand on his feet, and of this wound, received in the service of God, he died.

277. I must tell you of the Lord of Brancion. When he died he had taken part in thirty-six battles and fights in which he had won the prize for bravery. I saw him once in a troop of the Count of Chalon, whose cousin he was. It was a Good Friday, and he

came to me and my brother and said to us, " My nephews, come and give me your help, you and your men, for the Germans are breaking into the church." We went with him and attacked them with drawn swords, and, with great difficulty, after a hard fight we drove them out of the church.

278. Afterwards, the good man knelt in front of the altar and prayed out loud to Our Lord for His grace, saying, " Lord, have pity on me, I beg You, and take me from these wars between Christians, in which I have lived so long, and grant me the boon of dying in Your service, that so I may have Your Kingdom of Paradise." I tell you this because I believe it was God who, as you may see from what I have just told you, answered his prayer.

279. After this battle on the first Friday in Lent the King summoned all his barons before him and said to them, " We should be very grateful to God for the double honour He has granted us this week, of driving the enemy on Shrove Tuesday from their camp, where we are now lodged, and on the next Friday, which has just passed, of beating off their attack, though they were mounted and we were on foot." He spoke further, and the nobility of his words heartened them.

LVI

The Mamluks

280. To keep our story clear, we must digress a little in order to understand how the Sultans maintained the order and disposition of their troops. The truth is that they recruited the greater part of their cavalry* from foreigners whom merchants obtained abroad in order to re-sell them. The Sultans were ready buyers, and at a high price. The men whom the merchants brought to Egypt were obtained in the East; for when one Eastern king had overcome another he took the poor of the population he had conquered and sold them to the merchants. These came to Egypt to re-sell them.

281. The system was so organised that the children were brought up by the Sultan in his household, until their beards began to

grow. According to their age, he had bows made to fit their strength; and as soon as they grew stronger they returned the weaker bows to the Sultan's arsenal, and the master armourer gave them bows as strong as they could bend.

282. The Sultan's arms were *or*, and these young soldiers wore the same arms as he did. They were called *baharis*.* As soon as they were old enough to grow a beard the Sultan knighted them. They wore his arms, but with a difference—scarlet devices, for example, or roses, or bands, or birds, or other emblems, super-imposed at their choice on the golden shield.

283. The men of whom I am speaking were known as " of the Halca ",* for the *baharis* slept in the Sultan's tents. When the Sultan was in the camp the Halca guard were lodged around his quarters and maintained as his personal guard. There was a small tent by the door of the Sultan's lodging, in which lay his door-keepers and musicians, the latter with Saracen horns and drums and kettledrums. At sunrise and sunset they raised such a noise that those who were close to them could not hear one another speak, and they could be heard without difficulty anywhere in the camp.

284. But the musicians would never have dared to sound their instruments in the daytime without an order from the commander of the Halca. The arrangement was that when the Sultan had an order to give he sent for the Commander of the Halca and entrusted it to him. The Commander had the Sultan's instruments sounded and the whole army came to hear the order. The Commander announced it, and they all carried it out.

285. When the Sultan went to war he promoted the knights of the Halca, according to the merit they showed in battle, to be emirs and put them in charge of a company of two hundred or three hundred knights; the better their showing, the larger the command the Sultan gave them.

286. When these knights have reached the height of renown and wealth, and the Sultan is afraid that they may kill or dispossess him, the reward that then awaits them is to be arrested by him and put to death in his prisons, their wives, too, forfeiting every-thing they own. This is what the Sultan did to those who captured

the Count of Montfort and the Count of Bar. Boudendars
treated in the same way those who overcame the King of Armenia.
He was hunting wild beasts, when, thinking to have a reward,
they dismounted and approached him on foot with a salute. He
answered, " I have no salute for you," for they had interrupted his
hunt. And he had them beheaded.*

LVII

THE NEW SULTAN

287. But to return to our story. The Sultan who died had a son
aged twenty-five, clever, cunning, and minded to evil. Fearing
that he might dispossess him, he had given him one of his
dominions in the East. Now that the Sultan was dead, the emirs
sent for the son. No sooner had he arrived in Egypt than he
stripped his father's seneschal, and constable, and marshal, of
their golden rods of office, and gave them to men who had come
with him from the East.

288. When they saw what had been done to them they and all the
other members of the father's council were greatly angered by the
insult. Fearing, moreover, that he might treat them as his father
had treated the men who captured the Count of Bar and the Count
of Montfort (as I mentioned before), they came to an agreement
with the Halca—the Sultan's personal guard of whom I spoke—
by which the latter undertook, when called upon, to assassinate
the Sultan.

LVIII

DISTRESS IN THE CHRISTIAN CAMP

289. It was after the two battles I have described that our situation
in the camp began to look serious. At the end of nine days the
corpses of our dead rose to the surface of the water; this was said
to be caused by the putrefaction of the gall. They floated as far as

the bridge between our two camps, which they were unable to pass under, because the bridge touched the water. There were so many of them that the whole river was filled with corpses from one bank to the other, and as far back as you could throw a small stone. 290. The King had hired a hundred labourers, who spent a good week at the work. They threw the Saracen corpses, which were circumcised, over to the other side of the bridge and let the stream carry them away. The Christians they laid all together in deep trenches. There I saw the Count of Artois' chamberlains and many others searching for their friends among the dead, but I never heard that any had been recognised.

291. During the whole of Lent we ate no fish except eels; and the eels, which are ravenous feeders, fed on the corpses. It was this wretched diet and the unhealthiness of the country, where not a drop of rain falls, that brought upon us the " camp fever "* which caused the flesh on our legs to dry up completely and the skin to become covered with black and earth-coloured spots, just like an old boot. When we caught the disease the flesh on our gums began to rot away. Nobody recovered from it, and it was always fatal. Bleeding at the nose was a sure sign of the approach of death.

292. A fortnight later the Turks, in order to starve us out, took some of their galleys from above our camp—which was a surprise to many—dragged them over land, and placed them a good league below the camp in the river which was our communication with Damietta. These galleys caused a famine, for they made it impossible for anyone to come to us upstream from Damietta with provisions. We knew nothing of this blockade until a small vessel belonging to the Count of Flanders, which eluded them with the help of the current, brought us the news and told us that the Sultan's galleys had captured eighty of ours coming from Damietta and killed those on board.

293. Prices in the camp rose so much as a result of this that by Easter an ox cost eighty pounds, a sheep thirty, a pig thirty, an egg twelve deniers, and a measure of wine ten pounds.

LIX .

THE CRUSADERS RETIRE OVER THE RIVER

294. When the King and the barons realised our position they decided that the King should move his camp from the Babylon side of the river to the Duke of Burgundy's camp on the branch which runs to Damietta. In order to get his men across with greater safety the King had a barbican built in front of the bridge between the two camps, so constructed as to allow the passage of mounted men in either direction.

295. When the barbican was ready all in the King's camp armed themselves. The Turks made a heavy attack on them, but the King and his men did not fall back until all the baggage had been carried over. The King then crossed, followed by his own company, and then all the barons except my Lord Walter of Châtillon, who had the rearguard. Just as they were entering the barbican my Lord Erard of Valery* rescued his brother, my Lord John, whom the Turks were carrying off prisoner.

296. When the whole army had crossed over, those who stayed in the barbican were very hard pressed. The barbican was not high, and they were fully exposed to the fire of the mounted Saracens, while the foot soldiers were flinging clods of earth right in their faces. They would all have been lost had it not been for the Count of Anjou (who afterwards became the King of Sicily), who went to their rescue and brought them back to safety. Of all those who were in the barbican, the prize that day was won by my Lord Geoffrey of Mussambourc.

297. On the eve of Shrove Tuesday I witnessed a remarkable event, of which I must tell you. On that day my Lord Hugh of Landricourt, a knight banneret who was in my company, was buried. He lay on a bier in my chapel, and six of my knights were there, leaning on some sacks of barley. As they were talking loudly in my chapel and disturbing the priest by their noise, I went and told them to be quiet and that it was disgraceful for knights and gentlemen to talk while Mass was being sung.

298. They began to laugh and told me, laughing, that they were finding a new husband for his wife. I reproved them and told them that that was not a charitable or honourable way to speak and that it had not taken them long to forget their comrade. And such was the vengeance of God, that the next day was the great battle of Shrove Tuesday, in which all six were killed or mortally wounded; and it was their wives who needed new husbands.

LX

A TRUCE IS DISCUSSED

299. As a result of the wounds I received on Shrove Tuesday the camp fever attacked me in the mouth and legs; this was accompanied by a double tertian fever and so severe a cold in the head that phlegm ran out of my head through the nostrils. These attacks forced me at mid-Lent to take to my bed. My priest, accordingly, used to sing Mass in my tent, at the foot of my bed; and he was suffering from the same disease as I was.

300. Once he fainted at the Consecration. When I saw that he was going to fall I leapt out of bed barefoot—I was already wearing my tunic—and took him in my arms and told him to take his time and go through with the Consecration, for I should not leave him until he had done. He recovered from his faintness and completed the Consecration, and finished singing the whole Mass; and never again did he sing Mass.

301. It was after this that the King's Council and the Sultan's Council fixed a day on which to come to terms.* The conditions of the agreement were that Damietta should be surrendered to the Sultan, and that the Sultan should surrender to the King the Kingdom of Jerusalem. The Sultan was to look after the sick in Damietta, the salted meats (for the Saracens ate no pork) and the King's engines, until the King should be able to send and fetch them.

302. They asked the King's Council what security they could give them for the return of Damietta. The Council offered them as a

hostage for the surrender one of the King's brothers, either the Count of Anjou or the Count of Poitiers. The Saracens replied that they would not agree unless the King in person was left as a pledge. Of this the good knight, my Lord Geoffrey of Sargines, said that he would rather that they should all be killed or captured by the Saracens than that they should be reproached with having left the King as a pledge.

303. The epidemic in the camp began to grow worse; our men had so much dead flesh on their gums that the barbers had to remove it to enable them to chew food and swallow. It was most pitiful to hear all over the camp the moans of men from whom the dead flesh was being cut away, for they moaned just like women in the pains of childbirth.

LXI

THE RETREAT FROM MANSURA

304. When the King saw that to stay where we were meant death for himself and his people he gave orders and made arrangements to move at nightfall on the Tuesday after the Octave of Easter, in an attempt to reach Damietta. He sent word to the sailors in charge of the galleys to gather all the sick and convey them to Damietta; and he ordered Jocelyn of Cornaut and his brothers and the other engineers to cut the ropes which fastened the bridge between us and the Saracens; but this they failed to do.

305. We embarked on the Tuesday, in the afternoon after dinner, myself and the two knights that were left to me, and my servants. When night began to fall I told my sailors to raise the anchor so that we could go downstream; they answered that they were afraid to do so, because the Sultan's galleys, which were between us and Damietta, would kill us. The sailors had built large fires to give them light while they collected the sick into their galleys, and the sick had gathered on the river bank. While I was telling the sailors that we should be moving, the Saracens made their way into the camp, and by the light of the fires I saw them slaughtering the sick on the bank.

306. While my sailors were raising the anchor, those who were to bring off the sick cut the anchor-cables and mooring ropes of their galleys and ran alongside our little vessel, hemming us in on both sides, so that they nearly capsized us in the water. When we had extricated ourselves from this danger and were making our way downstream, the King, who was suffering from the camp fever and a very severe dysentery, could well have found safety in the galleys had he wished. But he said that, please God, he would not desert his people. That night he fainted several times, and his dysentery was so bad that it was necessary, so often was he obliged to go to the latrine, to cut away the lower part of his drawers.

307. As we were going downstream we were shouted at to wait for the King, and when we refused to do so we were fired on with crossbows. We had to stop, accordingly, until they gave us permission to sail.

LXII

THE KING IS CAPTURED

308. I must break off at this point and tell you how the King was captured, as he described it to me himself. He said that he had left his own division and, with my Lord Geoffrey of Sargines, joined that of my Lord Walter of Châtillon, who commanded the rearguard.

309. The King told me, too, that he was riding a cob, covered with a silken housing, and that behind him, of all his knights and men-at-arms, there remained only my Lord Geoffrey of Sargines, who led the King as far as the village in which he was taken. Speaking of the way in which he escorted him, the King told me that my Lord Geoffrey of Sargines protected him from the Saracens like a good servant protecting his master's cup from flies; every time the Saracens approached, he took his spear, which he kept between himself and his saddle-bow, couched it under his armpit, and charged them again and drove them away from the King.

310. So he conducted the King as far as the village. There they took him into a house and laid him in the lap of a woman, a Parisian,

and he almost like a dead man so that they thought that he would not see that night. There came my Lord Philip of Montfort* and told the King that he could see the emir with whom he had discussed the truce; if the King wished, he would go to him and arrange a truce again on the terms the Saracens offered. The King said that he agreed, and begged him to go. He went to the Saracen, who had his turban off his head and took the ring from his finger as an assurance that he would respect the truce.

311. Meanwhile a great misfortune had befallen our people. A treacherous man-at-arms called Marcel began to shout to them, " My Lords, knights, surrender yourselves, for it is the King's order, and do not cause the King to be slain! " They all believed that it was indeed the King's order and surrendered their swords to the Saracens. The emir saw that the Saracens were already leading off our men as prisoners and told my Lord Philip that there was no need for him to grant terms of truce to them, since he could see that they were already captured.

312. Although all our people were taken prisoner, my Lord Philip himself was left free in virtue of being an envoy. But they have a bad custom in the country of the infidels, by which when the King sends envoys to the Sultan, or the Sultan to the King, should the King or the Sultan die before their return the envoys are imprisoned or enslaved, to whichever party they may belong, Christian or Saracen.

LXIII

The Author is Intercepted by Saracen Galleys

313. While our people on land had the misfortune of being taken prisoner, the same happened to us on the river, as you will shortly hear. The wind was blowing in our direction from Damietta and deprived us of the advantage of the current. The knights, too, whom the King had embarked in his boats to protect the sick, fled. Our sailors missed the main stream of the river and took a backwater from which we had to return towards the Saracens.

314. A little before dawn broke, we who were going by water came

to the stretch in which were the Sultan's galleys which had prevented provisions from coming to us from Damietta. There was
a tremendous hubbub. They were firing such a quantity of bolts
armed with Greek fire at us and at those of our mounted men who
were on the river bank that it seemed as though the stars were
falling from the sky.

315. When our sailors had brought us back from the arm of the
river into which they had turned, we met—flying towards Damietta—the boats which the King had given us for the defence of
the sick. A wind then rose from that direction, of such force that
the current was of no service to us.

316. By both banks of the river there was a great number of our
people's vessels which were unable to go downstream and had been
held up and captured by the Saracens. They were killing the men
and throwing them into the water, and robbing our ships of their
chests and baggage. Their cavalry on the bank were firing bolts
at us because we were refusing to pull into them. My people had
put a jousting hauberk over me to save me from being wounded
by the bolts which were falling into our vessel.

317. At that moment my people who were forward in the bows
called out to me, " Sir, sir, the sailors are frightened by the
Saracens' threats and mean to put you on shore." Weak as I was,
I had myself hoisted up by the arms and drew my sword on them
and told them that if they put me on shore I should kill them.
They answered that I could make my own choice: either they could
put me on shore, or they could anchor for me in the middle of the
stream until the wind should fall. I told them that I would rather
they anchored than put me on shore where I could see our men
being slaughtered; and they accordingly anchored.

318. It was not long before we saw four of the Sultan's galleys
approaching, with a good thousand men on board. Then I called
my knights and my men and I asked them which they would
prefer that we should do: surrender to the Sultan's galleys or
surrender to the enemy on land. We all agreed that we should
prefer to surrender to the galleys, where we would be kept all
together, rather than to the Saracens on land, who would divide us
up and sell us to the Bedouins.

319. Then one of my store-keepers, who was born at Doulevant, said, " Sir, I cannot agree with that advice." I asked him to what he would agree, and he answered, " I think that we should all allow ourselves to be killed and thus we shall all go to Paradise." But we paid no attention to him.

LXIV

THE AUTHOR IS CAPTURED

320. When I saw that we were bound to be captured I took my jewel-box and jewels and threw them in the river, and my relics with them. One of my sailors then said to me, " Sir, unless you allow me to say that you are the King's cousin you will all be killed, and we too." I told him that he might say what he pleased. When the men in the first galley, who were preparing to ram our vessel, heard what he said, they anchored close by us.

321. It was then that God sent me a Saracen,* a man who came from one of the Emperor's possessions. He was dressed in a pair of drawers of unbleached linen and swam across the river to our vessel. He took me by the waist and said, " Sir, unless you look to yourself quickly, you are lost; you must jump from your vessel on to the beak of this galley; they will not notice you if you jump— their minds are on what they can loot in your ship." They threw me a rope from the galley, and by God's grace I jumped into the bows. But I may tell you that I was trembling so much that if the Saracen had not jumped after me and supported me I should have fallen into the water.

322. They took me into the galley, in which there were at least two hundred and eighty of their men, and all the time he held me firmly. Then I was thrown on the ground and they fell on me to cut my throat, for whoever murdered me would have thought to win honour for himself. But the Saracen continued to hold me firm and shouted, " The King's cousin! " In this way I was twice thrown to the ground, and once to my knees, and it was then I felt the knife at my throat. From this extremity God saved me through

the help of the Saracen, who brought me to the aftercastle in which were the Saracen knights.

323. When I came among them they took off my hauberk, and, taking pity on my condition, they threw over me a scarlet blanket I had, lined with miniver, which my Lady my mother had given me, and someone else brought me a white belt. I tied it round the blanket I had put on, in which I had made a hole. Another brought me a hood, which I drew over my head. But then, from the state of terror I was in, I began to tremble violently, though this was also due to my sickness. I asked them for something to drink, and they brought me some water in a jar, but as soon as I filled my mouth to swallow it, it poured out of my nostrils.

324. When I saw this I sent for my people and told them I was a dead man, for I had a tumour in my throat. They asked me how I knew, and I showed them; as soon as they saw the water pouring out of my mouth and nostrils they began to weep. When the Saracen knights who were present saw my folk weeping they asked the Saracen who had saved us why they were doing so. He answered that he thought that I had a tumour in my throat from which I should not recover. Then one of the knights told the man who had looked after us to console us, since he would give me something to drink which would cure me in two days. And this he did.

325. My Lord Raoul of Wanou, who was in my party, had had the muscles at the back of the knees cut through in the battle of Shrove Tuesday and was unable to stand on his feet; and I should tell you that an old Saracen knight, who was in the galley, used to carry him to the latrine hanging from his neck.

LXV

TREATMENT OF THE PRISONERS

326. The chief emir in command of the galleys sent for me and asked me if I were the King's cousin. I answered that I was not, and told him how and why the sailor had said that I was. He told

me that I had been wise, for otherwise we should all have been killed. Then he asked me whether I was any relation to the Emperor Frederick of Germany, who was then still alive. I answered that I thought my Lady my mother was his cousin,* and he said that he liked me the better for it.

327. As we were eating, he had a man brought before us, a Parisian. When the Parisian came, he said, " Sir, what you are doing? " " What am I doing? " I answered. " In God's name," he said, " you are eating meat on a Friday." When I heard this, I pushed my plate away. The emir asked my Saracen why I had done so; he told him, and the emir said that God would not hold it against me, because I had done it unknowingly.

328. The Legate, too, I should add, told me the same thing when we came out of prison. But even so, I always fasted on bread and water every Friday in Lent afterwards, which made the Legate very angry* with me, as I was the only man of any position who had stayed with the King.

329. The next Sunday the emir had me landed on the river bank, myself and the others who had been taken prisoner on the water. As they were dragging my Lord John, my good priest, out of the hold of the galley he fainted. He was killed and thrown into the river. His clerk, who also fainted from the camp fever from which he was suffering, was beaten over the head with a stone mortar, killed, and thrown into the river.

330. As they were landing the other sick from the galleys in which they had been imprisoned there were Saracens standing ready, with naked swords, and any who fell they killed and threw in. I told them, through my Saracen, that I thought they were doing a wicked thing, for it was contrary to the teaching of Saladin, who said that you should kill no man when once you have given him of your bread and salt to eat. The emir answered that the men were of no value since their disease had made them helpless.

331. He had my sailors brought before me and told me that they had all renounced their faith. I answered that he should not rely too much on their conversion: they would leave the Saracens as quickly as they had left us when time and place were opportune. The emir's reply was that he agreed with me, for Saladin used to

say that you never saw a good Saracen made of a bad Christian,
nor a good Christian of a bad Saracen.

332. After this, he mounted me on a pony and led me by his side.
We crossed over a bridge of boats and came to Mansura, where
the King and his people were held prisoner. We went to the
entrance of a large pavilion in which were the Sultan's clerks,
and there they wrote down my name. Then my Saracen said to me,
" Sir, I must leave you now for I can come with you no farther.
But I beg you, sir, always to hold by the hand this child you have
with you, so that the Saracens may not take him away." The
child was called Bartlemy, and he was a bastard son of the Lord of
Montfaucon.

333. When my name had been recorded the emir took me to the
pavilion in which were the barons and more than ten thousand
others with them. When I came in the barons were all so delighted
that you could not hear a word; they praised Our Lord and said
that they thought they had lost me.

LXVI

The Prisoners are Threatened, but Hear that the King has Arranged for their Release

334. We had been there but a short while, when they took away
one of the chief men who was with us and led us to another pavilion. The Saracens were holding many knights and others in a
courtyard which was shut in by an earthen wall. They had them
brought one by one from this enclosure in which they had confined them and asked them, " Will you renounce your faith? "
Those who refused were put on one side and their heads were cut
off; the renegades were put on the other side.

335. At this moment the Sultan sent his Council to speak with
us. They asked to whom they should address the Sultan's
message, and we told them that they should speak to the good
Count Peter of Brittany. There were men present called drago-
mans, who knew both Saracen and French and they translated

the Saracen into French for Count Peter. Their message was, " Sir, the Sultan sends us to you to know whether you wish to be set free." " Yes," answered the Count.

336. " And what will you give the Sultan in return for your freedom? " " Whatever we can reasonably do and afford," answered the Count. " Will you give," they said, " in return for your freedom, any of the castles which are in the hands of the overseas barons? " The Count answered that it was impossible for him to do so; they were held from the Emperor of Germany, who was still alive. They asked whether we would surrender, against our freedom, any of the castles belonging to the Temple or the Hospital. The Count said that that was impossible; that when wardens were appointed to the castles they were made to swear on the Holy Gospels that for no man's ransom would they surrender any castle. They answered that we seemed to have little desire for freedom; they would leave us and send those to us who would show us some swordplay, as they had to the others. Then they went away.

337. As soon as they had gone a great horde of young Saracens burst into our pavilion, swords in their belts. They brought with them a very old man, quite white, who had us asked whether we believed in a God who had been imprisoned, wounded, and killed for us, and on the third day had risen from the dead. We answered that we did, and he then told us that we should not lose heart at having suffered these trials for His sake, for, said he, " You have not yet died for Him as He died for you; and if He had the power to rise from the dead, you may be sure that He will set you free when it pleases Him to do so."*

338. Then he went away, and all the young men followed him. I was greatly relieved by this, since I thought for certain that they had come to cut off our heads. Shortly afterwards men came from the Sultan and told us that the King had arranged for us to be set free.

339. After the old man who had comforted us had gone the Sultan's Council came back to us and said that the King had arranged for our freedom and that we should send him four of our people to hear the terms. We sent my Lord John of Valery, that

excellent knight, my Lord Philip of Montfort, my Lord Baldwin of Ibelin, the Seneschal of Cyprus, and my Lord Guy of Ibelin, the Constable of Cyprus, than whom I have seen few knights of better parts and none who loved better the people of this country. These four lords came back and told us how the King had arranged for our release, and the story was as follows:

LXVII

St. Louis Threatened with Torture: Terms of Truce

340. The Sultan's Council tested the King in the same way as they had tested us, to see whether he would promise to surrender any of the castles of the Temple or the Hospital or of the Syrian barons. By God's will, the King gave them the same answer as we had done. They threatened him and said that as he would not agree they would have him put in the bernicles.*

341. The bernicles are the most cruel torture you can suffer. They consist of two pliable lengths of wood, armed at the end with teeth. They fit together and are lashed at the end with strong oxhide thongs. When they wish to put people in them they lay the victims on their sides and insert their legs between the teeth. Then they have a man sit on the planks. The result is that there is not six inches of unbroken bone left in the legs. To make the torture as severe as possible, at the end of three days, when the legs are swollen, they place them in the bernicles again and break them afresh. To these threats the King answered that he was their prisoner and that they could do with him as they wished.

342. When they saw that their threats could not master the good King, they asked him how much money he would pay the Sultan, Damietta to be surrendered in addition. The King answered that if the Sultan would accept a reasonable sum from him he would send and ask the Queen to pay it for their release. "How is it," they said, "that you will not undertake yourself to pay the ransom?" The King answered that the Queen was his lady and

mistress and he did not know whether she would be willing. The Council then went back to consult the Sultan and returned with a message to the King that he would set the King free if the Queen would pay one million gold besants, which was the equivalent of five hundred thousand pounds.

343. The King asked them, on their oath, whether the Sultan would release them for that sum if the Queen was willing. They went back to consult the Sultan, and when they returned they swore to the King that they would release him on those terms. As soon as they had sworn, the King spoke and promised the emirs freely to pay the five hundred thousand pounds for the freedom of his people, and Damietta for the release of his own person, since a man of his position should not be ransomed for money. When the Sultan heard this, he said, "By my faith, it is liberal of the Frank not to have haggled over so large a sum of money. Go tell him," said the Sultan, "that I make him a present of one hundred thousand pounds towards the ransom."

LXVIII

The Sultan's Lodging

344. Then the Sultan had the men of rank embarked on four galleys, to take them to Damietta. In the galley in which I was put were also the good Count Peter of Britanny, Count William of Flanders, the good Count John of Soissons, my Lord Humbert of Beaujeu, the Constable of France, the good knight my Lord Baldwin of Ibelin, and my Lord Guy, his brother.

345. Those who were taking us in the galley brought us opposite a lodging which the Sultan had had put up by the river. I will explain how it was made. In front of the lodging was a tower of fir-poles covered with dyed cloth. This was the entrance to the lodging. Beyond this door a pavilion was erected in which the emirs, when they went to speak with the Sultan, left their swords and equipment. Beyond this pavilion there was another entrance like the first, and through this one went into a large pavilion which

was the Sultan's hall. Beyond the hall was a tower like the first one, through which one entered the Sultan's chamber.

346. Behind the chamber was a courtyard, and in the middle of it a tower higher than the others; this the Sultan used to climb to look over all the countryside and the camp. From the courtyard an alley ran to the river, where the Sultan had had a pavilion erected in the water for bathing. The whole lodging was enclosed by wooden trellis-work covered with indigo cloth, so that those outside could not see within, and all four towers were also covered with cloth.

347. We arrived at this place in which the Sultan's quarters had been built on the Friday before the Ascension,* and the four galleys in which we were all confined together were anchored off it. The King was landed and taken to a pavilion close by. The Sultan had arranged that on the Saturday before the Ascension Damietta should be surrendered to him and he should release the King.

LXIX

THE SULTAN IS MURDERED

348. The emirs whom the Sultan had dismissed from his Council to make way for his own men whom he had brought from abroad took counsel together, and one of the Saracens whose opinion was respected spoke as follows, " My Lords, you are witnesses of the dishonour the Sultan has done us in removing us from the honourable offices to which his father* appointed us. We must realise that once he is in possession of the fortress of Damietta he will arrest us and put us to death in his prison, as his father did to the emirs who captured the Count of Bar and the Count of Montfort. Our best plan, I think, is to have him put to death before he escapes from our hands."

349. They approached the men of the Halca and called on them to kill the Sultan immediately after the dinner to which he had invited them. When, accordingly, they had eaten and the Sultan was going to his chamber, and had taken leave of his emirs, one of

the knights* of the Halca, the Sultan's sword-bearer, struck him on the palm of his hand with the Sultan's own sword, between his four fingers, and split his hand right up to the arm.

350. The Sultan turned to his emirs who had caused the attack to be made, and said to them, " My Lords, you see that the men of the Halca seek to kill me, and to you I appeal against them." With one voice, however, the knights of the Halca answered him, " Since you say that it is we who seek to kill you, it is better that we should indeed kill you than that you should kill us."

351. Then they had the trumpets sounded, and the whole army came to hear the Sultan's orders. They told them that Damietta had been taken, that the Sultan was going thither, and that it was his wish that they should follow him. Then all armed and spurred towards Damietta. When we saw where they were going, our hearts were greatly cast down, for we thought that Damietta was lost. The Sultan, who was young and nimble, took refuge in the tower he had had built, with three of his bishops [imams] who had dined with him. The tower, as I told you before, was behind his chamber.

352. The men of the Halca, who numbered five hundred mounted men, broke down the Sultan's pavilions and, making a cordon around the tower he had built, besieged him and the three bishops who had dined with him, and called out to him to come down. The Sultan said that he would do so if they would guarantee his life. They told him that they would fetch him down by force, and that he was not in Damietta. They attacked him with Greek fire, and it took hold on the tower, which was made of planks of pine and cotton cloth. The tower caught quickly, so that I never saw so fine and tall a blaze. When the Sultan saw the fire, he hurried down and fled towards the river, along the path I described to you.

353. The men of the Halca had broken down all the hedge with their swords, and as the Sultan ran by to reach the river one of them caught him between the ribs with his spear, and the Sultan ran into the river with the spear dangling. They waded out into the river, until they were swimming, and killed him in the stream, close by the galley in which we were. One of the knights, called Faraquataye,* split him open with his sword and pulled out his

heart from his chest. Then he came to the King, his hand dripping with blood, and said to him, "What will you give me? For I have killed your enemy who would have killed you, had he lived." But the King made him no answer.

LXX

The Prisoners are Close to Death; but the Emirs Confirm the Truce

354. Thirty of them boarded our galley, naked swords in their hands and Danish axes on their shoulders.* I asked my Lord Baldwin of Ibelin, who knew the Saracen tongue well, what these men were saying. He told me that they were saying that they had come to cut off our heads. Many of our folk then were confessing themselves to a Brother of the Trinity,* called John, who was attached to Count William of Flanders. For my part, I could not remember any sin I had committed. But I thought to myself that the more I struggled and defended myself the worse it would be for me.

355. Then I crossed myself and knelt at the feet of one of them, who held a carpenter's Danish axe, and said, " So died Saint Agnes." My Lord Guy of Ibelin, the Constable of Cyprus, knelt by me and confessed himself to me, and I said to him, " By such power as God has given to me, I absolve you of your sins "; but when I rose to my feet I could not remember a single thing he had said or told me.

356. They had us taken from where we were and confined us in the galley's hold. Many of our people thought they had done so because they did not wish to fall on us in one body, but to kill us one by one. Late that night we suffered greatly from being in the hold, for we were lying so closely packed that my feet were against the good Count Peter of Brittany and his were against my face.

357. In the morning the emirs had us released from our confinement, and their messengers told us that we were to confer with

them and renew the agreement which the Sultan had made with us. They told us also that we might be sure that had the Sultan lived he would have had the King beheaded, and all of us, too. Those of us who could, went to the meeting; the Count of Brittany, the Constable and I, who were seriously ill, stayed behind. The Count of Flanders went, with Count John of Soissons, the two brothers of Ibelin, and the others who could manage by themselves.

358. They agreed with the emirs that as soon as Damietta had been surrendered the emirs should release the King and the other men of importance whom they held. The lesser folk the Sultan had sent to Babylon, except for those whom he had had put to death. This he had done contrary to the agreement he had come to with the King, and for that reason it is probable that as soon as he was in possession of Damietta he would have had us put to death also.

359. The King was to swear also to pay a ransom of two hundred thousand pounds before he left the river, and two hundred thousand more when he reached Acre. By the terms which they had agreed with the King the Saracens were to keep the sick who were at Damietta, the crossbows, the munitions, the salt meats and the engines of war, until the King should send for them.

LXXI

The Truce is Sworn

360. The oaths which the emirs were to make to the King were put in writing, and this was their purport: If they did not respect the terms which they had agreed with the King they should be as shamed as a man who, for his sin, went on the pilgrimage to Mahomet, at Mecca, with his head uncovered: as shamed, too, as those who leave their wives and later take them to wife again. (They referred to the law of Mahomet by which a man who puts away his wife can never take her back again, unless he has first seen another man lie with her.)

361. Their third oath was this: that if they did not respect the terms which they had agreed with the King they should be as shamed as a Saracen who eats pig's flesh. The King was satisfied with these oaths of the emirs, for Master Nicholas of Acre, who knew the Saracen tongue well, told him that their religion recognised no more binding oath.

362. When the emirs had sworn, they had put in writing the oaths they required of the King. By the advice of renegade priests who had gone over to the Saracens they were expressed and written as follows: That if the King did not keep his agreement with the emirs he should be as shamed as a Christian who denies God and His Mother, and should be deprived of the fellowship of His twelve companions, and of all the saints. To this the King agreed. The second clause of the oath was that if he did not keep his agreement with the emirs he should be as shamed as a Christian who denies God and His law, and who in despite of God spits on the Cross and tramples it under foot.

363. When the King heard this, he said that such an oath, please God, he would never take. The emirs sent Master Nicholas, who knew the Saracen tongue, to the King, and he said to him, " Sir, the emirs take it very ill that they have sworn whatever you required, but you refuse to swear what they require. You may be sure that if you do not swear it they will have you and all your people beheaded." The King answered that they might do as they wished, but that he would rather die a good Christian than live in the anger of God and His Mother.

364. The Patriarch of Jerusalem, an old man of eighty years, had obtained a safe-conduct from the Saracens and come to the King to assist in arranging his release. Now the custom between the Christians and the Saracens is that when the King or the Sultan dies, those who are acting as messengers, whether to the pagans or the Christians, are imprisoned and enslaved. As the Sultan who had given the Patriarch the safe-conduct was dead, the latter was, like us, a prisoner. When the King had given his answer, one of the emirs told the infidels that he had acted on the Patriarch's advice, and added, " Trust me, I shall make the King take the oath: for I will send the Patriarch's head flying into his lap."

365. They would not do as he wished, but took the Patriarch away from the King and tied him with his hands behind his back to a tent-pole, so tightly that his hands swelled to the size of his head and the blood spurted out from his nails. The Patriarch cried out to the King, " Sir, for the love of God, I beg you take the oath. Have no fear, for, since you are firm in your desire to keep it, I will take on my own soul the whole sin of what you swear." I do not know how the oath was settled, but the emirs were satisfied with what was sworn to by the King and the other men of importance who were present.

LXXII

Surrender of Damietta

366. After the Sultan had been killed his instruments of music were brought before the King's tent, and the King was told that the emirs had been anxious to make him Sultan of Babylon and had discussed it. He asked me whether I thought that he would have accepted the throne of Babylon had they offered it to him. I told him that, since they had killed their ruler, he would have been mad to do so, but he told me that indeed he would not have refused it.

367. The story ran, I should add, that their plan went no further only because they said that the King was the most steadfast Christian you could find. They gave as an example of this that when he came out of his lodging he used to lie on the ground in the form of a cross and so made the sign of the Cross with his whole body. They said, too, that had Mahomet allowed such misfortunes to befall them they would never have kept their faith in him; and that if their people made him Sultan, either they would have to become Christians or he would put them to death.

368. After the terms between the King and the emirs had been settled and sworn, it was agreed that they should release us the day after Ascension Day; and that as soon as Damietta had been surrendered to the emirs the King himself and the persons of importance who were with him should, as was said before, be

released. On the Thursday evening, those in charge of our four galleys anchored in midstream, by the bridge at Damietta; there they had a pavilion erected, and the King landed.

369. At sunrise my Lord Geoffrey of Sargines went into the town and arranged for it to be handed over to the emirs. The Sultan's banners were hoisted on the towers. The Saracen knights entered the town; they began to drink the wine and soon they were all drunk. One of them came to our galley, drew his sword dripping with blood, and told us that for his own share he had killed six of our people.

370. Before Damietta was surrendered, the Queen, with all our people in the town except the sick, had been put on board our ships. By the terms of their oath the Saracens should have looked after the sick; they killed them all. The King's engines of war, also, which they should have kept for him, they broke to pieces; nor did they keep the salt meats, as, not being eaters of pork, they should have done. They made a pile of the engines, another of the salt meat, and another of the corpses, and set fire to them. The blaze was so huge that it lasted all the Friday, Saturday and Sunday.

LXXIII

The Prisoners' Death is Discussed

371. The King and us, whom they should have released at sunrise, they held until sunset. We had no food to eat, nor had the emirs, who spent the whole day in arguing. The spokesman of one party said, " My lords, if you will take my advice and that of those present who agree with me, we will kill the King and the men of importance who are here. Then we shall be safe for the next forty years, for their children are young; Damietta, too, is in our hands, and so we may do it with the greater assurance."

372. Another Saracen, called Sebreci, a Mauretanian by birth, argued on the other side, saying, " If we kill the King after having already killed the Sultan it will be said that the Egyptians are the vilest and most treacherous people in the world." The one who

wished us to be killed retorted, " It is indeed true that we did great wrong in murdering our Sultan to be rid of him, for we have broken the commandment of Mahomet, who bids us cherish our Lord as the apple of our eye. And here is the book with the commandment written plain. But listen," he said, " to the commandment of Mahomet which follows."

373. He turned over a leaf of the book which he held and showed them the other commandment, which read, " For the surety of the faith, slay the enemy of the law." " You may see, then, that we have sinned against the commandments of Mahomet in having killed our Lord; but we shall sin still more grievously if we do not kill the King, whatever assurance we may have given him; for he is the mightiest foe known to our pagan faith."

374. It was almost settled that we should die; so much so that one of the emirs who was hostile to us thought that we were all to be killed, and, embarking on the river, began to shout in Saracen to the men in charge of our galleys and took his turban off his head and signalled with it to them. They immediately raised the anchor and took us a good league back towards Babylon. Then we all thought that we were lost and many tears were shed.

LXXIV

The King and Other Prisoners are Released

375. By the will of God, who is never forgetful of His own, it was agreed, about sunset, that we should be released. We were brought back again and our four galleys moored at the bank. We then asked to be allowed to go, but they told us that they could not allow us to do so until we had eaten, " for the emirs would be shamed if you were to leave our hands fasting ".

376. We then asked to be given food, and we would eat, and they told us that food had been sent for from the camp. What they gave us was little round cheeses baked in the sun to keep the worm out, and hard-boiled eggs four or five days old; the shells of these they had painted, in our honour, in different colours.

377. We were landed and went to join the King, whom they were escorting to the river from the pavilion where they had held him. Twenty thousand Saracens at least, swords at their belts, marched on foot behind him. In the stream there was a Genoese galley, facing the King, and there appeared to be only one man on board. As soon as he saw the King on the bank he blew a whistle, and at the signal eighty or so fully armed crossbowmen, their bows at the ready, leapt out of the hold and straightway loaded their bolts in the notches. When the Saracens saw them, they scattered like sheep, until only two or three were left with the King.

378. A plank was passed to the shore for the King to come on board, with his brother the Count of Anjou, my Lord Geoffrey of Sargines, my Lord Philip of Nemours, the Marshal of France, who was known as du Mez, the Minister of the Trinity, and me. They were holding the Count of Poitiers in confinement until the King should have paid them the two hundred thousand pounds ransom that was due before he left the river.

379. On the Saturday after the Ascension, which was the day after that on which we were released, the Count of Flanders,* the Count of Soissons and several other men of note who had been captured in the galleys came to take their leave of the King. The King told them that he thought they would do well to wait until his brother, the Count of Poitiers, had been released. But they said that they could not delay, since the galleys were ready to put to sea. They embarked accordingly and went back to France, taking with them the good Count of Brittany, who was so ill that he survived only three weeks and died at sea.

LXXV

PAYMENT OF THE RANSOM

380. That Saturday morning, the business of making up the money was begun, and continued all day Saturday and Sunday, until Sunday evening. For the payment was made in scales by weight and each scale represented the value of ten thousand pounds.

At Vespers time on Sunday the King's men who were making up the money sent a message to the King that they were still a good thirty thousand pounds short. With the King were only the King of Sicily, the Marshal of France, the Minister of the Trinity, and I. All the others were at the weighing.

381. Then I told the King that he would do well to send for the Commander and the Marshal of the Temple (for the Master was dead) and ask them to lend him the thirty thousand pounds needed to release his brother. The King sent for them and asked me to speak to them. When I had given them the message, Brother Stephen of Otricourt, the Commander, said to me, " My Lord of Joinville, this advice you have given the King is neither good nor reasonable, for you know that we receive deposits only on the sworn understanding that we shall not hand them over to any person except those who deposited them in our keeping "—and this led to plenty of hard words and names between him and me.

382. Then Brother Renaud of Vichiers, who was the Marshal of the Temple, spoke. " My Lord," he said, " enough of this dispute between the Lord of Joinville and our Commander. As our Commander says, we could not hand over any money without being false to our oath. But when the Seneschal suggests that if we are unwilling to lend you the money you should simply take it there is nothing extraordinary in his suggestion, and you may do as you please about it. If you take any of our moneys we have sufficient of yours at Acre for you to reimburse us."

383. I told the King that I was ready to go if he wished, and he bade me do so. I went then to one of the Templars' galleys, the flag-ship, and as I was about to go down into the hold where the treasure was kept I asked the Commander of the Temple to come and see what I took, but he haughtily refused. The Marshal said that he would come and see what I took by force.

384. As soon as I had gone down to the place where the treasure was I asked the Treasurer of the Temple, who was there, to give me the keys of a chest which was facing me. Seeing how lean and wasted by disease I was, and that I was still wearing the clothes I had worn in captivity, he refused to give them to me. I saw a hatchet lying on the ground, picked it up, and said that I would

use that as a key for the King. Seeing this, the Marshal took me by the hand and said, " My Lord, we see that you are set on taking what you need by force: we will give you the keys." Then he ordered the Treasurer to have them given to me, which he did; and when he told him who I was the Treasurer was greatly disconcerted.

385. I found that the chest I opened belonged to Nicholas of Soisy, one of the King's men-at-arms. I turned out all the money I found inside it and went and sat in the bows of the boat that had brought me out. I put the Marshal of France and the Minister of the Trinity on board the galley and left the Marshal below with the money. Once on board, the Marshal handed the money up to the Minister, who passed it down to me in the boat. As we approached the King's galley I began to call out to him, " Sir, sir, see what I have got! " The Saint was overjoyed to see me, and we gave my load to the men who were weighing out the money.

LXXVI

THE KING SETS SAIL

386. When it had all been weighed the King's Council who had been in charge of the work came and told him that the Saracens refused to release his brother until the money was in their hands; some of them thought that the King should not actually pay the money until he had his brother back. The King answered that he would hand it over, as he had agreed to do, and if the Saracens wished to do what was right they should keep their part of the agreement. My Lord Philip of Nemours then told the King that in the count they had cheated the Saracens of one balance of ten thousand pounds.

387. The King was extremely angry and said that he wished the ten thousand pounds to be returned to them, since he had promised to pay the two hundred thousand before he left the river. I then trod on my Lord Philip's foot and told the King not to believe him, for he was mistaken, the Saracens being the most skilful reckoners

in the world. My Lord Philip said that I was right and that he had only been joking. The King said that such a joke was untimely. " I order you," he said to my Lord Philip, " on the faith you owe me, being my own man, if the ten thousand pounds have not been paid, to see that they are made up in full."*

388. Many had advised the King to transfer to his ship, which was waiting out at sea for him, so as to remove himself from Saracen hands; but he would have none of that advice, saying that he would not leave the river until, as he had agreed, he had paid them two hundred thousand pounds.* As soon as the payment was complete, without anyone suggesting it again, he told us that now he had fulfilled his oath and that we were to leave and go on board the ship, which was out at sea.

389. Our galley then got under way, but it was a good league before any of us spoke to the other, so distressed were we at the confinement of the Count of Poitiers. My Lord Philip of Montfort then came up in a barge and called out to the King, " Sir, sir, speak to your brother, the Count of Poitiers, who is in this other boat." Then the King cried, " Light up! Light up! "* The lights were lit and no joy could have been greater than ours. The King went on board his ship, and we followed him. A poor fisherman brought the news to the Countess of Poitiers that he had seen the Count released, and she had him given twenty pounds *parisis*.

LXXVII

OF BRAVE MEN IN EGYPT, AND OF A RENEGADE

390. But I must not forget some other things that happened while we were in Egypt. First of all I must tell you of my Lord Walter of Châtillon. A knight, called my Lord John of Monson, told me that he saw my Lord of Châtillon in a road in the village in which the King was captured. This road ran straight through the village, so that you could see the fields at each end, and in it was my Lord Walter of Châtillon, his naked sword in his hand.

391. When he saw the Turks entering the road he charged them,

sword in hand, and flung them out of the village. The Turks can shoot just as well to the rear as to the front, and as they fled from the village they covered him with their arrows. When he had driven them out, he shook off the arrows that clung to him, put on his surcoat again, and stood up in his stirrups, arms outstretched, brandishing his sword and crying, " Châtillon, knights! Where are my champions? " When he turned and saw that the Turks had entered the other end of the village, again he charged them, sword in hand, and pursued them; three times he did this.

392. When the emir in charge of the galleys had brought me to the prisoners who had been captured on land I enquired of those who had been with my Lord Walter's company, but I found no one who could tell me how he had been taken, except the good knight, my Lord John Fouinon, who told me that he himself had been taken as a prisoner to Mansura; there he met a Turk who was riding my Lord Walter of Châtillon's horse, and the crupper was dripping with blood. He asked the Turk what he had done with the horse's rider, and the Turk told him that he had cut his throat while he was actually riding it, and showed him in evidence the blood-soaked crupper.

393. There was a very brave man in the army, by name my Lord James of Castel, Bishop of Soissons.* He was a man with a great desire to go to God, and when he saw that our men were falling back on Damietta he had no wish to return to the land of his birth, but made all haste to be with God, and, spurring his horse, he fell alone upon the Turks, who killed him with their swords and so sent him to join the fellowship of God, in the number of the martyrs.

394. While the King was waiting for his men to pay the Turks the money for the release of his brother, the Count of Poitiers, a Saracen, finely dressed and of a handsome presence, came to him with a present, from the children of Nasac,* who had been Sultan of Babylon, of milk in jars and flowers of different kinds and colours, and when he gave them to him he spoke in French.

395. The King asked him where he had learnt French. He answered that he used to be a Christian. " Be off with you," said the King, " I will not speak to you." I drew the man aside and

asked him to tell me his story. He was born in Provins, he said,
and had come to Egypt with King John;* there he had married
and become a rich man. " Do you not realise," I asked him, " that
were you to die in your present state you would be damned and
go to Hell? "

396. " Yes," he said, for he knew well that no religion was as
good as the Christian, " but I dread the poverty and reproaches I
shall have to support if I go back to you. Every day they will say
of me, ' There goes the renegade.' I prefer to live in wealth and
comfort than to put myself in such a position as I foresee would
be mine." I told him that on the Day of Judgment, when every
man would see his sin, there would be worse reproaches than those
of which he spoke. I gave him much good advice, but it was of no
avail. He left me, and I never saw him again.

LXXVIII

THE QUEEN'S DISTRESS

397. You have already heard of the great hardships which the
King and we had to suffer. The Queen, as you will now hear, did
not escape equal hardship. Three days before she was brought to
bed the news reached her of the King's capture. She was so
terrified by this news that whenever she was asleep in bed she
thought that her room was full of Saracens, and called out, " Help,
help! " In order, then, that the child she was carrying might not
be lost, she had an old knight, eighty years of age, sleep by her
bed and hold her hand. Whenever the Queen called out, he would
say, " Do not be frightened, Lady; I am here."

398. Just before she was brought to bed, she had all, except this
knight, sent out of her room; she knelt before him and asked him a
boon. The knight swore that he would grant it. Then she said to
him, " I beg you, by the faith you have pledged to me, if the Saracens capture this town, to cut off my head before they take me."
The knight answered, " You may be assured that I shall certainly
do so, for I had already decided to kill you before we were captured."

399. The Queen gave birth to a boy, whose name was John; but, for the great sorrow in which he was born, he was called Tristan.* On the very day he was born she was told that the Pisans and Genoese and those of the other free cities had decided to leave the town. The next day she summoned them all to her bedroom, which they filled completely, and said to them, " For the love of God, sirs, do not abandon this town. You can see that if it were lost my Lord the King would be lost, too, and all the prisoners. If this does not move you, take pity on the weak little creature who lies here, and wait till I can rise from my bed."

400. " Lady," they answered, " how can we do so? In this town we are dying of hunger." She told them that the famine was no reason for their leaving. " For I shall buy all the provisions in the town, and from now on I engage you all at the King's charges." They consulted among themselves and came back to her and agreed to stay. The Queen (God grant her His mercy) bought all the provisions in the town, which cost her three hundred and sixty thousand pounds* and more. She was obliged to leave her bed before her time; the town had to be surrendered to the Saracens, and she went to Acre to await the King.

LXXIX

THE VOYAGE TO ACRE

401. While the King was waiting for his brother's release he sent Brother Raoul, the Friar Preacher, to an emir called Faracataie,* one of the most honest Saracens I ever met. The King told him that he was astonished that he and the other emirs allowed the terms of their truce to be so flagrantly broken by killing the sick whom they were to look after, breaking up the engines of war, and burning the corpses of the sick and the salt meat, which they should also have kept for him.

402. The answer which Faracataie gave to Brother Raoul was, " Tell the King, Brother Raoul, that my religion makes it impossible for me to help him, and I am sorry. Tell him, too, from

me, not to show his anger at this so long as he is in our hands, or he will be a dead man." And he advised the King to take the matter up again as soon as he reached Acre.

403. When the King came on board his ship he found that his people had nothing ready for him, no bed and no clothes; and until we arrived at Acre he had to lie on the bedding which the Sultan had given him and wear the clothes which he had had made and given him; they were of black satin, lined with ermine and grey squirrel, and with a profusion of buttons of solid gold.

404. I was sick for the six days we were at sea and sat all the time beside the King. It was then he told me how he was taken prisoner, and how, by the help of God, he had arranged his own ransom and ours. He made me tell him how I had been captured on the river. Afterwards he told me that I should be very thankful to Our Lord for having saved me from such great dangers. He was much grieved by the death of the Count of Artois who, he said, would never have let anything prevent him, like the Count of Poitiers, from coming to see him in the galleys.

405. He complained to me also of the Count of Anjou, who was in the same ship, that he gave him none of his company. One day he asked what the Count was doing and was told that he was playing backgammon with my Lord Walter of Nemours. Tottering with weakness from his disease, the King took the dice and the board and threw them into the sea. He was very angry with his brother for so soon taking to playing with dice. But my Lord Walter had the best of it, for he scooped all the money on the board—and there was a great pile of it—into his lap and went off with it.

LXXX

ARRIVAL AT ACRE

406. Now I must tell you of the many hardships and tribulations I suffered at Acre, from which God, in whom I trusted as I trust in Him now, delivered me. I shall have these written down that those who hear them may also put their trust in God when they

suffer hardship and sorrow, and so God will help them as He helped me.

407. First, then, when the King arrived at Acre, all the people came joyfully in procession to meet and welcome him on the sea-shore. They brought me a pony, but as soon as I was mounted my heart gave way, and I told the man who brought it to hold me in case I should fall. With great difficulty I was brought up the steps of the King's hall; I sat down by a window, and beside me was a child, about ten years old, called Bartlemy, who was a bastard son of my Lord Ami of Montbeliard, Lord of Montfaucon.

408. While I was sitting there without anyone noticing me a servant in a scarlet tunic with two yellow stripes came up to me. He saluted me and asked me if I recognised him. I told him that I did not, and he said that he came from Oiselay, my uncle's castle. I asked him in whose service he now was. He said that he had no master and would stay with me if I wished. I told him that I should be pleased if he would, and immediately he went and fetched me some clean caps and combed my hair thoroughly.

409. The King then sent for me to dine with him. I joined him at table, wearing the tunic which had been made for me in prison out of pieces cut from my blanket; the blanket I left with the child Bartlemy, and four yards of woollen camlet I had been given in prison for the love of God. Guillemin, my new servant, came and carved before me and arranged for the child to have food while we dined.

410. My new servant told me that he had found me a lodging close to the baths so that I could wash from myself the filth and sweat I had brought from prison. That evening, when I was in the bath, my heart gave way and I fainted, and it was with difficulty that I was carried from the bath to bed. In the morning an old knight, by name my Lord Peter of Bourbonne, came to see me; I kept him with me, and he was my security in the town for what I lacked of clothing and equipment.

411. It was four days or so before I was provided with what I needed. I then went to see the King, and he scolded me for being so long in coming to see him. He bade me, as I valued his love,

to breakfast and dine with him every day until he had decided whether we were to go to France or stay.

412. I told the King that my Lord Peter of Courtenay owed me four hundred pounds of my pay and was refusing to pay it. The King said that he would see that I was paid from the money which he owed to the Lord of Courtenay, and did as he promised. On the advice of my Lord Peter of Bourbonne we took forty pounds for our expenses and entrusted the rest to the keeping of the Commander of the Palace of the Temple. When I had spent the forty pounds, I sent the father of John Caym of Sainte Menehould, whom I had taken into service overseas, to fetch another forty. The Commander told him that he held no money of mine and that he did not know me.

413. I went to Brother Renaud of Vichiers, who in return for his courtesy to the King in his captivity (of which I have spoken) had, with his assistance, become Master of the Temple, and complained to him of the Commander of the Palace's refusal to pay me back the money I had entrusted to him. When he heard my story he was greatly disconcerted and said to me, " My Lord of Joinville, it is true that I am a friend of yours; but you may be sure that I shall no longer be one, unless you withdraw this claim; for you are trying to give people to understand that our brethren are thieves." I told him that, please God, I should certainly not withdraw my claim.

414. For four days I was sick at heart, like a man who has no money at all to spend; but then the Master came to me with a smiling face and told me that he had traced my money; he found that he had changed the Commander of the Palace and sent him to a village called Le Saffran,* and it was this man who gave me back my money.

LXXXI

The Author is Sick

415. The Bishop of Acre at that time, who was a native of Provins, lent me the house of the priest of the Church of St. Michael; I

had retained Caym of Sainte Menehould, who served me very well for two years, better than any man I had about me out there, and I had also engaged several others for my household. Just by the head of my bed was a little door which led into the church.

416. Then, however, I succumbed, and all my people too, to a continual fever which forced me to take to my bed; and there was never a day all that time on which I had anyone to help me or lift me up. I felt that only death awaited me, from a sign that was constantly close to my ear; for there was no day on which twenty or more dead were not carried into the church, and from my bed, as each was carried in, I heard the chant of *Libera me, Domine*. Then I wept and gave thanks to God, and said to Him, " Blessed may You be, Lord, for this suffering You have sent me, for in my rising and in my going to bed I have been used to too much ceremony; but help me, Lord, I pray You, and deliver me from this sickness." And this He did, both for me and for my people.

417. Afterwards I asked Guillemin, my new squire, to show me his accounts. He produced them, and I found that he had robbed me of ten pounds *tournois* or more. When I asked for the money he told me that he would pay me when he could. I dismissed him, but told him that I made him a present of what he owed me, for he had certainly earned it. When the Burgundian knights, who had brought him out with them, returned from captivity I learnt from them that he was the most obliging thief that ever was; for if a knight lacked a knife or a belt, gloves, spurs, or anything else, he used to go and steal it and give it to him.

418. While the King was at Acre his brothers took to playing at dice. The Count of Poitiers was so gracious a player that when he won he would have the door of the hall thrown open and call in any gentlemen and ladies who were there and give away in handfuls his own money as well as what he had won; if he lost he bought back the money, guessing its value, from those he had been playing with, his brother the Count of Anjou and others, and gave it all away, his own as well as the others'.

LXXXII

THE KING SUMMONS A COUNCIL

419. One Sunday, while we were at Acre, the King sent for his brothers and the Count of Flanders and the other men of note, and said to them, " My Lords, my Lady the Queen has written to me, urging me as strongly as she can to return to France, for, since I have neither truce nor peace with the King of England, my Kingdom is in great danger. Those of this country to whom I have spoken of it have told me that, if I leave, this country is lost, for they will all follow me from Acre, none being prepared to stay with so small a force. I bid you, then, consider this matter. As it is of great moment, I shall give you until today week to tell me what you think best."

420. During the week the Legate came to me and told me that he could not understand how the King could stay, and urged me strongly to leave in his ship. I answered that it was impossible for me to do so, for, as he knew, I had nothing: I had lost everything when I was captured on the river.

421. It was not because I should not have been glad to accompany him that I gave this answer, but because of something which my cousin, my Lord of Bourlemont (God grant him His mercy) said to me when I was going overseas. " You are going overseas," he said. " Take care, then, how you come home, for no knight, poor or rich, can come home without disgrace, if he leaves in Saracen hands the humble folk of Our Lord, in whose company he went." The Legate was angry with me and told me that I should not have refused his offer.

LXXXIII

THE COUNCIL DEBATES WHETHER THE KING SHOULD RETURN TO FRANCE OR STAY IN PALESTINE

422. The next Sunday, we waited again on the King. He asked his brothers, the other barons, and the Count of Flanders what was

their opinion: should he stay, or should he go? They all replied that they had deputed my Lord Guy Mauvoisin to announce the advice they wished to give him. The King asked him to deliver the message that had been entrusted to him, and my Lord Guy spoke as follows:

423. " Sir, your brothers and the men of note who are here present have considered your position and are convinced that you cannot stay in this country without prejudice to yourself and your Kingdom. Of all the knights that came with you, and you brought two thousand eight hundred to Cyprus, there are not one hundred left in this town. They advise you then, sir, to return to France and raise men and money with which you can shortly come back here and take your revenge on the enemies of God who held you in captivity."

424. The King was not satisfied with what my Lord Guy Mauvoisin said. He asked the Count of Anjou, the Count of Poitiers, the Count of Flanders, and the other great men who were sitting below them, but they all agreed with my Lord Guy Mauvoisin. The Legate asked Count John of Jaffa, who came next, what he thought of the matter. The Count begged to be excused, " for ", he said, " my castle is on the border; and if I advised the King to stay it might be thought it was self-interest that prompted me ".

425. The King then insisted that he should speak his mind. The Count answered that if the King could contrive to keep the field for another year his stay would do him great honour. The Legate then questioned those who were seated below the Count of Jaffa, but they all agreed with my Lord Guy Mauvoisin.

426. Of those seated in front of the Legate I was fourteenth. He asked me my opinion. I answered that I fully agreed with the Count of Jaffa. The Legate then asked me angrily how the King could possibly keep the field with so small a force. I answered with an equal show of anger, for I thought his question was meant to sting me, " Since you wish it, I will tell you.*

427. " It is said, sir, though I do not know whether it is true, that the King has not yet spent any money of his own, but only the clergy's.* Let him, then, spend his own, and let him send to the Morea and overseas for knights: when it is known that the

King is paying well and liberally, knights will come to him from all parts. So, please God, he will be able to keep the field for a year, and his stay will enable the poor prisoners, who were taken in God's service and the King's, to have their freedom, who will never have it if he leaves." There was none there who had not some dear friend in captivity; none, then, took me up, but all began to weep.

428. After me, the Legate asked my Lord William of Beaumont, who was then Marshal of France, his opinion. He said that I had spoken well, " and ", he added, "I will tell you why". The good knight my Lord John of Beaumont, who was his uncle and was eager to return to France, railed at him most rudely. " You filthy brute! " he said. " What are you trying to say? Sit down and hold your tongue! "

429. " My Lord John," the King said to him, " you are in the wrong. Let him speak." " Indeed, sir, I will do no such thing." The Marshal was forced to hold his tongue, and not one of them after agreed with me, except the Lord of Châtenay.* The King then said to us, " Sirs, I have listened to what you have said. This day week I will let you know my decision."

LXXXIV

The Author is Blamed for His Advice: the King's Kindness to Him

430. When we came out they began to attack me on all sides. " My Lord of Joinville, the King must indeed be out of his mind if he prefers your advice to that of the whole Council of the Kingdom of France." When the tables were set, the King bade me sit by him at dinner, in the place he always gave me when his brothers were absent. All during dinner he did not speak a word to me, though it was his usual custom to be free with me* at table. I thought, indeed, that he was angry with me for saying that he had not yet spent any of his own money and that he should not be sparing of it.

431. While the King was hearing grace I went to a barred window in an alcove by the head of the King's bed. I passed my arms

through the bars and was thinking that if the King returned to France I should follow the advice the Lord of Bourlemont gave me and go to the Prince of Antioch (who counted me a kinsman and had sent for me) until I could join another expedition or peace was confirmed and the prisoners released.

432. As I stood there, the King came and leant on my shoulders and put his two hands on my head. I thought it was my Lord Philip of Nemours, who had already tormented me a great deal that day on account of the advice I had given the King. " Leave me in peace, my Lord Philip," I said. It happened, as I turned my head, that the King's hand slipped down in front of my face, and I recognised him by an emerald he wore on his finger. " Keep quite still," he said. " I want to ask you something: how could a young man like you be so bold as to advise me to stay, in the face of all the great and wise of France who told me to go? "

433. " Sir," I said, " even if I had that evil thought in my heart, I would never at any price have given you such advice." " Do you mean," he said, " that I should do wrong to leave? " " God help me, sir, I do." Then he added, " If I stay, will you also stay? " I told him that I would, either at my own or at another's charges. " Be easy, then," he said, " for I am indeed pleased by your advice. But say no word of it to any man during this week."

434. I was consoled by what he told me, and I defended myself more vigorously against my opponents. The natives who live in the country are nicknamed " Colts ".* My Lord Peter of Avalon, who lived at Tyre, heard that I was being called a colt because I had urged the King to stay with the colts. He accordingly sent me a message that I should counter those who gave me that name by telling them that I would rather be a colt than a broken-down hack like them.

LXXXV

THE KING DECIDES TO STAY

435. The next Sunday we all waited on the King again. When he saw that we were all present he made the sign of the Cross on his

lips, and after he had invoked the help of the Holy Spirit (so at least, I think; for my Lady my Mother used to tell me that whenever I had something to say I should invoke the Holy Spirit and cross my lips) he spoke as follows:

436. " My Lords," he said, " I give my hearty thanks both to those who have advised me to return to France and to those who have advised me to stay. But I have decided that if I stay there is no serious danger of my Kingdom suffering, since my Lady the Queen has ample forces to defend it. I have considered also that the barons of this country assure me that if I go the Kingdom of Jerusalem is lost, since when I am gone none will dare to stay.

437. " Hence it has seemed good to me that on no account should I desert the Kingdom of Jerusalem which I came to win and hold. Thus I am resolved for the present to stay here. And I bid you great barons here present, and all you other knights who are willing to stay with me, to come forward and speak freely to me. I shall so repay you that it will be your fault and not mine if you do not stay." Many who heard this speech were dismayed, and there were many, too, who wept.

LXXXVI

ENGAGEMENT OF MORE KNIGHTS

438. The King gave orders, so it is said, that his brothers should return to France. Whether it was at their request or by his wish I do not know. The speech in which he announced that he was staying was made around St. John's Day.* On the Feast of St. James,* then (whose pilgrim I was and who had granted me many favours), the King came back from Mass to his chamber and summoned such of his Council as were remaining with him—that is to say, my Lord Peter the Chamberlain,* who was the truest and most upright man I ever saw in a king's household,* my Lord Geoffrey of Sargines, a good knight and true, and my Lord Giles le Brun, a good knight and true, to whom he had given the

Constableship of France after the death of my noble Lord Humbert of Beaujeu.

439. The King said to them in a loud and angry voice, " My Lords, it is already a month that it has been known that I am staying, and yet I hear no news of your having engaged any knights for me." " Sir," they answered, " it is impossible for us to do so. Every man sets so high a price on himself, being anxious to go home, that we dare not pay what they ask." " Whom, then," asked the King, " can you find who is cheaper? " " Indeed, sir," they said, " there is the Seneschal of Champagne, but even to him we dare not pay what he asks."

440. At that moment I was in the King's chamber. The King said, " Call the Seneschal to me." I went up and knelt to him. He made me sit down, and said to me, " Seneschal, you know that I have loved you well, and now my people tell me that they are finding you a hard man to deal with. How is that? " " Sir," I answered, " I cannot help myself. You know that I was taken prisoner on the river, everything I had was taken from me, and I have nothing left." He asked me how much I was asking, and I told him that for the two-thirds of the year that remained till Easter I was asking two thousand pounds.

441. " Tell me, then," he said, " have you engaged any other knights? " " Yes, sir," I answered. " My Lord Peter of Pontmolain, and two other knights bannerets, and their charges until Easter amount to four hundred pounds each." The King counted on his fingers. " What your new knights will cost, then," he said, " comes to twelve hundred pounds." " Consider, sir," I added, " that it will cost me at least eight hundred pounds to mount and arm myself and feed my knights; for you would not have us feed at your lodging." " Indeed," said the King to his officers, " I cannot see that his charge is excessive "; and to me, " I engage you."

LXXXVII

THE KING'S BROTHERS LEAVE: ENVOYS ARE SENT TO DAMASCUS

442. It was after this that the King's brothers and the other chief men in Acre prepared their squadron. When they were leaving the town, the Count of Poitiers borrowed jewels from those who were returning to France, and generously gave them to those of us who were staying. Both the brothers begged me to take care of the King, and told me that there was no man left on whom they could count more surely. When the time came for the Count of Anjou to embark, the grief he displayed astonished us all, but none the less he went back to France.

443. Shortly after the departure of the King's brothers from Acre the envoys of the Emperor Frederick came to the King, bringing letters of credence, and told him that they had been sent by the Emperor to assist in our release. They showed the King the letters which the Emperor was sending to the Sultan who was dead (of which the Emperor was ignorant), in which he told him that he could confidently treat with these envoys for the King's release. There were many who said that it was as well that the envoys did not find us still in captivity, because it was believed that the Emperor's real purpose in sending them was rather to hinder than to assure our release. Finding that we were free, the envoys returned.

444. While the King was at Acre the Sultan of Damascus* sent envoys to him, with a bitter complaint against the Egyptian emirs, who had murdered his cousin the Sultan. In return for the King's help, he promised to surrender to him the Kingdom of Jerusalem, which was in his hands. The King decided to send envoys of his own to the Sultan of Damascus to take back his answer. With them went Brother Yves le Breton, of the order of Friars Preachers, who knew the Saracen tongue.

445. On their way from their lodging to that of the Sultan Brother Yves saw an old woman crossing the street; in her right hand she was carrying a bowl full of fire, and in her left hand a jug of water.

" What are you going to do with those? " Brother Yves asked her. She answered that with the fire she was going to burn Paradise, so that it should exist no more, and with the water extinguish Hell, so that there should be no more Hell. " And why," he asked, " do you wish to do that? " " Because I want no one ever to do good in order to have the reward of Paradise, or for fear of Hell, but only to have the love of God, who is so precious and can give us all that there is of goodness."

LXXXVIII

JOHN THE ARMENIAN: VIRTUE OF ALMSGIVING

446. John the Armenian, the King's armourer, also went to Damascus, to buy horns and glue to make crossbows. He saw a very aged old man sitting in the bazaar, who called him and asked him whether he was a Christian. He replied that he was. Then the old man said, " You Christians must hate one another bitterly, for I have seen a time when King Baldwin* of Jerusalem, the one who was a leper, beat Saladin, though he had but three hundred men in arms against Saladin's three thousand. But now your sins have brought you to such a pass that we round you up in the fields like cattle."

447. Then John the Armenian told him that he should not speak of the sins of the Christians, for the sins of which the Saracens were guilty were much greater. The Saracen said that that was a foolish answer. John asked him why. The old man said that he would tell him, but that first he had a question to ask him. Had he, he asked, any child? " Yes," answered John, " a boy." He then asked him which would grieve him the more, to receive a blow from him or from his son. John said that he would be more angry with his son, if he struck him, than with the old man.

448. " Here, then," said the Saracen, " is my answer. You Christians say that you are sons of God, and it is from His name of Christ that you are known as Christians. He has done you the kindness of giving you teachers from whom you may learn when

you are doing right and when you are doing wrong. Thus God is more angry with you when you commit a small sin than with us when we commit a grievous sin, for we do not know what we are doing; we are so blind that we think that all our sins are remitted if we can wash in water before we die, Mahomet telling us that at death we shall be saved by water."

449. Once when I was going to Paris, after my return from overseas, John the Armenian was with me. As we were dining in a pavilion a crowd of poor folk begged alms of us for the love of God. They were making a great noise, and a man who was in our company said to a servant of ours, " Get up and drive these paupers away."

450. " Oh! " said John the Armenian. " That was a bad thing to say. If the King of France were now to send to each of us a hundred silver marks, you would not drive away the messengers who brought it. Yet you are driving away these envoys who are offering you the greatest of all gifts; they are begging from you, that is, for the love of God; which means that if you give them your alms they will give you God. And God has told us with His own mouth that they have the power to give Him to us; the saints tell us also that the poor can bring us back to God's favour, for as water quenches fire, so almsgiving quenches sin. Never let it happen, then," said John, " that you drive away the poor like this; but give to them, and God will give to you."

LXXXIX

THE OLD MAN OF THE MOUNTAIN

451. During the King's stay at Acre messengers came to him from the Old Man of the Mountain.* When the King came back from his Mass he had them brought to his presence and sat them down, with an emir in front, finely clothed and appointed; behind this emir was a well-appointed squire who held three knives in his hand, each with its blade inserted into the handle of another. These, had the emir met with a refusal, he would have presented

to the King as a token of defiance. Behind the squire who held the knives was another who held a sheet of fine linen* wrapped round his arm, which he would also have given the King for a burial shroud had he rejected the demand of the Old Man of the Mountain.

452. The King told the emir to speak his mind. The emir gave him his letters of credence and said, " My Lord sends me to ask you whether you know him." The King answered that he did not know him, because he had never seen him, but that he had indeed heard tell of him. " Since you have heard tell of my Lord," said the emir, " I am amazed that you have not sent to him such tribute as would have won his friendship, as the Emperor of Germany, the King of Hungary, the Sultan of Babylon and the others do every year, for they well know that their lives depend on my Lord's pleasure.

453. " But if you do not wish to do this, then relieve him of the tribute which he owes to the Temple and the Hospital, and he will be satisfied with you." At that time he was paying a tribute to the Temple and the Hospital, who had no fear of the Assassins, since the Old Man of the Mountain could gain nothing by having the Master of the Temple or of the Hospital assassinated. He knew well that if he had one Master killed another equally good would be appointed. For this reason he was unwilling to lose his assassins to no purpose. The King's answer was that the emir should return in the afternoon.

454. When the emir came back he found the King seated with the Master of the Hospital on one side of him and the Master of the Temple on the other. The King then told him to repeat what he had said in the morning. The emir refused to do so except in the presence of the same persons as were with the King before. Then the two Masters said to him, " We order you to speak." He told them that since it was their order he would do so. The two Masters then had him told in his own language to come back the next day and speak to them in the Hospital, which he did.

455. There the Masters told him that it was indeed bold of his Lord to dare to send so peremptory a message to the King, and added that it was only out of respect to the King, as envoys to

whom they had come, that they did not have them drowned in the filthy water of the harbour at Acre, to their Lord's shame. " And we order you to return to your Lord and be back here in a fortnight, bringing the King such letters and jewels from him as may satisfy him and win you his favour."

XC

Of the Same

456. Within the fortnight the envoys of the Old Man of the Mountain returned to Acre, bringing the King the Old Man's shirt; they told him from their Master that it was a symbol that, as the shirt is closer to the body than any other garment, so the Old Man wished to hold the King closer in his love than any other King. He sent also his ring of fine gold with his name engraved on it; by sending the ring he meant again that he wedded the King, for he wished for the future to be as one with him.

457. Among other jewels which he sent the King were an elephant finely made of crystal, and an animal, also of crystal, called a giraffe; crystal apples, too, of different sorts, and games of backgammon and chess. All these were scented with ambergris,* the ambergris being fastened to the crystal by fine golden filigree. As soon as the envoys opened the boxes which held them, the scent was so sweet that the whole room seemed full of fragrance.

458. The King sent the envoys back to the Old Man, and in return a great abundance of jewels, draperies of scarlet, golden cups and silver bridles. With them he sent Brother Yves le Breton, who knew Saracen. Brother Yves found that the Old Man of the Mountain did not believe in Mahomet, but in the law of Ali, Mahomet's uncle.

459. It was this Ali who brought Mahomet to his high position; but when Mahomet had gained the supreme power over the people he turned against his uncle and dismissed him. When Ali saw this he gathered around him such people as he could and taught them a different faith from that of Mahomet. Hence it now comes that all

those who hold the law of Ali call those who hold that of Mahomet unbelievers, while those who hold Mahomet's say the same of the followers of Ali.

460. One of the points of the law of Ali is the belief that when a man meets death in the fulfilment of his Lord's order his soul enters into a body which is happier than that which it inhabited before; it is for this reason that the Assassins do not shrink from incurring death at their Lord's bidding, believing that after their death they will be much happier than they were before.

461. The other point is that they believe that no man can die before the day which has been appointed for him. This belief no man should hold, since God has the power either to prolong or to cut short our lives. The Bedouins also hold it, and they accordingly refuse to wear armour when they go into battle, believing that to do so would be to transgress their law. When they rail at their children they say to them, " The curse of the Frank on you, who wears armour because he is afraid of death."

462. By the head of the Old Man's bed Brother Yves found a book in which were written some of Our Lord's sayings to Saint Peter when he was on earth. Brother Yves said to the Old Man, " Ah, sir, in God's name, study this book often, for it is excellent doctrine." The Old Man said that it was his custom to do so. " For I am devoted to my Lord Saint Peter, since at the beginning of the world the soul of Abel, after his murder, passed into the body of Noah; and after Noah's death into that of Abraham; and after Abraham's death it passed, when God came on earth, into the body of Saint Peter."

463. Hearing this, Brother Yves showed him that his faith was mistaken, and taught him much of the good truth; but the Old Man refused to believe. When he came back to us Brother Yves explained this to the King. When the Old Man rode he had a crier preceding him, carrying a Danish axe with a long handle all mounted with silver, and many knives fastened in the handle, who called out, " Make way for him who holds in his hands the death of kings! "

XCI

RETURN OF MORE PRISONERS FROM EGYPT

464. I had forgotten to tell you of the answer which the King gave to the Sultan of Damascus. It was as follows: That he had no intention of joining him until he knew whether the Egyptian emirs were going to give him satisfaction for the treaty they had broken. He would summon them to do so, and if they refused to put the matter right he would willingly help him to avenge his cousin, the Sultan of Babylon, whom the Egyptians had murdered.

465. During his stay at Acre the King sent my Lord John of Valenciennes to Egypt; he called on the emirs to make good the outrages and damage they had done the King. They answered that they were ready to do so, provided the King would enter into an alliance with them against the Sultan of Damascus. My Lord John of Valenciennes protested vigorously against their gross breach of faith with the King (which I have already described) and advised them that it would be well for them, if they wished to soften the King's heart, to return to him all the knights they held in confinement. This they did, and in addition sent him all the bones of Count Walter of Brienne, that they might be laid in consecrated ground.

466. When my Lord John of Valenciennes came back to Acre with two hundred knights, not counting other persons whom he brought from captivity, my Lady of Sayette,* who was a cousin of Count Walter and sister of my Lord Walter, Lord of Reynel (whose daughter John, Lord of Joinville, married after his return from overseas)—my lady of Sayette took Count Walter's bones and had them buried at the Hospital at Acre. She arranged that at the service every knight should give a candle and a silver penny at the offertory, and the King a candle and a golden besant, all at her own expense. Men were surprised at the King's so doing, as he had never been seen to offer any money except his own; but out of courtesy he did so.

XCII

THE KING GOES TO CAESAREA

467. Among the knights whom my Lord John of Valenciennes brought back I found a good forty from the Court of Champagne. I had green tunics* and cloaks made for them, and brought them to the King's presence, where I begged him to pay them whatever they needed to stay in his service. The King listened to their requests and was silent.

468. One of the knights of his Council, however, said that I was wrong in making such a suggestion to the King, since their claim was at least seven thousand pounds too high. I told him that he might come to no good by speaking so; that we of Champagne had lost at least thirty-five knights of the Court of Champagne, all bannerets: and I added, " So great is the King's need of knights that he will not do well to be persuaded by you."   After I had spoken I began to weep bitterly; the King told me to be quiet and he would give them all I had asked; he engaged them as I wished, and put them in my division.

469. The answer which he sent to the Egyptian envoys was that he would make no treaty with them unless they sent him all the heads of Christians which had been hung round the walls of Cairo since the time when the Count of Bar and the Count of Montfort were captured; in addition they must send him all the children they held who had been taken in infancy and had lost their faith, and must also remit the two hundred thousand pounds he still owed them. With the envoys of the Egyptian emirs he sent my Lord John of Valenciennes, a brave and prudent man.

470. At the beginning of Lent* the King prepared, with all his forces, to renew the fortifications of Caesarea, which the Saracens had torn down. It lay twelve leagues from Acre, in the direction of Jerusalem. My Lord Raoul of Soissons, whom sickness had kept at Acre, was with him in this work. I do not know how it was that during all that year the Saracens gave us no trouble, except that it was by the will of God. While the King was fortifying

Caesarea, the envoys to the Tartars returned, and I will tell you what news they brought us.

XCIII

The Envoys Return and Tell of the Tartars

471. As I said before, it was during the King's stay in Cyprus, that envoys came to him from the Tartars* and gave him to understand that they would help him to win the Kingdom of Jerusalem from the Saracens. The King sent his envoys in return, and with them a chapel that he had had made for them of scarlet. In this chapel, to attract them to our faith, he had had embroidered all that we believe: the Annunciation by the Angel, the Nativity, the Baptism in which God was baptised, the whole of the Passion, the Ascension and the coming of the Holy Ghost. He sent chalices, too, and books, and all that is needed for singing Mass, and two Friars Preachers to sing Masses for them.

472. The King's envoys arrived at the port of Antioch.* From Antioch to the great Tartar King they found that it was a good twelve months' journey, riding ten leagues a day. They found that all the country was subject to the Tartars, and saw many cities which they had destroyed, and great piles of dead men's bones.

473. They asked how they had attained the power to kill and conquer so many people; according to the report they gave the King it came about as follows: the Tartars originally came from a vast sandy plain, where nothing useful could grow. This plain began at a huge and astounding cliff of rocks which mark the eastern end of the world. No man, so the Tartars witness, has ever crossed these rocks; and they said that within them was confined the people of Gog and Magog, who will emerge at the end of the world when Antichrist comes to bring universal destruction.

474. The Tartar people lived in this plain, under the rule of Prester John* and the Emperor of Persia,* whose country lay next to his, and of various infidel Kings, to whom they were obliged to pay annual tribute and service in return for pasture for

their cattle, which were their only livelihood. This Prester John and the Emperor of Persia, and the other Kings, so despised the Tartars that when they brought their tribute they refused to receive it face to face and turned their backs on them.

475. They had among them a wise man who travelled throughout the plains, speaking to the wise men in the plains, and in the different places, and urged them to consider how they might escape from the slavery in which they were held. He finally assembled them all at the edge of the plain by the country of Prester John and explained their position. Let him devise a plan, they answered, and they would carry it out. He told them that they could not be successful unless they had a King and a Lord over them; he explained to them how they might do this, and they were ready to take his word.

476. The arrangement was that each of their fifty-two tribes should bring an arrow marked with its name. With the consent of the whole people it was agreed that these fifty-two arrows should be placed before a five-year-old child, and the King should be appointed from the tribe whose arrow the child first took hold of. When the child had taken one, the wise man had all the other tribes withdrawn, and it was arranged that the tribe from whom the King was to be appointed should elect from themselves fifty of their best and wisest men. When they had been elected, each brought an arrow marked with his name.

477. Then they agreed that the man whose arrow the child picked up should be made King. The child picked one up, and it was that of the wise man who had instructed them. The whole people was overjoyed, but he silenced them and said, " My Lords, if you wish me to be your King, you shall swear to me by Him who made Heaven and earth to keep my commands." And this they swore.

478. The laws which he gave them were designed to keep the people at peace. They were: that no man should steal from another, nor strike another, on pain of losing his hand; and that no man should consort with the wife or daughter of another, on pain of losing his hand or his life. He gave them many other good laws for the keeping of the peace.

XCIV

OF THE TARTARS

479. After he had given them law and order, he said to them, " My lords, the greatest of our enemies is Prester John, and I command you all to be ready tomorrow to attack him. If it happens (which God forbid) that he overcomes us, then let each man do the best he can for himself; but if we overcome him, it is my order that the affair* last for three days and three nights, and that no man be so bold as to lay hand on any plunder, but shall confine himself to slaughter; when victory is ours I shall divide the booty so freely and fairly that all will be satisfied." To this they all agreed.

480. The next day they fell on their enemies and, by the will of God, they overcame them. All whom they found armed and able to defend themselves they killed; those who wore religious clothing, priests and other religious, they spared. The other nations in Prester John's territories who were not present at the battle submitted to the Tartars.

481. A prince of one of the tribes I spoke of before was lost for three months, and there was no news of him. When he returned, he was neither hungry nor thirsty, thinking that at the most he had been away for a night. The news he brought back was that he had climbed a very high mountain and at the top had found a multitude of people, the finest he had ever seen, the best clothed, and the best adorned. At the top of the hill he saw a King sitting, on a golden throne, finer than the others, more richly clothed and adorned.

482. On his right hand sat six crowned Kings, finely adorned with precious stones, and the same number on his left. Close by his right hand knelt a Queen, who spoke to him and begged him to take thought for her people. On his left knelt a man of great beauty, with two wings that shone like the sun, and round the King was a great throng of grand winged beings.

483. The King called the prince and said to him, " You have come from the army of the Tartars." " Indeed, sir," he answered,

" I have." " You shall go to your King and tell him that you have seen Me, who am Lord of Heaven and earth; and you shall tell him to give thanks to Me for the victory I gave him over Prester John and his people. Tell him, too, from Me, that I grant him the power to subdue all the world." " Sir," said the prince, " how shall he believe my word? "

484. " You shall tell him that by these signs he may believe you: that you will go to do battle with the Emperor of Persia with no more than three hundred of your people; and that your great King may know that I have the power to do all things, I shall give you victory over the Emperor of Persia, though he will bring against you three hundred thousand men-at-arms and more. Before you go out to do battle with him you shall ask your King to give you the priests and the men of religion whom he took in the battle; and what they shall witness to you, that shall you and all your people firmly believe."

485. " Sir," said he, " I shall not know my road hence unless you give me a guide." The King turned to a great throng of knights, so finely armed that it was a wonder to look on them, and called one of them, saying, " George, come." This knight came and knelt, and the King said to him, " Rise, and lead this man safely to his encampment." And this he did one morning at the break of dawn.

486. As soon as his people saw him they and the whole camp made such a joy that no man could describe it. He asked the great King for the priests; he gave them to him, and their doctrine was so readily accepted by the prince and all his people that they were all baptised. Afterwards, he took three hundred men at arms; he had them shriven and equipped, and went to give battle to the Emperor of Persia, whom he overcame and drove from his Kingdom. The Emperor in his flight reached the Kingdom of Jerusalem, and it was he who beat our people and captured Count Walter of Brienne, as you will hear later.*

XCV

MORE OF THEIR HABITS

487. The people of this Christian prince were so numerous that the King's envoys told us that they had in their camp eight hundred chapels on wagons. Their mode of life was such that they ate no bread but lived on meat and milk. Their favourite meat is horseflesh; they let it soak in brine* and dry it, until they can cut it like black bread. Their favourite drink, and the strongest, is mares' milk brewed with herbs. The great King of the Tartars was given a present of a horse laden with flour, which had come from a distance of three months' journey. He gave it to the King's envoys.

488. Among their subjects are many Christians who follow the Greek obedience, both those of whom I have spoken and others. It is these they employ against the Saracens when they are at war with them, while against Christians they employ Saracens. All the childless women accompany their army to battle; they pay the women a soldier's wage according to their vigour, in the same way as the men. The King's envoys reported also that the paid soldiers, men and women, eat together in the lodging of their own commanders; and the men dared not touch the women by reason of the law which their first King gave them.

489. They eat the meat of every sort of animal that dies in their camp. The women who have children bring them up and look after them, and prepare food for those who do the fighting. They lay the raw meat between their saddles and their saddle-cloths. When the blood has all been pressed out they eat it raw. What they cannot eat at the moment they put in a leather bag, and when they are hungry they open the bag, and always eat the oldest piece first. Thus I saw a Khwarizmian, who belonged to the Emperor of of Persia's people, and guarded us in prison; when he opened his bag we had to stop our noses; we could not bear the putrid stench which came out.

490. To return, however, to our story. When the Great King of

the Tartars had received the envoys and presents, he sent under safe-conduct for several Kings who had not yet recognised his suzerainty; he had the chapel erected for them and spoke to them. " Sirs," he said, " the King of France has submitted himself to our mercy and acknowledged himself our subject. See here the tribute he sends us. If you do not submit also, we shall send for him to destroy you." Many of them, from fear of the King of France, made their submission.

491. His envoys accompanied the King's when they returned, and brought the King of France letters from their Great King which said, " Peace is good; for when a country is at peace those who go on four feet eat the grass in peace, and those who go on two feet till the ground, from which good things come, in peace.*

492. " This we send you for a warning, for you cannot have peace if you are not at peace with us. Prester John rose against us, and such and such kings (giving the names of many) and all we have put to the sword. We bid you, then, every year to send us of your gold and of your silver so much as may win you our friendship. If you do not do this we shall destroy you and your people, as we have done to those we have named." The King, you may be sure, repented of having sent him his ambassadors.

XCVI

How the Norwegians Hunted Lions

493. To continue. While the King was fortifying Caesarea my Lord Alenard of Senaingan arrived in the camp and told us that the ship in which he came he had built in the Kingdom of Norway, which is at the extreme Western end of the world. On his journey to the King he had rounded the whole of Spain and had had to pass through the Straits of Morocco. He had been through great danger before he reached us. The King engaged him and nine other knights with him. He told us, too, that in the country of Norway the summer nights are so short that every evening you

saw the light of that day's sunset at the same time as that of the next day's dawn.

494. He and his men were in the habit of hunting lions; sometimes they took great risks in killing them, for they used to shoot at them while they were galloping as hard as they could. When they fired, the lion attacked them and would have caught and eaten the hunters if they had not let fall some old piece of cloth; the lion stopped and tore and ate the cloth, thinking it was a man he held. While he was tearing it another hunter shot at him; again the lion dropped the cloth and charged him. As soon as this man let another piece of cloth fall, the lion mauled it again, and by this method they killed him with their arrows.

XCVII

The Coman Burials

495. While the King was fortifying Caesarea my Lord Philip of Toucy* joined him. The King counted him a cousin, for he was descended from one of the sisters of King Philip, whom the Emperor Andronicus had married. The King engaged him, with nine other knights under him, for a year, after which he left and returned to Constantinople, whence he had come. He told the King that the Emperor of Constantinople* and the other chief men of the city had formed an alliance with a people known as the Comans, in order to have their assistance against Vataces,* who was then Emperor of the Greeks.

496. To ensure good faith on both sides in their alliance, the Emperor and the other chief men of his party were obliged to draw blood from themselves into a large silver cup. The King of the Comans and the chief men of his party did the same. They mixed their blood with that of our men and diluted it with wine and water; both they and our men drank from it, and then they said that they were blood-brothers. In addition they made a dog run between our men and theirs and cut it to pieces with their swords,

our men doing the same; so, they said, might they, too, be cut to pieces if they failed one another.

497. He told us another astonishing thing he had seen while he was in their camp: a rich knight had died, and they had dug a wide and deep trench for him in the ground. In this he was placed, sitting on a chair and dressed with great nobility; with him were placed the best horse he had and the best soldier, both alive. Before the soldier was placed in the trench with his Lord he bade farewell to the King of the Comans and the other great Lords, and while he was doing so they put in his scarf a great sum of silver and gold, saying, " When I arrive in the other world you shall give back to me that which I entrust to you." " With all my will ", he answered, " shall I do so."

498. The Great King of the Comans gave him a letter addressed to their first King, in which he told him that this hero had lived the life of a good man and had served him well, and prayed him to give him the reward of his service. When this had been done, they placed the soldier, still alive, in the trench with his master and the horse, and laid over the mouth of the trench planks of wood carefully fitted together. Then the whole army ran to fetch stones and earth, and before they went to sleep that night they had raised, in memory of those they had buried, a great mound over them.

XCVIII

THE AUTHOR'S LIFE IN PALESTINE

499. While the King was fortifying Caesarea I went to his lodging to see him. As soon as he saw me enter his room, where he was talking to the Legate, he rose and drew me to one side and said to me, " You know that I engaged you only until Easter; now tell me, pray, what I must pay you to remain in my service until Easter of next year." I told him that I did not wish him to pay me any more of his money than he had already done, but that I did wish to make another bargain with him.

500. " Since ", I said, " you are angry when anyone asks you for

anything, I want you to have a contract with me that if I ask you for anything all this year you will not be angry; and on my side I shall not be angry if you refuse me." He began to laugh heartily when he heard me, and told me that he retained me on those conditions. Taking me by the hand, he led me towards the Legate and his Council and told them of the bargain we had made. As I was the man of most importance in the camp, they were more than pleased.

501. I will now tell you how I settled and arranged my affairs during the four years* I stayed, after the King's brothers had gone. I had two chaplains with me who recited the Hours for me, one of them saying Mass for me as soon as the dawn appeared, the other waiting until my own knights and those of my division had risen. When I had heard my Mass I went out with the King. If he wished to ride, I accompanied him; sometimes it happened that messengers arrived for him, and it was necessary for us to work all morning.

502. My bed was so placed in my tent that no one could enter without seeing me in bed; this I did to avoid any scandal about women. At the approach of the feast of St. Remy I bought pigs for my sty and sheep for my fold, and flour and wine to furnish my establishment throughout the winter; this was because provisions rise in price during the winter, the sea being then more dangerous than in the summer.

503. I bought a hundred barrels of wine, of which I always had the best drunk first. The servants' wine I had mixed with water, the squires' with less water. At my own table the knights were served with a large flask of wine and another of water, so that they could mix it to their taste.

504. The King had put me in charge of a division of fifty knights. Whenever I ate, I had ten of these knights at my table with my own ten. They ate facing one another,* as is the custom of the country, seated on mats on the ground. Whenever there was a call to arms I sent out one of the fifty-four knights who were called *diseniers*, each one being in command of nine other men. When we rode out under arms all fifty knights ate in my lodging on our return. On every feast day of the year I invited all the chief men

in the camp, so that sometimes the King was obliged to borrow some of my guests.

XCIX

SOME OF THE KING'S JUDGMENTS

505. Now you must hear some of the sentences and judgments I heard pronounced during the King's stay at Caesarea. First I will tell you of a knight who was found in a brothel. By the custom of the country he was given a choice: either to be led through the camp by the whore, in his shirt, with a cord tied round his genitals, or to forfeit his horse and armour and be expelled from the camp. The knight chose to forfeit his horse and arms to the King, and left the camp.

506. I went and asked the King to give me the horse for a poor gentleman in the camp. The King said that my request was unreasonable, the horse being still worth eighty pounds. I replied, " How comes it that you have broken your bargain by being angry at my request? " The King said to me with a laugh, " You may say what you please, but I am not getting angry! " Still, I did not get the horse for the poor gentleman.

507. The second sentence was as follows: the knights of our division were hunting a wild animal called a gazelle, which is much like a deer. The Brothers of the Hospital attacked our men, handled them roughly and drove them off. I complained to the Master of the Hospital, and the Master answered that he would give me satisfaction according to the custom in the Holy Land, which was that he would make the brothers who were guilty of the offence take their meals sitting on their cloaks until those who had been wronged should allow them to rise.

508. The Master kept his word: when we saw that they had for some time been taking their meals in this way, I went to him, and, finding him at dinner, I asked him to allow the brothers who were forced to eat sitting on their cloaks in front of him to rise. The knights, too, on whom the attack had been made, made the same request. He answered that he would not do so, as he did not wish

his brothers to illtreat men who came on pilgrimage to the Holy
Land. When I heard his refusal I sat down myself with the
brothers and began to eat with them, and told him that I should
not get up until they did. The Master said that I was forcing his
hand, and granted my request. He had me and the knights that
accompanied me dine with him and the brothers went and ate
with the others sitting up at a table.

509. The third sentence I saw pronounced at Caesarea was this:
one of the King's men-at-arms, who was known as the Glutton,
laid hands on a knight in my division. I went and complained to
the King. He told me that I could well overlook it, he thought, as
the man-at-arms had only pushed him. I told the King that I
should not overlook it, and that if he did not give me satisfaction
I should leave his service, seeing that his men-at-arms could push
knights about.

510. He gave me satisfaction, and, by the custom of the country,
in this way: the man-at-arms came barefoot to my lodging, in shirt
and drawers, and no more, with a naked sword in his hand;
kneeling in front of the knight, he took the sword by the point and
presented the hilt to him, saying, " Sir, I make amends to you
for laying hands on you, and I have brought this sword, so that,
if you wish, you may cut off my hand." I asked the knight to
forgive his offence, and he did so.

511. The fourth punishment was this: Brother Hugh of Jouy, the
Marshal of the Temple, was sent by the Master of the Temple to
the Sultan of Damascus to negotiate with the Sultan an agreement
about a large tract of country which the Temple used to hold and
which the Sultan wished to divide between the two of them. The
division was agreed to, subject to the King's approval. Brother
Hugh brought back an emir representing the Sultan, with the
agreement written in legal form.*

512. The Master reported the matter to the King. The King was
astounded that he should have been so bold as to negotiate or
have any discussion with the Sultan without consulting him, and
wished for satisfaction. This he arranged as follows: the King
had the sides of three of his tents raised and any of the common
people in the camp who wished were allowed to enter. Then

the Master of the Temple and all his Brotherhood came barefoot through the camp, their own lodging being outside the
camp boundaries. The King had the Master and the Sultan's
envoy seated in front of him, and said in a loud voice to the
Master,

513. " Master, you will tell the Sultan's envoy that you repent of
having made any treaty with him without consulting me; and
since you did not consult me, you release him from any agreement
he made with you and return him his contract in its entirety."
The Master took the agreement, handed it back to the emir, and
said to him, " I give you back the agreement which I did wrong
to make, and of which I repent." Then the King told the Master
to rise and to allow all the brothers to rise. This he did. " And
now," said the King, " kneel and make amends to me for going
against my will."

514. The Master knelt and offered the end of his cloak to the
King, and surrendered to him all their possessions, to take from
them such indemnity as he might decide. " In the first place,"
said the King, " I pronounce that Brother Hugh, who made the
treaty, shall be banished from every part of the Kingdom of
Jerusalem." Neither the Master, who, with the King, was god-
father to the Count of Alençon,* born at Châtel-Pèlerin, nor the
Queen, nor any one else, could do anything to help Brother Hugh,
and he was obliged to leave the Holy Land and the Kingdom of
Jerusalem.

C

ALLIANCE WITH THE EGYPTIANS AGAINST THE SULTAN OF
DAMASCUS

515. While the King was fortifying Caesarea the envoys returned
to him from Egypt bringing him the treaty, the King's terms for
which I have already described. It was agreed between the two
parties that on a given day the King was to go to Jaffa; on the
same day the Egyptian emirs undertook on oath to be at Gaza, to
win for the King the Kingdom of Jerusalem. The King and the

chief men in the army swore to the terms of the treaty which the envoys had brought, and took an oath that we would help the Egyptians against the Sultan of Damascus.

516. When the Sultan of Damascus heard of our alliance with the Egyptians he sent to Gaza, where they were expected, four thousand well-equipped Turks, knowing that if once the Egyptians could join forces with us he might well be lost. Nevertheless, the King did not abandon his march to Jaffa. When the Count of Jaffa saw that the King was on the way, he so furnished his castle that it indeed had the appearance of a fine stronghold; at each battlement (and there were a good five hundred) hung a shield with his arms and a pennon, and, his arms being *or* with a cross *patée gules*, it was a noble sight to see.

517. Our camp was in the fields round the castle, which is built by the sea, reaching the shore on both sides. The King immediately began to build a fortification from shore to shore, encircling the new town which lies round the old castle. Often I saw him, to gain the indulgence, himself carrying a basket of earth at the entrenchments.

518. The Egyptian emirs, fearing to advance on Gaza, which was held by the forces of the Sultan of Damascus, failed to keep their agreement with us. Nevertheless they fulfilled their undertaking in sending the King all the Christian heads which they had hung from the walls of the castle of Cairo after the capture of the Count of Bar and the Count of Montfort. These the King had buried in consecrated ground. They sent him also the children who had been captured at the same time as the King, although, the children having already abjured the faith, they were loth to do so; and with these they sent him an elephant,* which he sent to France.

519. While we were at Jaffa an emir from the Sultan of Damascus's force came to cut the corn in a village three leagues from the camp. It was decided to attack him, but he fled at our approach. During his flight a young squire of good birth joined in the pursuit, brought down two of his knights without breaking his lance, and struck the emir with such force that he broke it in his body.

520. The envoys from the Egyptian emirs asked the King to fix a day for their joining him and they would come without fail. The

King decided not to reject their offer, and named a day, by which they promised, on oath, to be at Gaza.

CI

THE PRINCE OF ANTIOCH

521. While we were waiting for the day he had arranged with the Egyptian emirs, the Count of Eu, who was still a squire, arrived at the camp, bringing with him the good knight my Lord Ernoul of Guines, who had nine knights under him, including his two brothers. The Count remained in the King's service, and the King knighted him.

522. It was just at this time that the Prince of Antioch* and the Princess, his mother, returned to the camp. The King paid him great honour and knighted him with high ceremony. He was no more than sixteen years old, but I have never seen so sensible a boy. He asked the King to give him audience in his mother's presence. The King agreed, and, with his mother present, the Prince addressed the King as follows:

523. " Sir, it is true that my mother should act as regent for me for another four years. But that does not mean that she should allow my territory to be lost or weakened. I tell you this, sir, because while it is in her hands the city of Antioch is being lost. I beg you, then, sir, to ask her to give me men and money that I may go to the help of my people in Antioch and assist them. This, sir, she can well afford to do, for if I stay with her in the city of Tripoli it can only be at great expense, and I shall cause that great expense to no purpose."

524. The King listened favourably to him and did all that he could to induce his mother to hand over to him as much as he could extract from her. As soon as the Prince left the King he went to Antioch, where he acquitted himself well. As the King had knighted him, he allowed him, by his favour, to quarter his arms, which are gules, with the arms of France.

525. The Prince was accompanied by three minstrels from

Greater Armenia. They were brothers and were going on pilgrimage to Jerusalem; they had three horns, so curved that the sound came back into their own faces.* When they began to blow you would have said that it was the song of the swans rising from the lake; and they played melodies so sweet and graceful that it was wonderful to hear them.

526. These three were marvellous acrobats.* A towel was laid under their feet and they turned a standing somersault, landing upright with their feet on the towel. Two of them did it backwards; the third, the eldest, did the same; but when he was made to do a forward somersault he used to cross himself first, fearing that he might break his neck as he went over.

CII

THE GREAT COUNT WALTER OF BRIENNE

527. Since it is good that the memory of the Count of Brienne,* who was Count of Jaffa, should not be forgotten, I will now tell you about him, for he held Jaffa for many years and for a long time defended it by his vigour, and to a great extent lived on what he won from the Saracens and the enemies of the faith. Thus he once defeated a large force of Saracens with a rich convoy of cloth of gold and silk. He seized it all and, bringing it to Jaffa, divided it among his knights, retaining nothing for himself. It was his habit, when he left his knights, to shut himself in his chapel, where he spent a long time in prayer before he went at night to lie with his wife,* who was a lady of great goodness and wisdom, a sister to the King of Cyprus.

528. The Emperor of Persia, whose name was Barbaquan,* had been defeated, as I told you before, by one of the Tartar Princes. He invaded the Kingdom of Jerusalem with all his forces and took the castle of Tiberias, which had been fortified by my Lord Eudes of Montbéliard, the Constable, who was Lord of Tiberias by right of his wife. He inflicted great losses on our people, ravaging all he found outside Châtel-Pèlerin and Acre and Safad, and also

outside Jaffa. After these raids, he moved towards Gaza to join the Sultan of Babylon, who was to come there to harass and plunder our people.

529. The Syrian barons and the Patriarch decided to engage him before the Sultan of Babylon should arrive. They sent for assistance from the Sultan of La Chamelle,* one of the best knights that ever was among the infidels; at Acre they paid him the honour of spreading cloth of gold and silk in his path. Our men went to Jaffa, and the Sultan with them.

530. The Patriarch had excommunicated Count Walter for refusing to surrender to him a tower in Jaffa known as the Patriarch's tower. Our men asked Count Walter to march with them against the Emperor of Persia. He said that he would be glad to do so, provided the Patriarch would give him absolution until their return. The Patriarch refused, but nevertheless Count Walter accompanied them. Our men divided themselves into three corps, of which one was led by Count Walter, one by the Sultan of La Chamelle, and the third by the Patriarch and the barons of the country. In the Count of Brienne's corps were the Hospitallers.

531. They rode until they sighted the enemy. As soon as our men saw them they halted, and the enemy also formed up in three corps. While the Khwarizmians were drawing up their corps, Count Walter came to our men and called out, " For God's sake, my Lords, let us get at them! Our halt is giving them the time they need. " But he was unable to persuade any of them to move.*

532. Seeing this, Count Walter went to the Patriarch and asked him, as I described before, for absolution. The Patriarch refused. But with the Count of Brienne was a stout priest, the Bishop of Ramleh, who had done many fine deeds of knighthood in company with the Count. " Do not let your conscience be uneasy," he told him, " that the Patriarch will not give you absolution; he is in the wrong, and you are right, and I absolve you in the name of the Father, and of the Son, and of the Holy Ghost. Now, at them! "

533. Then they spurred to attack the Emperor of Persia's corps, which was the rearmost. On both sides there was terrible slaughter, and it was there that Count Walter was captured, all our men running so shamefully that many of them in desperation took to

the sea and were drowned. Their panic was caused by an attack that one of the Emperor of Persia's corps made on the Sultan of La Chamelle. Although the Sultan fought back desperately, when he left the field, of the two thousand Turks in his force there were only two hundred and eighty survivors.

CIII

Death of Count Walter

534. The Emperor decided to besiege the Sultan in the castle of La Chamelle, thinking that, having lost so many men, he would not be able to hold out for long. When the Sultan saw this he went to his men and told them that he was going out to give battle, since it would be fatal to allow himself to be besieged. His plan was to send those of his force who were not well armed to hide in a valley. As soon as they heard the beat of the Sultan's drums they attacked the Emperor's camp from the rear and began to slaughter the women and children.

535. When the Emperor, who had come out into the open country to attack the Sultan, whose force was in sight, heard the cries of his people, he immediately turned back to the camp to assist the women and children. Then the Sultan and his force fell on them, to such effect that of twenty-five thousand not one man nor woman escaped death by the sword.

536. Before moving on La Chamelle, the Emperor of Persia brought Count Walter before the walls of Jaffa. They hung him by the arms from a gibbet and said that they would not take him down until the castle of Jaffa was in their hands. While he was so hanging, the Count called out to those in the castle not to surrender the town, no matter what torture they might inflict on him, and that if they did surrender it he would put them to death himself.

537. Seeing this, the Emperor sent Count Walter to Babylon and made a present to the Sultan of him and the Master of the Hospital and of a number of other prisoners he had taken. There were three hundred men to escort the Count, and these escaped

the slaughter when the Emperor fell before La Chamelle. These Khwarizmians fought against us on the Friday* when we received the enemy's attack on foot. Their banners were scarlet, with deep indentions running back to the lance, and on the lances they had heads, made of hair,* which looked like the heads of devils.

538. Some of the merchants of Babylon appealed to the Sultan to give them satisfaction from Count Walter for the great damage he had done them. The Sultan allowed them to take their revenge on him. They went and killed him in prison and martyred him; and thus we do right to hold that he is numbered with the martyrs in Heaven.

539. The Sultan of Damascus led the force he had at Gaza to invade Egypt. The emirs marched out to engage him. The Sultan's own corps worsted the emirs whom he attacked, while the other Egyptian corps got the better of his rearguard. The Sultan accordingly fell back to Gaza, wounded in the head and hand. Before he left Gaza the Egyptian emirs sent envoys to him and made peace, so breaking all their agreements with us. In future we had neither truce nor peace with either Damascus or Babylon; and you should mark that at the most we never had a force of more than fourteen hundred men-at-arms.

CIV

A RAID

540. While the King was encamped before Jaffa, the Master of Saint Lazarus* had discovered near Ramleh, at a distance of ten to twelve miles, cattle and other valuables which he thought would provide him with fine plunder. He kept no discipline* in the camp, but did as he pleased; and, without consulting the King, he went to the spot. When he had collected his booty, the Saracens fell on him and handled him so roughly that of his whole force only four men escaped.

541. As soon as he reached the camp he began to raise the alarm. I went to arm myself and asked the King to allow me to go. He

gave me permission and told me to take the Templars and the Hospitallers with me. When we arrived we found that some more Saracens of another tribe had come down into the valley in which the Master of Saint Lazarus had been beaten. While these new-comers were examining the dead, the Master of the King's Cross-bowmen fell on them, and before we came up our men had worsted them and killed a number.

542. One of the King's men-at-arms and a Saracen brought each other to the ground with a blow from a lance. Another of the King's men-at-arms saw this, took the two horses and led them off to steal them. In order not to be seen he went between the walls of the city of Ramleh. As he was leading the horses, an old cistern he was crossing gave way beneath him, and he and the three horses fell to the bottom. Being told of this, I went to see, and found that the cistern was still collapsing on them and that both the man and the horses were close to being buried. Then we returned, with no loss apart from that incurred by the Master of Saint Lazarus.

CV

A Skirmish on St. John's Day

543. As soon as the Sultan of Damascus had made peace* with the Egyptians he ordered his force at Gaza to return to him. On their way they passed within less than two leagues of our camp, and although they numbered twenty thousand Saracens and ten thousand Bedouins they did not dare attack us. Before they came by our camp the Master of the King's Crossbowmen and his division kept them under observation for three days and nights, for fear that they might make a surprise attack on the camp.

544. On Saint John's Day, which was after Easter, the King was hearing his sermon. Before the preacher had finished, one of the men-at-arms of the Master of the King's Crossbowmen came armed into the King's chapel and told him that the Saracens had cut off the Master Crossbowman. I asked the King for per-mission to go, and he granted it; he told me to take with me up to

four or five hundred men-at-arms, naming those whom he wished me to take. As soon as we came out of the camp, the Saracens, who had got between it and the Master of the Crossbowmen, joined forces with an emir who was on a hill facing him, with at least a thousand men-at-arms.

545. Fighting then began between the Saracens and the Master's force, which numbered about two hundred and eighty men. Whenever the emir saw that his men were hard pressed he sent them sufficient reinforcements to throw our men-at-arms back on the Master's division; and when the Master saw that his men were similarly pressed he sent a hundred or a hundred and twenty men-at-arms, who flung the enemy back into the emir's force.

546. While we were there, the Legate and the barons of the country who had stayed with him told the King that he was very foolish to hazard me; by their advice, the King sent to recall me, and the Master of the Crossbowmen, too. The Turks retired, and we went back to camp. There were many who wondered that the enemy did not attack us, and some said that the only reason they refrained was that they and their horses had been famished in Gaza, where they had been for nearly a year.

CVI

FIGHTING OUTSIDE ACRE

547. After leaving the neighbourhood of Jaffa, these Saracens came before Acre and sent word to the Lord of Arsuf,* who was Constable of the Kingdom of Jerusalem, that unless he sent them fifty thousand besants they would destroy the gardens of the town. He sent them back a message refusing any payment. They then drew up in battle order and passed along the sands of Acre,* so close to the town that they were well within range of a swivel cross-bow. The Lord of Arsuf came out of the town and placed himself on St. John's Hill, where the cemetery of St. Nicholas is, to defend the gardens. Our infantry came out from Acre and began to harass the enemy with bows and crossbows.

548. The Lord of Arsuf called a Genoese knight, my Lord John le Grand, and ordered him to collect the lightly armed troops* who had come out of Acre, so that they should not endanger themselves. While he was leading them back a Saracen began to shout to him in Saracen that he would joust with him if he were willing. My Lord John said that he would be glad to accept his challenge. While he was riding towards the Saracen to joust with him he looked to his left and saw a group of Turks, about eight of them, who had stopped to see the jousting.

549. He left his duel with the Saracen who had challenged him, turned towards the group, who were standing still to watch it, struck one of them through the body with his lance and threw him down dead. Seeing this, the others fell on him as he was coming back to our ranks, and one of them struck him a great blow with his mace on his steel cap. As the Turk went by him, my Lord John caught him with his sword on the turban he wore twisted round his head and sent it flying into the field. They wore these turbans when they were going into battle, because they can stand a heavy blow from a sword.

550. Another Turk spurred at him and tried to catch him with his lance between the shoulders. My Lord John saw the lance coming, and swerved. As the Saracen went by he gave him a back-handed blow with his sword on his arm, sending the lance flying, and so came safely back, and brought in his infantry. These three fine blows he gave under the eyes of the Lord of Arsuf and the great men in Acre and of the ladies who were on the walls watching the Saracens.

CVII

THE SARACENS SACK SAYETTE

551. When this large Saracen force before Acre, which dared not face either us or the garrison of Acre in battle, heard, as was true, that the King was having the city of Sayette fortified, and that with few good troops, they moved off in that direction. Hearing of their approach, my Lord Simon of Montceliard,* the Master of

the King's Crossbowmen and commander of the royal garrison in Sayette, withdrew into the castle of Sayette, which is exceedingly strong and surrounded on all sides by the sea. He did this, realising that he had not the strength to stand up to them. With him he sheltered as many as he could; but the castle was too small to hold more than a few.

552. The Saracens burst into the town; it was not completely enclosed, and they met with no resistance. They killed more than two thousand of our people and returned to Damascus with the plunder they had taken. When the King heard the news he was greatly angered and would have given much to make good the loss.* The barons of the country, however, profited by it, since the King was anxious to fortify a hill on which formerly, in the time of the Machabees, there had been an old castle. This castle lies on the road from Jaffa to Jerusalem.

553. The overseas barons did not hold with the rebuilding of this castle; it is five leagues from the sea, and it would thus be impossible to send us provisions from the sea without their being intercepted by the Saracens, who were stronger than we were. When the news of the destruction of the town of Sayette reached the camp the barons approached the King and told him that it would be more profitable for him to rebuild the fortifications of Sayette, torn down by the Saracens, than to build a new fortress; and to this the King agreed.

CVIII

THE KING REFUSES, AS KING RICHARD REFUSED, TO LOOK ON JERUSALEM

554. While the King was at Jaffa he was told that the Sultan of Damascus would allow him to visit Jerusalem under a safe-conduct. The King held a full Council, the result of which was that no one was in favour of his going, since he would be obliged to leave the city in Saracen hands.

555. They pointed out to the King as an example that when the great King Philip left the siege of Acre to return to France he left

all his people behind in the camp with Duke Hugh of Burgundy,* the ancestor of the duke who has recently died. While the Duke was at Acre, and King Richard of England with him, news was brought to them that it would be possible for them on the next day to capture Jerusalem, if they wished, because all the Sultan of Damascus's knights had returned to him to take part in a war in which he was engaged with another Sultan. They prepared their force, the King of England leading the first division, while the Duke of Burgundy took the second, including the force of the King of France.

556. They were well set, they thought, for seizing the city, when word came from the Duke's division to King Richard not to advance farther, because the Duke was retiring; the only reason being that they did not wish it to be said that the English had taken Jerusalem. As they were talking, one of King Richard's knights called to him, " Sir, sir, come just here and I will show you Jerusalem." When the King heard him he threw his surcoat over his eyes and prayed, with tears, to Our Lord. " Dear Lord God, I beg You not to allow me to see Your Holy City, since I am not able to deliver it from the hands of Your enemies."*

557. They quoted this example to the King, to show him that if he, who was the greatest of Christian Kings, fulfilled his pilgrimage without delivering the city from the enemies of God, all the other Kings and pilgrims who came after him would feel that they were justified in making their pilgrimage in the same way as the King of France had made it, and would be little concerned with the deliverance of Jerusalem.

558. While he was overseas, King Richard wrought such feats of arms that when the Saracens' horses shied at a bush their masters used to say to them, " What do you take it for, King Richard of England? " And when their children wailed, the mothers said, " Quiet, quiet, or I shall fetch King Richard to eat you up."

CIX

THE KING FORTIFIES JAFFA

559. The Duke of Burgundy, of whom I spoke, was a very fine knight of his hands, but he was never thought to have the virtue of prudence in either sacred or secular matters, as is shown by the story I have just quoted. It was for this reason that the great King Philip, being told that Count John of Chalon had had a son, who was called Hugh after the Duke of Burgundy, said that he hoped God would make him as brave (*aussi preu*) a man as the Duke after whom he was named.

560. The King was asked why he had not said as brave and good (*aussi preudome*). "For this reason," he answered. "There is a world of difference between a brave man (*preu home*) and a brave and good man (*preudome*). There are, in Christian and Saracen lands, many brave knights, who have never believed in God nor His Mother. And that is why I say that God gives a great gift and a great grace to the Christian knight whom He permits both to be bodily brave and to be His servant, preserving him from mortal sin; and it is the man who so orders himself that one should call *preudome*, since his prowess is a gift from God. But those of whom I spoke before, one should call *preuz homes*, since they are physically brave, but take no heed either of God or of sin."

561. It is impossible to reckon the enormous sums of money the King spent in fortifying Jaffa; it was beyond any estimate. He built a wall with twenty-four towers round the town, from the sea on one side to the other, and the mud was cleared out of both the inner and outer ditches. There were three gates, one of which, with a section of the wall, was made by the Legate.

562. To show you how much the King spent, I can tell you that I asked the Legate how much this gate and the section of wall had cost him. He asked me how much I thought they cost. I reckoned that the gate he had built had cost him five hundred pounds and the section of wall three hundred. He told me that, God help him, the gate and wall together had cost him a good thirty thousand pounds.*

CX

FORTIFICATION OF SAYETTE

563. When the King had finished the fortifications of the town of Jaffa he decided to rebuild those of the city of Sayette, which the Saracens had destroyed. He set out for Sayette on the feast of Saints Peter and Paul, and he and his army camped before the castle of Arsuf, a place of great strength. That night the King summoned his people and told them that if they agreed he proposed to seize a Saracen city called Naplus, which the ancient Scriptures call Samaria.

564. The Templars and Hospitallers and the barons of the country unanimously answered that, though it would be well to try and seize the city, they did not agree that he should go in person, since if anything happened to him the whole country would be lost. The King replied that he would not allow them to go unless he accompanied them himself. The matter was left there, as the local lords refused to agree to his going.

565. By daily marches we reached the sands of Acre, where the King and his army encamped. It was there that a crowd of pilgrims to Jerusalem from Greater Armenia, who were paying a heavy toll to their Saracen escort, came to me and asked me, through an interpreter who knew our language and theirs, to let them see the holy King.

566. I went to the King, who was sitting in a tent, leaning against the tent-pole; he was seated on the sand, without a carpet or anything under him. " Sir," I said to him, " there is a crowd of people outside from Greater Armenia, who are on their way to Jerusalem. They are asking me, sir, to let them see the holy King; but I do not want to kiss your bones just yet." The King laughed out loud and told me to fetch them. When they had seen him, they commended him to God, and he them.

567. The next day the army lay at a place called Passe Poulain [Colts' Crossing], where there is excellent water which is used to irrigate the plant from which sugar is made. While we were

camped there one of my knights said to me, " Sir," he said, " I have given you a better site than you had yesterday." Another knight who had chosen my camping ground the time before flung himself furiously on him and shouted, " How dare you criticise my work! " He attacked him and seized him by the hair. I jumped at the man and punched him between the shoulders, and he let go. Then I said to him, " Now, get out of my camp, for God help me, you shall be in my company no more."

568. The knight went off very unhappily and brought my Lord Giles le Brun, the Constable of France, to see me. Seeing how bitterly the knight repented of his foolishness, he begged me most earnestly to take him back into my camp. I answered that I would not have him back unless the Legate released me from my oath. They went to the Legate and told him the story. He answered that it was impossible for him to release me, since the oath was a reasonable one, the knight having well deserved it. I tell you this, so that you may beware of making an oath when it is unreasonable to do so; for, as the sage says, " Quick to swear, quick to forswear."

CXI

EXPEDITION TO BANIYAS

569. On the next day the King went and camped before the city of Sur,* which in the Bible is called Tyre. There he summoned the chief men in the army and asked them whether it would be well to go and take the city of Belinas* before going to Sayette. We were all of the opinion that the King should send a force, but no one thought that he should go in person. It was only with great difficulty that the King was dissuaded, and it was agreed that the Count of Eu should go, with my Lord Philip of Montfort (the Lord of Sur), my Lord Giles le Brun (the Constable of France), my Lord Peter the Chamberlain, the Master of the Temple, the Master of the Hospital and their brethren.

570. At nightfall we armed ourselves, and a little before daybreak we reached a plain lying in front of the city which is now known

as Belinas, and in the ancient Scriptures is called Caesarea Philippi. A spring rises in this city called *Jor*; and in the middle of the plain before the city rises another very beautiful spring called *Dan*. Thus it is that when the streams from these two springs come together it is called the river Jordan, in which God was baptized.

571. By agreement between the Temple, the Count of Eu, the Hospital and the barons of the country who were present, it was decided that the King's division (to which I then belonged, the King having himself engaged the forty knights who were in my troop) and the good knight my Lord Geoffrey of Sargines, should advance between the castle and the city. The local barons were to make their way into the city on the left, the Hospitallers on the right, while the Templars were to enter straight ahead of the road by which we had come.

572. Our division advanced until we were close to the city, when we found that the Saracens in the town had got the better of the King's men-at-arms and thrown them out. Seeing this, I went to the good knights who were with the Count of Eu and said to them, " My lords, unless you go where we were told, between the city and the castle, the Saracens will slaughter those of our men who go into the town." It was a dangerous spot to reach, for in the ground we had to go over was the obstacle of three double dry walls to be crossed; the hill, too, was so steep that a horse could hardly keep its footing, and the hill which was our objective was held by a large force of Turkish cavalry.

573. While I was talking to them I saw that our infantry were breaking down the walls. Seeing this, I told the men to whom I was speaking that the King's division had been ordered to go to the position held by the Turks, and that, as those were the orders, I should go. I and two of my knights went to join the men who were breaking down the walls. I saw a mounted man-at-arms trying to cross, and his horse fell on him. Seeing this, I dismounted and took the horse by the bridle. By the grace of God, when the Turks saw us coming they abandoned the position we were to take, from which a precipitous cliff dropped down to the city.

574. When we had reached this place, and the Turks had left it, the Saracens in the city were worsted and abandoned it to our

men without further struggle. While I was there, the Marshal of the Temple heard that I was in danger and came up the hill towards me. I was still on the hill, when the Germans in the Count of Eu's division joined me. Seeing the Turkish cavalry retreating to the castle, they moved off in pursuit of them. I said to them, " My Lords, you are doing wrong; this is where we were told to go, and you are going beyond your orders."

CXII

PART OF THE DETACHMENT, INCLUDING THE AUTHOR, IS HARD PRESSED

575. The castle that overlooks the city is called Subeiba;* it lies a good half-league up into the mountains of Lebanon, and the hill that runs up to it is strewn with rocks as big as cupboards. When the Germans saw the folly of their pursuit they returned. Seeing this, the Saracens attacked them on foot, standing on the rocks and hitting them great blows with their maces and tearing off the housings of their horses.

576. The men-at-arms who were with us, seeing how the Germans were mauled, showed signs of panic. I told them that if they ran I should see that they were dismissed from the King's service for good. " Sir," they answered, " the game is too one-sided for us: you have a horse and can run, but we are on foot and the Saracens will kill us." " I assure you, sirs," I said, " that I shall not run. I shall stay with you, on foot." I dismounted and sent my horse back to the Templars, who were at long crossbow range to the rear.

577. As the Germans were retiring, the Saracens hit one of my knights with a bolt through the throat, and he fell dead right in front of me; this was my Lord John of Bussey. My Lord Hugh of Ecot, whose nephew he was, a man who proved himself well in the Holy Land, said to me, " Sir, come and help us to carry my nephew back down the hill." " Bad luck," I answered, " to the man who gives you a hand. You went up there without my orders, and if you

ran into trouble it was what you deserved. Carry him down to the refuse-heap yourself; I shall not leave until I am sent for."

578. When my Lord John of Valenciennes heard of our awkward position he went to my Lord Oliver of Termes,* and the other leaders of Languedoc and said to them, " My Lords, I beg and command you, by the King's authority, to help me to bring back the Seneschal." While he was making the arrangements for this my Lord William of Beaumont came to him and said, " You are giving yourself trouble for nothing; the Seneschal is dead." " Dead or alive," he answered, " I shall let the King know how he stands." He then moved off towards the position to which we had climbed on the mountain, and as soon as he reached us he sent for me to come and speak with him, which I did.

579. Oliver of Termes then told me that we were very dangerously situated : if we descended by the route up which we had come we could do so only at great risk; the hilly ground was very difficult and the Saracens would attack us from above. " But if you will trust me," he added, " I can bring you away without loss." I asked him to explain his plan and I would follow it.

580. " I will tell you," he said, " how we can get away. We shall go right along this slope* as though we were making for Damascus; the Saracens who are on it will think that we are going to take them in the rear. But when we reach the plain we shall gallop round the city and we shall have crossed the stream before they can overtake us. At the same time we will be able to do great damage to them by setting fire to the threshed corn in those fields."

581. We did as he advised, and he had us take hollow canes (the sort from which flutes are made), put live coals inside them and thrust them into the threshed corn. So God made use of Oliver of Termes' wits to bring us back to safety. I should tell you also that when we came back to where our men were camped we found that nobody had been concerned about us, and they had all put off their arms. So on the next day we returned to Sayette, where the King was.

CXIII

St. Louis Buries the Dead: the Count of Eu

582. We found that the King himself had had the Christians buried whom the Saracens, as I described before, had killed. With his own hands he carried the rotting and stinking corpses to be laid in the earth in trenches, and never stopped his nose as the others did. He gathered labourers from all parts and set himself to refortifying the city with high walls and strong towers. When we reached camp we found that the King in person had marked out our camping ground: he put me next to the Count of Eu, knowing that the Count liked my company.

583. I must tell you of the jokes the Count of Eu played on us. I had a building made in which I and my knights took our meals, by the light from the door. The door was on the Count of Eu's side, and the ingenious fellow made a little catapult with which he shot into the building.* He would watch until we had sat down to eat and then enfilade the table, breaking our jugs and glasses. I had laid in a stock of hens and capons. Someone, I do not know who, had given him a young she-bear:* he let it loose on my hens and it had killed a dozen before anyone could reach it. The woman who looked after the hens beat it off with her distaff.

CXIV

The Tartars Capture Bagdad

584. While the King was fortifying Sayette, merchants came to the camp who told us how the King of the Tartars had captured the city of Bagdad and the Saracen Pope, the Lord of the city, who was known as the Caliph of Bagdad. The merchants described to us the way in which they took the city and the Caliph. It was as follows: When they had invested the Caliph's city, the Tartar King sent a message to the Caliph saying that he would be

willing to arrange marriages between his own children and the Caliph's. The Caliph's councillors advised him to agree to the marriage.

585. The King of the Tartars then told him to send no less than forty of his Council and of the men of most standing to swear to the marriage. The Caliph did this, and the King then told him to send another forty of his best and richest subjects. Again the Caliph did so. A third time the King told him to send forty of the best men in his own household, and the Caliph obeyed. When the King of the Tartars saw that he held all the important men of the city, he felt that the common folk would be unable to defend themselves without leaders. He had all the hundred and twenty chief men beheaded, and then assaulted and captured the town, and took the Caliph prisoner.*

586. To mask his treachery and to throw on the Caliph the blame for his seizing the city he had the Caliph arrested and placed in an iron cage. There he kept him without food for as long as one can keep a man, short of death, and then asked him if he was hungry. The Caliph answered that he was, which was little wonder. Then the Tartar King had a great golden dish brought to him, loaded with jewels and precious stones, and said to him, " Do you recognise these jewels?" " Yes," the Caliph answered, " they were mine." The King then asked him if he loved them, and he answered, " Yes."

587. " Since you love them so much," said the Tartar King, " come, help yourself to your taste, and eat." The Caliph answered that he could not do so, for it was not food that one could eat. Then the King told him, " Now you can see where your defence lay; for had you given your treasure—so useless now—to soldiers, in so spending what fails you now in your greatest need, you would have provided yourself with a firm defence against us."

CXV

THE AUTHOR SUSPECTS AN ASSASSIN

588. One day, while the King was fortifying Sayette, I went to his Mass at dawn. He told me to wait for him, because he wished to ride out, and I did so. In the open country we came by a little church and, still mounted, we saw a priest singing Mass. The King told me that this church had been built in honour of the miracle which God wrought in casting out the devil from the body of the widow's daughter, and said that, if I pleased, he would go in and hear the Mass which the priest had begun. I told him that I thought we should do so.

589. When it came to the kiss of peace, I noticed that the clerk who served was a big man, dark, lean and hairy, and I was afraid that if he took the pax* to the King he might perhaps be a blackguardly assassin and kill the King. I went and took the pax from him and gave it to the King. When Mass was over and we had mounted our horses, we met the Legate out in the fields. The King went up to him, and, calling me, he said to him, " I have a complaint to make to you about the Seneschal; he brought me the kiss of peace himself, and would not allow the poor clerk to do so."

590. I told the Legate why I had done so, and he said that I had been quite right. The King answered, " Indeed, no." There was a great argument between them, but I kept quiet. I have told you this story to illustrate the King's great humility. The Gospel speaks of this miracle which God worked on the widow's daughter, saying that at the time of the miracle God was *in parte Tyri et Syndonis,* for in those days the cities of Sur and Sayette, of which I have spoken, were called Tyre and Sidon.

CXVI

The Queen Returns to Sayette

591. While the King was fortifying Sidon envoys came to him from a great Lord in far Greece who called himself the Great Comnenus* and Lord of Trebizond. They brought presents to the King of various jewels. Among other things they brought him bows made of horn,* the nocks of which were screwed into the bows and though you thought they were on the outside, you found they were on the inside, neatly tapered and very well made.

592. The envoys asked the King to send their Lord a lady from his household for him to take to wife. The King answered that he had brought none with him from over the sea and advised them to go to the Emperor at Constantinople, his cousin, and ask him to give their Lord a wife who would be of the Emperor's lineage and his own. This he suggested so that the Emperor might have this great and important man as an ally against Vataces, who was then the Emperor of the Greeks.

593. The Queen, who had recently risen after the birth of Lady Blanche,* whom she had borne at Jaffa, arrived at Sayette, having come by sea. When I heard of her arrival, I got up from the King's presence and went to meet her and brought her back to the castle.

594. When I returned to the King, who was in his chapel, he asked me if the Queen and the children were well and I told him that they were. He said to me, " When you got up and left me I knew that you were going to meet the Queen, and so I have delayed the sermon for you." I tell you this, because I had been with him then for five years without his ever, to my knowledge, mentioning the Queen or his children to me or to anyone else; and I do not think it was kindly so to be a stranger to his wife* and children.

CXVII

A Poor Knight and His Children

595. On All Saints' Day I invited all the great men in the camp to my lodging, which was beside the sea. A poor knight landed from a barge, with his wife and his four sons. I brought them to dine in my lodging. After dinner I called on the rich men who were with us and said, " Let us do a great act of charity and relieve this poor man of his children. Let each choose his own, and I will take one, too." They all chose a child and argued as to who should have him. When the poor knight saw this he and his wife began to weep with joy.

596. Later, when the Count of Eu came back from the King's lodging, where he had dined, he came to see the great men in my lodging and took my child from me, who was twelve years old. The boy served the Count so well and faithfully that when we returned to France he arranged a marriage for him and knighted him. Whenever I was with the Count he could hardly tear himself away from me and used to say, " Sir, God reward you! For it was you that gave me the honourable station I hold." What happened to his three brothers I do not know.

CXVIII

Pilgrimage to Tortosa

597. I asked the King to allow me to go on a pilgrimage to Our Lady of Tortosa, which was a great place for pilgrims, being the first altar in the world to be built in honour of the Mother of God. There Our Lady used to work great miracles. Among others, there was a maniac who was possessed by the devil. When his friends who had brought him prayed to the Mother of God to give him back his health the Enemy within him answered, " Our Lady is not here: she is in Egypt, to help the King of France and

the Christians who today will land on foot in that country in the teeth of the mounted infidels."

598. The day was noted in writing and given to the Legate, who told me of it himself with his own mouth. And you may be sure that Our Lady did help us, and would have given us still more help, had we not angered both her and her Son, as I told you before.

599. The King gave me leave to go, and asked me privately to buy for him a hundred lengths of camelhair cloth* of different colours, to give to the Franciscans when we should arrive in France. This cheered my heart, for I thought that he would not be staying long. When we arrived at Tripoli, my knights asked me what I meant to do with the camelhair and begged me to tell them. " Perhaps," I answered, " I stole it to make some money."

600. The Prince of Tripoli* (God grant him His mercy) received us with all the joy and honour he could show us, and would have loaded me and my knights with gifts had we been willing to accept them. We would not, however, take anything except some of his relics, a number of which I brought back to the King with the camelhair I had bought for him.

601. In addition I sent the Queen four lengths of camelhair. The knight who gave them to her carried them wrapped in a white towel. When the Queen saw him enter her room she knelt before him, and the knight in turn knelt to her. The Queen said, " Rise up, Sir Knight; you should not kneel, for you are carrying the relics." But the knight answered, " Lady, they are not relics, they are lengths of camelhair which my Lord is sending you." When the Queen and her ladies heard this they began to laugh, and the Queen said to my knight, " Tell your Lord that I wish him bad luck for making me kneel to camelhair cloth."

602. While the King was at Sayette he was brought a stone which flaked off in scales: it was the most wonderful thing in the world, because when you lifted a scale you found between the two pieces of stone the shape of a sea fish. The fish was made of stone, but it was complete in shape, the eyes, the bones, the colour and every- thing just as if it were alive. The King gave me a stone, and inside I found a tench, brown, and made exactly as a tench should be.

CXIX

DEATH OF QUEEN BLANCHE

603. At Sayette news came to the King of his mother's death. He was so overcome by grief that for two days no one could speak to him. He then sent one of the servants of his chamber to fetch me. When I came to him in his room, where he was alone, and he saw me, he flung out his arms and said to me, " Ah, Seneschal, I have lost my mother! "

604. " Sir," I said, " I do not wonder at that, for she had to die; but I do wonder that you, who are a man of sense, should have shown such grief. For you know what the wise man says, that a man should not show in his face the sorrow he has in his heart; for to do so is to make his enemies happy and his friends sad." Overseas he had many grand services held for her, and afterwards he sent to France a pack-horse loaded with letters asking for prayers to be said for her in the churches.

605. My Lady Mary of Vertus, a very good lady and a very holy woman, came and told me that the Queen was overcome by grief and asked me to go and comfort her. When I came to her I found her weeping and told her that the man who said that one should not rely on a woman spoke the truth. " For it is the woman you most hated who is dead, and yet you are making such a show of grief." She told me that it was not for the Queen she wept, but for the sorrow of my Lord the King and for his daughter* (who was afterwards Queen of Navarre) who was left to the care of men.

606. Queen Blanche treated Queen Margaret with great harshness; so much so that as far as she could she prevented her son from being in his wife's company, except at night when he slept with her. The palace in which the King and Queen liked best to live was Pontoise, because the King's room was over the Queen's on the next floor.

607. They had a plan by which they used to talk together on a winding staircase which led from one room to the other, and they arranged that when the ushers saw Queen Blanche going to her

son's room they knocked on the doors with their rods; the King then used to run up to his room so that his mother might find him there; and when the ushers at Queen Margaret's door saw Queen Blanche coming they did the same so that she might be found in her own room.

608. Once the King was with the Queen, his wife, who was in great danger of death in childbed. Queen Blanche came, and, taking her son by the hand, said to him, " Come away, you can do no good here." When Queen Margaret saw her taking the King away she cried out, " Alas! You will not allow me, dead or alive, to see my Lord." Then she fainted and it was thought she was dead. The King, who thought she was dying, came back, and with great difficulty she was revived.

CXX

The King Decides To Go Home

609. Just when the fortification of Sidon was nearly completed the King arranged several processions in the camp, at the end of which the Legate had prayers said that God might order the King's affairs in accordance with His will, so that the King should do whichever was the more pleasing to God—return to France or stay abroad.

610. After the processions were over, I was sitting with the notables of the country, when the King called me into a courtyard and made me turn my back to them; then the Legate said to me, " Seneschal, the King sets great store by your service and would be glad to increase your profit and honours; and to set your mind at rest, he has told me to tell you that he has arranged to return to France this coming Easter." I answered, " God grant that therein he may do His will."

611. The Legate then rose and asked me to accompany him to his lodging, which I did. Then he shut himself, alone with me and no other, in his private room, took my two hands in his, and began to weep bitterly. When he could speak, he said to me, " Seneschal,

I am indeed glad, and I thank God that the King and you and the other pilgrims are escaping from the great danger in which you have been in this country. But my heart is deeply grieved that I shall be obliged to quit your godly company and go to the Court of Rome, among the faithless folk who frequent it."

612. " But I will tell you what I purpose to do: I still intend to arrange to stay here for a year after you, and I mean to spend all my money on fortifying the suburbs of Acre, so that the Romans will see that I am not bringing back any money, and then they will not pester me to see what they can get from me."

613. Once I told the Legate of two sins of which one of my priests had told me. His answer was this: " No one knows as well as I do the wicked sins that are committed in Acre; God should take such vengeance for them that the city of Acre should be washed in the blood of its inhabitants, and other folk should then come and live in it." This good man's prophecy has been partly fulfilled, for the city has indeed been washed in the blood of its inhabitants, but those who should live in it have not yet come. May God send good men and such as live according to His will.*

CXXI

PREPARATIONS FOR DEPARTURE

614. It was after this that the King sent for me and told me to go and arm myself—and my knights, too. I asked him why, and he told me that it was to escort the Queen and his children to Sur, a distance of seven leagues. I did not answer a word, and yet it was a dangerous assignment, for at that time we had no truce nor peace with either the Egyptians or the Damascenes. By the mercy of God, we arrived in perfect safety, without hindrance, at nightfall, although we had twice been obliged to dismount in hostile country to light a fire and cook food, and to feed and suckle the children.

615. When the King left the city of Sayette, which he had fortified with high walls and towers and with deep ditches on both

sides, well cleaned out, the Patriarch and the barons of the country came to him and addressed him as follows:

616. " Sir, you have fortified the city of Sayette, and that of Caesarea, and the town of Jaffa, which is of great service to the Holy Land; and you have greatly strengthened the city of Acre by the walls and towers you have built. Sir, we have consulted among ourselves and we do not see that your further stay can in any way benefit the Kingdom of Jerusalem. Hence we urge and advise you to go to Acre this coming Lent and prepare your crossing so that you may leave for France after this Easter." On the advice of the Patriarch and the barons the King left Sayette and went to Sur, where the Queen was; and from Sur, at the beginning of Lent,* we went to Acre.

617. All during Lent the King was preparing his ships, of which he had thirteen, including galleys, for his return to France. The preparation of the ships and galleys was completed in time for the King and Queen to embark after Easter, on the vigil of Saint Mark, and we had a favourable wind for our sailing. On Saint Mark's day* the King told me that he was born on that day, and I told him that he might well add that he was born again on that day, for his escape from that dangerous country was certainly a second birth.

CXXII

The Ship Strikes Off Cyprus

618. On the Saturday, we made the island of Cyprus, and sighted a mountain on it, called the Mountain of the Cross. On that Saturday a mist rose from the land and came down over the sea, and thus our sailors, seeing the mountain through the mist, thought we were further from Cyprus than we were. They accordingly sailed boldly on, with the result that our ship struck on a submerged sandbank. As it happened, had we not chanced to hit that little patch of sand we should have struck a pile of covered rocks on which our ship would have been broken to pieces and we should all have been wrecked and drowned.

619. Immediately our ship struck, a huge cry went up on board. Everyone was calling out "Alas!"; the sailors and the passengers, all terrified of drowning, were beating their hands. Hearing the noise, I got up from my bed on which I was lying and went to the poop with the sailors. When I arrived, Brother Raymond, who was a Templar and in command of the sailors, said to one of his men, "Cast your lead!" The man did so, and as soon as he had cast it he called out, "Alas, we are aground." When Brother Raymond heard this he tore his tunic right down to his belt and began to pull out his beard and shout, "Woe, oh, woe is me!"*

620. At this moment one of my knights, by name my Lord John of Monson, the father of Abbot William of Saint Michael, did me a great kindness; without saying anything he brought me a fur-lined surcoat of mine and threw it on my back (I had only my tunic on). I called to him and said, "What do I want with this surcoat of yours that you are bringing me just as we are drowning?" "On my soul, sir," he said, "I would rather we were all drowned than that you should catch your death of cold."

621. The sailors shouted, "Galley ahoy! To pick up the King!" But not one of the four galleys the King had with him drew alongside; and in this they were very wise, for there were a good eight hundred persons on board the ship, and they would all have jumped into the galleys in an attempt to save their lives, and so the galleys would have been swamped.

622. The man who had cast the lead made another cast and came back to Brother Raymond and told him that the ship was no longer aground. Brother Raymond then went to tell the King, who was lying prostrate in the form of a cross on the ship's bridge, bare-footed, just in his tunic, his hair dishevelled, before the Body of Our Lord which was reserved in the ship; he was like a man who expected to drown at any moment. As soon as it was daylight, we saw in front of us the rock on which we should have struck had we not hit the sandbank.

CXXIII

St. Louis Refuses To Leave The Damaged Ship

623. In the morning the King sent for the master-mariners of the ships, who sent four divers down into the water. They dived overboard, and when they came on board again the King and the masters questioned them one by one, so that none of the divers knew what the other had reported. However, they learnt from the four of them, that with the ship's grating on the sand, the sand had torn away four fathoms of the keel on which the ship was built.

624. The King then called the masters before him and asked what would be their advice about the damage the ship had suffered. They consulted together and advised the King to leave the ship he was in and embark in another.

625. " And we give you this advice, because we are sure that all the timbers of your ship have started, which makes us fear that when it is out at sea it will not be able to stand the shock of the waves without going to pieces. When you sailed from France, a ship struck in the same way, and when she was on the high seas she could not stand the shock of the waves and went to pieces, and all who were in her were lost, except a woman and her child who were saved on a fragment of the ship." I can witness myself to the truth of what they said, for I saw the woman and child in the city of Paphos, at the lodging of the Count of Joigny, who charitably looked after them for the love of God.

626. The King then asked my Lord Peter the Chamberlain and my Lord Giles le Brun, the Constable of France, and my Lord Gervase of Escraines, the King's Master Cook, and the Archdeacon of Nicosia, who carried his seal and was afterwards a Cardinal, and me, what was our advice in the matter. We answered that in all practical affairs of the world one should trust those who knew most about them: " Therefore, for our part, we advise you to do what the sailors propose."

627. Then the King said to the sailors, " Tell me, by the loyalty

you owe me, if the ship was yours and laden with your goods, would you abandon it?" Without exception they all answered No, that they would rather take the risk of drowning than buy another ship for four thousand pounds or more. " Why, then, do you urge me to leave her?" " Because," they said, " the stakes are not equal: neither gold nor silver can equal in value your own person and that of your wife and children who are on board. That is why we urge you not to imperil yourself nor them."

628. Finally the King said, " My Lords, I have heard your opinion and that of my own men. Now I will tell you mine. It is this: If I leave the ship, it means that there are five hundred persons or more on board who will stay on the island of Cyprus, out of fear for the danger in which they stand (for there is no one here who does not love his life as much as I do mine), and who perhaps will never get back home. Hence, I would rather put myself and my wife and my children in the hands of God than cause such distress to so many persons as are on board."

629. The great distress the King would have caused to the people in his ship can be seen by what happened to Oliver of Termes, who was also on board. He was one of the bravest men I have ever seen, and none made a better showing than he did in the Holy Land, but he would not stay with us, for fear of drowning. He remained in Cyprus, where he met with such difficulties that it was a year and a half before he could get back to the King; and he was a man of position and rich, and well able to pay his passage. Imagine, then, what would have happened to humble folk who had no money with which to pay, when a man like him had such trouble.

CXXIV

A STORM AT SEA

630. After this danger, from which God delivered us, we fell into another. The wind which had thrown us on Cyprus, where we were nearly drowned, got up with such strength and ferocity that

it drove us back by force on to the island. The sailors put out anchors to hold us against the wind, but were unable to check the ship until they had got out five. They were obliged to break down the bulwarks of the King's cabin, and there was no one who dared to stay in it for fear of being blown into the sea by the wind. The Constable of France, my Lord Giles le Brun, and I were sleeping there, and just then the Queen opened the door, thinking to find the King in his cabin.

631. I asked her what she was looking for, and she told me that she had come to speak to the King and ask him to promise God, or one of His saints, to make a pilgrimage, so that He might deliver us from the danger in which we stood; for the sailors had said that we were in danger of drowning. I said to her, " Lady, promise the pilgrimage to my Lord Saint Nicholas* of Varangéville, and I pledge my word for him that God will bring you back to France, with the King and your children." " Seneschal," she said, " indeed I will gladly do so. But the King is so difficult that if he knew that I had made the promise without asking him he would never let me go."

632. " There is one thing you can do," I told her. " If God brings you back to France, promise him a ship made of silver, five marks* in weight, for the King, and yourself, and your three children; and I can be your surety that God will bring you back to France, for I promised Saint Nicholas that if he saved us from the danger in which we have been tonight I would walk barefoot from Joinville to say my prayers to him." She told me that she promised Saint Nicholas the silver ship, five marks in value, and that I would be her surety for it, and I said that I should willingly do so. Then she went, and had only been gone a moment, when she came back to us and said to me, " Saint Nicholas has saved us from the danger; the wind has dropped."

633. When the Queen (God grant her His mercy) was back in France she had the silver ship made in Paris. In the ship were the King, the Queen and the three children, all in silver; silver sailors, and masts, and rudder and rigging, and the sail all sewn with silver thread. The Queen told me that it had cost a hundred

pounds to make. When it was finished, she sent it to me at Join-ville so that I could have it taken to Saint Nicholas, which I did; and I saw it again at Saint Nicholas when we escorted the King's sister* to Haguenau, to the King of Germany.

CXXV

St. Louis Speaks of God's Warnings

634. But to come back to our story: I must tell you that after our escape from these two dangers the King sat down on the rail of the ship, made me sit at his feet, and said to me, " God has indeed shown us how mighty He is, for one of those petty winds (not one of the master winds) came close to drowning the King of France, his wife and his children, and all his company. So we should be grateful to Him and give Him thanks for the danger from which He has delivered us."

635. " Seneschal," said the King, " when people are visited by such trials, or great sicknesses, or other hardships, the saints say that they are Our Lord's warnings; for just as God says to those who recover from great sickness, '.Now you realise that I might well have killed you, had I wished , so can He say to us, ' Now you realise that I might have drowned you, had I wished.' "

636. " We should, then," said the King, " examine ourselves in case there is anything in us which is displeasing to Him, for which He has given us such a fright, so that we may cast it out of our-selves; if we do not do so after the warning He has given us His hand will be heavy on us and punish us with death, or some other great distress of bodily or spiritual injury."

637. " Seneschal," he continued, " the Saint says, ' Lord God, why do You warn us? For had You caused us all to perish, you would not be the poorer for it; nor would You be the richer by keeping us all.' So may we see, says the Saint, that the warnings which God gives us are not to advance His profit nor to save Him loss; it is only for the great love He bears us that He rouses us by His warnings, so that we may examine our faults closely and rid

ourselves of what is displeasing to Him.   And if we do so," he added, " we shall do wisely."

CXXVI

LAMPEDUSA

638. After taking in fresh water and other things we needed, we left the island of Cyprus and arrived at an island called Lampedusa,* where we caught a great number of rabbits. Among the rocks we found an old hermitage and the garden which the hermits who used to live there had made many years before. There were olive trees, fig trees, vine stocks, and other trees in the garden, and through it ran a stream from the spring. We went with the King to the end of the garden, and found an oratory; the first vault was whitewashed, with a cross of red earth.

639. We went into the second vault, and found two dead men's bodies, the flesh completely rotted away; the ribs still held together, the bones of their hands were crossed on their breasts, and they lay facing the east, just as they are arranged for burial in the ground. As we were going on board again, we missed one of our sailors. The Ship's Master thought that he had stayed behind to become a hermit, and Nicholas of Soisy, who was the King's chief steward,* left three bags of biscuit on the shore so that he might find them and have something to live upon.

CXXVII

PANTELLARIA: SOME YOUNG MEN DELAY THE FLEET AND ARE PUNISHED

640. After leaving Lampedusa, we sighted a large island in the sea called Pantellaria.* It was inhabited by Saracens, subjects of the King of Sicily* and the King of Tunis. The Queen asked the King to send over three galleys to get fruit for her children; he agreed, and told the master of the galleys to be ready to come

alongside as the King's ship was passing by the island. They landed at the port, but as the King's ship passed by it we could see nothing of our galleys.

641. The sailors then began to mutter to one another. The King called them up and asked them what they thought had happened. They answered that they thought the Saracens had captured his men and the galleys. " But we urge and advise you, sir, not to wait for them, since you are between the Kingdoms of Sicily and Tunis, neither of which is friendly to you. If you allow us to sail on we shall before night have taken you out of danger—we shall have got you through the narrows."

642. " In truth," said the King, " I shall not be persuaded to leave my men in the hands of the Saracens without at least doing what I can to rescue them. I order you to shift your sails; we shall attack the Saracens." When the Queen heard this she began to be greatly distressed, saying, " Poor wretch, this is all my doing! "

643. While they were changing course on the King's ship and the others we saw the galleys leaving the island. When they reached the King he asked the sailors why they had delayed. They answered that they could not help it; those to blame were some young Parisians. Six of these were eating fruit in the gardens; they could not get them to come, and did not wish to leave them behind. The King ordered these six to be put in the ship's boat. They began to cry and wail, " Sir, for the love of God, fine us all we have, but do not put us where murderers and robbers are put, for it will always be a reproach to us."

644. The Queen and we did all we could to induce the King to relent, but he would not listen to any of us. They were put in the boat and stayed there until we landed, in terrible discomfort, because when there was a high sea the waves dashed over their heads and they had to crouch down for fear the wind should blow them into the sea. But it served them right, because through their greediness we were delayed a full week* by the King's making the ships turn right back on their course.

CXXVIII

Fire in the Queen's Cabin

645. Here is another adventure that happened to us at sea before we reached land. When one of the Queen's waiting women had helped the Queen to bed she was careless and threw her headscarf down by the iron candlestick in which the Queen's nightlight was burning. After she had gone to bed herself in the cabin below the Queen's, where the women slept, the candle flared up and caught the scarf, and from the scarf it spread to the sheets which were laid over the Queen's clothes.

646. When the Queen woke up, she found the cabin full of flames. She jumped up naked, took the scarf and threw it still burning into the sea, and, picking up the sheets, she beat out the flames. The men in the ship's boat shouted in a half-hearted way,* " Fire! Fire! " I raised my head and saw the scarf still burning brightly on the surface of the sea, which was very calm. I put on my tunic as quickly as I could and went and joined the sailors where they were sitting.

647. As I was sitting there, my squire, who slept at the foot of my bed, came and told me that the King had woken up and had asked where I was. " I told him that you had gone to the heads, and the King said to me, ' You are lying.' " As we were talking, along came Master Geoffrey, the Queen's clerk, who told me not to worry, because it had happened as I have described. " Master Geoffrey," I said to him, " go and tell the Queen that the King is awake and that she should go and set his mind at rest."

648. The next day, the Constable of France, my Lord Peter the Chamberlain, and my Lord Gervase, the Master Cook, asked the King, " What happened in the night, that we heard talk of a fire? " I did not say a word. The King answered, " It must be that unhappily the Seneschal is more secretive than I am; so I will tell you how it was that we were all nearly burnt last night."

649. He told them how it had happened, and then said, " Seneschal, I order you in future not to go to bed until you have put out

all the fires on board, except the main galley fire in the hold;* and I warn you that I shall not go to bed until you have reported to me." I did this all the time we were at sea, and the King went to bed after I had reported.

CXXIX

A Squire is Saved from Drowning

650. We had another adventure at sea. My Lord Dragonet, one of the chief men of Provence, was sleeping one morning in his ship, which was a good league ahead of ours. He called one of his squires and told him, " Shut this port—the sun strikes on my face." The squire saw that he could do so only from the outside, so he went over the side. As he was closing the port his foot slipped and he fell into the water. It was a small ship and had no boat, and he was quickly left behind. We saw him from the King's ship, and thought it was a bundle or a barrel, for the man who had fallen into the water was making no attempt to save himself.

651. One of the King's galleys picked him up and brought him on board our ship, where he told us how it had happened. I asked him how it was that he did not try to save himself by swimming or otherwise. He answered that there was no need at all for him to bother himself, for as soon as he began to fall he commended himself to Our Lady of Vauvert and she held him up by the shoulders from the time he fell until the King's galley picked him up. In honour of this miracle I have had a picture of it painted in my chapel at Joinville and in the windows at Blécourt.

CXXX

Arrival off Hyères

652. After being ten weeks at sea we made land at a port two leagues from a castle called Hyères, which belonged to the Count

of Provence,* who was afterwards King of Sicily. The Queen
and all the Council were agreed that he should land there, since it
was in his brother's territory. The King answered that he would
not disembark until he arrived at Aigues Mortes, in his own
territory. All the Wednesday and Thursday he insisted against us
on this point, and we could not persuade him.

653. In these Marseilles ships there are two steering oars, attached
so cleverly to two tillers that you can turn the ship to right or
left as easily as you can turn a horse. On the Friday the King
was sitting on one of these tillers, when he called me and said,
" Seneschal, what do you think about this business? " " Sir," I
answered him, " it would serve you right if it happened to you
as it did to my Lady of Bourbon, who refused to land here and
put back again to sea, meaning to go on to Aigues Mortes, and
was another seven weeks at sea."

654. The King then called his Council and told them what I had
said and asked them what they thought he should do. They all
advised him to land, saying that, having once survived the dangers
of the sea, it would be rash again to expose his own person, and his
wife and children, to them. The King agreed to our advice, at
which the Queen was greatly pleased.

CXXXI

They Land at Hyères

655. The King landed from the sea, with the Queen and his
children, at the castle of Hyères. While he was at Hyères waiting
to get horses to go to France, the Abbot of Cluny, who was afterwards Bishop of Oliva, gave him a present of two ponies, which
would nowadays be worth at least five hundred pounds, one for
himself and one for the Queen. After presenting them, he said to
the King, " Sir, tomorrow I shall come and talk to you about my
affairs." The morrow came and the Abbot returned. The King
listened to him attentively for a long time. After the Abbot had
gone I went to the King and said to him, " I have a question to ask

you: did you give the Abbot of Cluny a more gracious reception because he gave you those two ponies yesterday? "

656. The King thought for a long time, and then said, " To speak the truth, the answer is Yes." " Do you know, sir," I asked him, "why I asked you that question? " " Why? " he said. " Because, sir," I answered, " I strongly urge you, when you are back in France, to forbid any of your sworn councillors to accept any gifts from persons who have business to put before you, for you may be sure that if they accept anything they will listen more readily and attentively to the givers, just as you did to the Abbot of Cluny." Later the King summoned all his Council and the first thing he told them was what I had said, and they agreed that I had given him good advice.

CXXXII

Brother Hugh Preaches to the King

657. The King heard of a Grey Friar called Brother Hugh; his reputation was such that he sent for him, wishing to see him and hear him speak. The day the friar came to Hyères we were watching the road by which he was coming, and saw a great crowd of men and women following him on foot. The King heard him preach. He began his sermon by speaking of religious, saying, " My Lords, I see too many religious at the King's Court and in his household "; and added, " To begin with, I am one too many myself;* and I say that, unless the Holy Scriptures lie to us, which is impossible, they are in no state to save their souls.

658. " For the Holy Scriptures tell us that the monk cannot live outside his cloister without mortal sin, any more than a fish can live out of water. And if the religious who live with the King say that they are living in a cloister, then I tell them that it is the widest I have ever seen—for it stretches right across the sea. If they say that in this cloister a man can live an austere life for his soul's salvation, I do not believe them; but I can tell you that in their company I have eaten great store of different flesh meats and drunk good wines, strong and clear; and so I am certain that

had they been in their cloister they would not have enjoyed such comfort as they do with the King."

659. In his sermon he taught the King that he should act in accordance with the will of his people; and he finished by saying that he had read the Bible and books that correspond to the Bible, and he had never, either in Christian or infidel books, seen any kingdom or lordship lost, or transferred from one government or king to another, except through some lack of justice. " The King, then," he said, " should be careful, now that he is returning to France, to do such justice to his people that he may thereby retain the love of God, so that God may not deprive him of his Kingdom during his lifetime."

660. I told the King that he should do all he could to keep Brother Hugh with him. He told me that he had already asked him, but Brother Hugh would not listen to him. Then the King took me by the hand and said, " Come, let us go and ask him again." We went to Brother Hugh and I said to him, " Sir, do as my Lord asks you, and stay with him while is he in Provence." He answered me very angrily, " Indeed, sir, I will not do so. I will go to a place where God will love me better than in the King's company." He stayed one day with us, and went on the next. I have since heard that he is buried at Marseilles, where he works many fine miracles.

CXXXIII

St. Louis Rates His Servant

661. The day the King left Hyères he came down on foot from the castle, as the hill was very steep. After he had walked a long way, his own pony not having arrived, he was obliged to mount on mine. When his own came, he rounded on the squire, Ponce, most bitterly. When he had rated him severely, I said to him, " Sir, you should put up with a great deal from Ponce the squire, for he has served your grandfather and your father and you."*

662. " Seneschal," he answered, " he has not served us. It is we that have served him, by allowing him to stay with us in spite of

his bad habits. My grandfather King Philip told me that in re-warding your servants you should give one more and one less, according to their service. And he used to say also that no man could govern a country well if he could not refuse as boldly and bluntly as he could give. I tell you this," said the King, " because people are now so greedy in their demands that there are few who look to the salvation of their souls and the honour of their persons, so long as they can by right or wrong lay their hands on other people's property."

CXXXIV

THE AUTHOR GOES HOME, BUT REJOINS THE KING LATER

663. The King crossed the county of Provence to the city called Aix-en-Provence, where it was said that the body of Mary Mag-dalen* was buried. We went into a very high rock cavern, in which it is said that Mary Magdalen lived as a hermit for seventeen years. When the King arrived at Beaucaire, and I saw him on his own land and in his own dominion, I took my leave of him, and on my way home I visited the Dauphine of Vienne, my niece,* and the Count of Chalon, my uncle,* and his son the Count of Burgundy.
664. After I had been some little while at Joinville and had put my affairs in order, I set out to rejoin the King, whom I found at Soissons, and he gave me such a welcome that all who were present were amazed. There I found Count John of Brittany and his wife,* the daughter of King Thibaut, who offered to do homage at the King's hands for all the rights that should be due to her in Champagne. The King adjourned her case, and that of King Thibaut II of Navarre, who was also present, to the Parliament at Paris, to hear and do justice to both parties.
665. To that Parliament came the King of Navarre and his Council—and the Count of Brittany, too. There King Thibaut asked for the hand of my Lady Isabel in marriage. In spite of what our folk of Champagne said behind my back, because of the love they had seen the King of France show for me at Soissons, I did not refrain from waiting on him and speaking of this marriage.

" Go," said the King, " and make your peace with the Count of Brittany, and then we will arrange our marriage." I told him that he should not delay it simply for that. But he answered that nothing would induce him to arrange the marriage until peace was made; he would not have it said that he married his children at the expense of his barons' inheritance.

666. I told this to Queen Margaret of Navarre and her son, and to the rest of their Council; and when they heard the King's message they were quick to be reconciled. After the reconciliation the King of France gave his daughter to King Thibaut. The wedding was at Melun, very grand and solemn. From there King Thibaut brought his bride to Provins, escorted by a large number of barons.

CXXXV

ST. LOUIS' MANNER OF LIFE: HIS RELATIONS WITH THE CLERGY

667. After his return from overseas, the King led so devout a life that he never again wore ermine or miniver, or scarlet, or gilt stirrups or spurs. His clothing was of undyed or dark blue wool.* The lining of his blankets and clothing was of doeskin, or fur from the legs of hares, or lambs'-wool; he was so temperate at table that he ordered no dishes beyond what his cook prepared; it was placed before him, and he ate it. He mixed his wine with water in a glass goblet, adding water in proportion to the strength of the wine, and while the wine was being watered behind his table, he held the glass in his hand. Every day he fed his poor, and after dinner provided money to be given to them.

668. In the houses of the great, when their minstrels came in after dinner with their viols, he waited to hear grace until the minstrel had finished his song; then he rose and the priests stood before him and said grace. When we were at home in private, he used then to go and sit on the foot of his bed; and if the Dominicans or Franciscans who lived with him recommended some book that he ought to listen to he would say to them, " No, you are not to read it to me; after dinner there is no book so good as *quodlibet*, that is,

conversation where every man says what he pleases." When any
great men from abroad dined with him he was good company.

669. I must tell you of his power of judgment. It was sometimes
said that he had no adviser so shrewd as his own self. For example,
when a matter was mentioned to him he used not to say, "I shall
take advice about that ", but, seeing clearly and precisely what was
the right thing to do, he gave an immediate answer, without any
deliberation. Such an answer, for example, I heard he gave to all
the prelates of the Kingdom of France when they put the following
request to him.

670. Bishop Guy of Auxerre was their spokesman. " Sir," he said,
" the Archbishops and Bishops here present have charged me to
tell you that under your rule Christendom is falling into decay and
dissolution; and it will fare still worse unless you put your mind
to the matter, since nowadays no man has any respect for excommunication. We call on you, then, sir, to order your judges
and officers to force those who have been under sentence for a
year and a day to give satisfaction to the Church." The King
answered, without taking any advice, that he would willingly order
his judges and officers to do as they asked provided he received
sufficient evidence to judge whether the sentence was justified or
not.

671. The Bishops consulted among themselves and replied to the
King that they would not submit to his judgment a matter that
concerned the Christian faith.* The King in turn answered that
he would not submit to their judgment a matter that was only his
own concern, and refused to order his officers to force the ex-
communicate, right or wrong, to obtain absolution. " Were I to
do so, I should be acting against God and justice. I will give you
an example: the bishops of Brittany held the Count of Brittany
under a sentence of excommunication for seven years, which was
later quashed by the Court of Rome. Thus I should have been
wrong in putting pressure on him after the first year."

CXXXVI

COMPLAINTS OF THE CLERGY

672. After our return from overseas, it happened that the monks of St. Urban elected two Abbots. Bishop Peter of Châlons (God give him His mercy) expelled them both, and blessed as Abbot my Lord John of Mymeri and gave him the crozier. I refused to accept him as Abbot, because he had wronged Abbot Geoffrey, who had appealed against him and gone to Rome. I kept the Abbey in my own hands until Geoffrey won the crozier, the Bishop's nominee losing the case. While the matter was in dispute the Bishop excommunicated me. There was, accordingly, at a Parliament held in Paris, a violent quarrel between me and Bishop Peter of Châlons, and between Countess Margaret of Flanders and the Archbishop of Rheims, whom she accused of lying.

673. At the next Parliament that was held all the prelates asked the King to come and speak alone with them. When he returned from doing so he came to us where we were waiting in the court-room; he laughed as he told of the trouble he had had with the prelates. In the first place the Archbishop of Rheims had said to him, " Sir, what are you going to do about the wardenship of St. Remy of Rheims, of which you are robbing me? For by the relics we venerate here I would not, for all the Kingdom of France, have such a sin on my soul as you have." " By these same relics," answered the King, " I swear you are so covetous that you would do so for Compiègne alone: so one of us must be forsworn. "

674. " The Bishop of Chartres," he then said, " called on me to surrender what I held of his. I refused to do so until my dues had been paid, and told him that he had sworn homage at my hands, and that his behaviour in trying to defraud me was neither good nor loyal."

675. " The Bishop of Châlons," he went on, " asked me, ' What are you going to do about the Lord of Joinville, who is robbing this poor monk of the Abbey of St. Urban? ' " " My Lord Bishop,"

answered the King, " you have laid it down between you that no excommunicated person should be heard in a lay court; I have seen a letter sealed with thirty-two seals which says that the Lord of Joinville is excommunicated, and I shall not hear his case until he has obtained absolution." I quote these stories to show you that the King needed only his own shrewdness to decide what action he should take.

676. After I had arranged matters for Abbot Geoffrey of St. Urban, he returned me evil for good and appealed against me. He gave St. Louis to understand that his Abbey was in the King's ward. I asked the King to find out the truth, whether the ward was his or mine. " Please God, sir," said the Abbot, " you shall not do so, but let the matter be properly tried in your Court between us and the Lord of Joinville, for we would prefer our Abbey to be in your ward rather than in that of the freeholder." The King then asked me, " Are they right in saying that the ward is mine? " " Certainly not, sir," I said; " it is mine."

677. The King answered, " It may well be that the freehold is yours, but that you have nothing to do with the wardenship of your Abbey. It must, however, if you please [he said to the Abbot], according to what both you and the Seneschal say, rest either with me or with him. Whatever you may say, I shall certainly find out for myself the truth of the matter, for if I made the Seneschal plead his case in court I should be doing him an injustice. He is my liegeman* and it would be unfair to make him argue in court a matter of which he is willing to explain to me the exact truth." The King found out the rights of the case, and when the truth was known he handed over to me the wardenship of the Abbey and gave me his charter for it.

CXXXVII

St. Louis' Love of Peace

678. It was through St. Louis' negotiations that the King of England, with his wife and children, came to France to discuss

the peace between the two Kingdoms. His Councillors were much opposed to this peace and said to him, " Sir, we are astonished that you should have decided to surrender to the King of England so large a part of your territory which you and your predecessors obtained from him by your conquest and his forfeiture. Our opinion of the matter is that if you do not think that you have a right to the territory you are not making proper restitution to the King of England unless you surrender all your predecessors' conquests; but if you do believe that you have a right to them, then we think that you are simply throwing away all the territory which you are ceding to him."

679. To this St. Louis replied, " My Lords, I know quite well that it was with complete justice that the King of England's predecessors lost the possessions which I hold; and the territory which I am giving him I am not giving because I am under any obligation to him or his heirs, but simply to foster love between his children and mine, who are first cousins. Moreover, I think that I am obtaining this advantage from my gift, that before the King of England was not my liegeman, but now he owes me homage."

680. There was no man in the whole world who worked harder for peace among his subjects, and particularly between great men who were neighbours, and the princes of the blood; as, for example, between the Count of Chalon, uncle of the Lord of Joinville, and his son, the Count of Burgundy, who, when we returned from overseas, were engaged in a bitter war. He sent some of his Council to Burgundy, at his own expense, to make peace between the father and the son, and his efforts were successful.

681. Later there was serious fighting between King Thibaut II of Champagne and Count John of Chalon, and his son, the Count of Burgundy, about the Abbey of Luxeuil. To put an end to this war, my Lord the King sent my Lord Gervase of Escraines, at the time Master Cook of France, whose efforts resulted in peace.*

682. After this war, which was settled by the King, another broke out between Count Thibaut of Bar and Count Henry of Luxembourg, who had married Thibaut's sister; they fought a battle near Prény in which Count Thibaut of Bar captured Count Henry of

Luxembourg and took the Castle of Ligny, which belonged to
Count Henry in his wife's right. To bring them to terms, the King
sent, at his own expense, my Lord Peter the Chamberlain, the man
whom of all he most trusted, and again the King was successful in
making peace.

683. Some of his Council said of foreigners whom he had reconciled that the King was unwise not to allow them to fight one
another, since if he left them to impoverish themselves they would
not be so ready to attack him as when they were rich. The King
answered that they were wrong. " For if these neighbouring
princes see that I am leaving them to fight, they might put their
heads together and say, ' It is from malice that the King is leaving
us to fight one another '; thus the ill will they bore me might lead
them to attack me, and I might well be beaten, besides incurring
the hatred of God, who says, ' Blessed are the peacemakers '."

684. Thus it was that the Burgundians and Lorrainers, whom the
King had reconciled, loved and obeyed him, so much that I have
seen them appear before him, at the royal court at Rheims and
Paris and Orleans, when they had disputes between one another.

CXXXVIII

His Hatred of Blasphemy

685. So great was the King's love for God and His sweet Mother
that he severely punished all whom he could convict of speaking
blasphemously of them or with a filthy oath. At Caesarea, for
example, I saw him put a goldsmith in the pillory, in his shirt and
drawers, with the guts and lights of a pig round his neck, such a
heap of them that they came right up to his nose. After I was back
from overseas, I heard it said that he branded the nose and lips* of
a citizen of Paris, but I did not see it myself. " I would willingly,"
St. Louis said, " be branded with a hot iron if all filthy oaths
could be abolished in my Kingdom."

686. Twenty-two years was I with him; and I never heard him
swear by God or His Mother or His saints. When he wished to be

emphatic, he used to say, " In truth it was so ", or " In truth it is so ".

687. Never did I hear him name the devil, unless it was in some book in which he had to read his name, or in the life of the saints of whom the book spoke; and it is a great disgrace to the realm of France and to the King that he allows it to be that men can hardly open their mouths without saying, " Devil take it!" It is, too, a great sin of speech when a man consigns to the devil a man or woman who from their baptism has been given to God. In my house at Joinville, any one who uses such an expression gets a clout or a box on the ears, and there this bad language has almost been stamped out.

CXXXIX

His Foundations And Endowments

688. Once the King asked me whether I washed the feet of the poor on Maundy Thursday. I told him no, it did not seem to me a good thing to do. He told me that I should not despise it, for God had done it. " You would, then, be most revolted at doing what the King of England does, who washes the feet of lepers and kisses them."

689. Before going to bed, he used to have his children brought to him and tell them stories of good kings and good emperors, telling them that they should take such men as examples. He told them stories, too, of wicked men of high estate, who, by their licentiousness and robberies and avarice, had lost their kingdoms. " I remind you of these things," he said, " so that you may be careful to avoid them and not incur the anger of God." He made them learn the Office of Our Lady and recite the day Hours to him, to accustom them to hearing the Office when they ruled their own possessions.

690. The King was so generous in almsgiving that wherever he went in his Kingdom he gave gifts to poor churches, to lazar-houses, almshouses and hospitals, and to poor gentlemen and gentlewomen. Every day he fed a crowd of poor, in addition to

those who ate in his chamber; and often have I seen him with his own hand cut their bread and pour their drink.

691. Many abbeys were built in his time; Royaumont, the abbey of Saint Antony by Paris, the abbey of le Lys, the abbey of Maubisson, and many other convents of Friars Preachers and Grey Friars. He built the hospitals at Pontoise and Vernon, the hospital for the blind in Paris, the convent of the Franciscan nuns at Saint-Cloud, which his sister my Lady Isabel founded with his authority.

692. When any benefice of Holy Church fell in to the King, before bestowing it he consulted with worthy religious and lay-men, and when he had heard their advice he gave the benefices in good faith and honestly and in accordance with the will of God. He refused to give any benefice to a cleric unless he resigned any other ecclesiastical benefices he held. In any town in his Kingdom in which he had not been before he visited the Friars Preachers and Grey Friars, if there were any there, to ask for their prayers.

CXL

How The King Reformed His Judges, His Provosts, and Mayors; and How He Made New Ordinances; and How Stephen Boileau was His Provost of Paris*

693. After his return to France from overseas King Louis bore himself with great devotion to Our Lord and great justice to his people. He took thought, then, and decided that it would be an excellent work to reform the Kingdom of France. In the first place, he laid down a general ordinance for his subjects throughout the Kingdom, which ran as follows:

694. We, Louis, by the grace of God King of France, do ordain that all our judges, viscounts, provosts, mayors, and all other officers, in whatever matter it may be, and whatever office they may hold, shall take oath that so long as they hold their office or judgeship, they shall do justice to all men, without exception of person, to poor as well as to rich, to strangers as well as to

natives, and shall keep the usages and customs that are good and proved.

695. And should it happen that the judges or viscounts or others, as officers or forest rangers, should violate their oaths, and should so be convicted, it is our wish that they be punished in their goods, or in their persons should the misdeed require it; the judges shall be punished by us, and the others by the judges.

696. Again, the other provosts, judges and officers, shall swear that they will loyally guard our revenues and our rights, and that they will not allow our rights to be stolen or taken away or diminished; with this they shall swear that they will not take or receive, either themselves or through others, gold nor silver nor any indirect benefits, nor anything else, other than fruit, or bread, or wine, or other such present up to the value of ten *sous*, which sum shall not be exceeded.

697. With this, they shall swear that they will not accept, nor cause to be accepted, any gift of no matter what nature, for their wives, or children, brothers, or sisters, or for any other person of however close a degree of kinship; and as soon as they shall know that such gifts have been accepted, they shall cause them to be returned as quickly as possible. And with this they shall swear that they will receive no gift, no matter what it may be, from any man in their jurisdiction or from any others who have a suit to bring or a cause to plead before them.

698. Again, they shall swear that they will not give nor send any gift to any person who is of our Council, nor to their wives nor children, nor to any person who belongs to them; nor to any who receive their accounts on our behalf, nor to any inspectors whom we may send to their bailiwicks or provostships to make enquiry concerning them. And with this they shall swear that they will not take part in any sale that may be made of our revenues, or of our judgeships, or of our coinage, or of any other things which are our property.

699. And they shall swear and promise that if they know of any officials, officers, or provosts, under them, who are disloyal, extortionate, usurious, or prone to any other vices prejudicial to our service, that they shall not, for any gift or promise or friend-

ship or for any other thing, give them their support, but shall punish and judge them in good faith.

700. Again, our provosts, our viscounts, our mayors, our forest rangers and our other officers, mounted or on foot, shall swear that they will give no gift to their superiors, nor to their wives or to the children who belong to them.

701. And since we would have these oaths carry full weight, it is our will that they be taken in full assize, before all, clergy and laity, knights and men-at-arms, even though they may already have sworn before us; that so they may fear to fall into the sin of perjury, not only through dread of God and of us, but also through public shame.

702. We will and ordain that all our provosts and judges shall refrain from any speech which is disrespectful to God, Our Lady or any of the saints, and that they shall abstain from dicing and taverns. We will that the manufacture of dice be forbidden throughout our Kingdom and that loose women be expelled from their houses, and that whoever lets a house to a loose woman, shall pay to the provost or judge one year's rent of the house.

703. Next, we forbid our judges to buy beyond reason, or cause to be bought, either of themselves or through others, any possessions or lands in their own bailiwick, or that of another, so long as they are in our service, without our permission; and if such purchases are made, it is our will that they be forfeited to us and remain in our hands.

704. We forbid our judges, so long as they are in our service, to marry any of their sons or daughters, or other persons who belong to them, to any other person in their bailiwick, without our particular permission; and with this, we forbid them to put them into any religious house in their bailiwick or to acquire for them any benefice of Holy Church or any property; furthermore, we forbid them to obtain provisions or rights of lodging* in or near a religious house, at the expense of the religious. The above-mentioned prohibition of marriages and the acquisition of property, we do not wish to be extended to provosts nor mayors nor other subordinate officers.

705. We order that neither judges nor provosts nor any others shall maintain too many sergeants or beadles, so that the people may not be over-burdened; and it is our will that the beadles shall be nominated in full assize or else shall not be accepted as beadles. When our sergeants are sent to any distant place or abroad, it is our will that they shall not be recognised without letters from their superiors.

706. We order that neither judge nor provost in our service shall oppress honest folk in his jurisdiction by excessive sentences, beyond what is right; and that no subjects of ours shall be imprisoned for debt, except the debt be owed to us.

707. We ordain that none of our judges shall impose any fine for a debt owed by our subjects, nor for any misdemeanour, except in open court, where the fine can be judged and assessed, and with the advice of honest men, even though it has already been paid to them.

708. And if it happens that a man who is accused of any offence does not wish to await the judgment of the Court which is offered to him, but offers a certain sum of money as a fine, such as has commonly been accepted, it is our wish that the Court accept the sum if it is reasonable and appropriate: but if not, it is our wish that the fine be assessed, as said above, even though the accused submit himself to the ruling of the Court. We forbid the judges, or mayors, or provosts to constrain our subjects by threats, or fear, or by any sharp practice, to pay a fine in secret or openly, or to bring charges against them without reasonable cause.

709. And we ordain that those who hold provostships, viscountships, or other offices of authority, cannot sell them to others without our permission; and should several persons jointly buy the above-mentioned offices, it is our will that one of the buyers shall perform the duties of the office on behalf of all the others, and that he alone shall benefit by the privilege connected with posting-houses, taxes or common charges, as the custom is.

710. And we forbid them to sell the said offices to their brothers, nephews, or cousins, once they have bought them from us; or themselves to claim through their own Court any debt owed to them, except such debts as pertain to their office; but their own

personal debts they must claim through the authority of the judge, just as though they were not in our service.

711. We forbid our judges and provosts to burden our subjects who have brought cases before them by moving from one place to another; they are to hear the business brought to them in the place where they have customarily sat, so that our subjects may not be forced by trouble and expense to abandon their search for justice.

712. Again, we order that they shall not dispossess any man of seisin he holds, without a full examination of the matter or without our special order; nor shall they burden our people with new impositions or taxes or new tolls; nor shall they summon them to ride to arms in order to obtain money from them; for it is our wish that no man from whom military service is due be summoned to the army without necessary cause, and those who are willing to join the army in person shall not be obliged to compound in money for their service.

713. Next, we forbid our judges and provosts to prohibit the export of corn or wine or other merchandise from our Kingdom without necessary cause; and when such a prohibition is needful, it is our wish that it be made in the open Council of tried men, with no suspicion of fraud or deceit.

714. Again, it is our wish that all former judges, viscounts, provosts, and mayors, shall, after they are out of office, remain for forty days either in person or by proxy in the district in which they held office, that they may answer to the new judges for any injustice they may have done against those who wish to bring complaints against them.

719.* In all these things which we have ordained for the well-being of our subjects and our Kingdom, we reserve to ourselves the power to explain, amend, add, or diminish, as we shall be advised.

The state of the Kingdom was greatly improved by this ordinance.

CXLI*

STEPHEN BOILEAU IS MADE PROVOST OF PARIS

715. At that time the provostship of Paris used to be sold to the citizens of Paris or to any persons; those who bought it shielded their children and nephews in their misdeeds, the young people relying on the protection of their parents and friends who held the provostship. The humbler people were accordingly greatly down-trodden and were unable to assert their rights against the rich, for the rich gave large presents and gifts to the provosts.

716. In those days, if a man spoke the truth to the provost or wished to respect his oath and not be perjured, in a matter that concerned a debt or anything else for which he was summoned to appear, the provost used to impose a fine on him, and the man was punished. Because of the great injustice and extortion for which the provostship was responsible, humble folk were afraid to remain in the King's dominions, and moved to other provostships and lordships, and the King's dominions were so deserted that when the provost held his court no more than ten or a dozen persons appeared.

717. In addition there were so many criminals and thieves in Paris and elsewhere that the whole country was full of them. The King, who always laboured for the protection of the poor, knew the truth. He refused accordingly to have the provostship of Paris sold, and gave a generous salary to those who should hold it in future. He stamped out all the evil customs by which the people could be oppressed, and everywhere throughout the Kingdom he had enquiries made to find a man who would deal out fair and firm justice, sparing the rich no more than the poor.

718. Stephen Boileau,* then, was brought to his notice; and he maintained and upheld the provostship so effectively that there was no malefactor or thief or murderer who dared to remain in Paris who was not forthwith hanged or exterminated. Neither kinship, nor birth, nor gold, nor silver could save him. The state of the King's realm began to improve, and people came to it for

the good justice to be obtained. Population and prosperity so increased that the revenue from sales of land, death duties, commerce and other sources was double what the King received before. From this ordinance the Kingdom of France derived great benefit, as many old and experienced men can witness.

CXLII*

St. Louis' Charity

720. From his childhood the King was very compassionate to the poor and suffering. It was always the custom, wherever he went, every day for six score poor persons to be fed in his house with bread and wine and meat or fish. In Lent and Advent a larger number were fed; and it sometimes happened that the King served them himself and set their meat before them, carving it for them, and when they left giving them money with his own hand.

721. In particular, on the high vigils of solemn feasts, he served all this food to the poor before he ate or drank himself. Moreover, every day at dinner and supper he had with him old and decrepit men to whom he gave the same food as he ate himself, and after they had fed they took with them a sum of money.

722. In addition to all this, the King daily gave countless generous alms, to poor religious, to poor hospitals, to poor sick people, to other poor convents, to poor gentlemen and gentlewomen and girls, to fallen women, to poor widows and women in childbed, and to poor minstrels who from old age or sickness were unable to work or follow their trade. So we may well say that he was happier than Titus,* the Emperor of Rome, of whom the old books tell us that he was greatly cast down and grieved on any day when he had done no act of charity.

723. From the time he first held his Kingdom and was of full discretion he began to build churches and many religious houses, among which the Abbey of Royaumont is pre-eminent in honour and dignity. He built several hospitals: at Paris, at Pontoise, at Compiègne and Vernon, which he endowed richly. He founded

the convent of Saint Matthew at Rouen, where he installed Dominican nuns, and that at Longchamps for Franciscan nuns, and gave them large endowments for their support.

724. He authorised his mother to found the Abbey of le Lys by Melun-sur-Seine, and that near Pontoise, which is known as Maubisson, and gave them also large endowments and properties. He built the hospital for the blind near Paris to receive the blind poor of the city of Paris, and built a chapel for them to hear divine service. The good King also built the Charterhouse outside Paris called Vauvert, and assigned to its monks, who served Our Lord, a sufficient revenue.

725. Soon afterwards he built another house outside Paris, on the road to St. Denis, which was called the House of the Daughters of God, and in this hostel he installed a large number of women who through poverty had abandoned themselves to the sins of the flesh, and gave them a revenue of four hundred pounds for their maintenance. In several places in his kingdom he built and endowed houses of Béguines and ordered that in them should be received women who wished to devote themselves to a life of chastity.

726. Some of his household grumbled at his giving such generous alms and spending so much on them. He answered, " I would rather my extravagance should be in almsgiving for the love of God than in the pomp and vain glory of this world." In spite, however, of the King's great expenditure in almsgiving, his daily household expenses were none the less very high. He was liberal and generous at the Parliaments and meetings of barons and knights, and entertained them at his court with greater courtesy and prodigality than had been seen for a long time at the courts of his predecessors.

CXLIII*

His Kindness to Religious

727. The King loved all who devoted themselves to the service of God and wore the religious habit, and none such came to him

and failed to find what he needed for his support.* He provided
for the Brothers of Carmel and bought them a place on the Seine
near Charenton, built their house and bought them vestments,
chalices and such things as are needed for the service of God.
Afterwards he provided for the brothers of St. Augustine, and for
these he bought a farm belonging to a citizen of Paris, with all
its appurtenances, and built them a church outside the Mont-
martre gate.

728. He provided also for the Brothers of the Sacks and gave
them a place on the Seine near St. Germain des Pres, where they
lived. But they did not stay long, for they were soon suppressed.
After the Brothers of the Sacks had been installed, another sort
of Friars came, known as the Order of the White Mantles, who
asked the King to help them to stay in Paris. The King bought
them a house to live in with some old outbuildings round it, near
the old Temple Gate in Paris, quite close to the Weavers. These
White Mantles were suppressed at the Council of Lyons, held by
Gregory X.

729. Later arrived another sort of Friars, who called themselves
Brothers of the Holy Cross, and wore a cross on their breast.
They asked the King for his support. He granted it readily, and
lodged them in a street which was then called the Temple Cross-
roads but is now known as Holy Cross Street. Thus the good King
surrounded the city of Paris with men of religion.

CXLIV

St. Louis Takes the Cross Again

730. One Lent, after the events I have already described, the
King summoned all his barons to Paris. I sent him my excuses,
pleading a quartan fever* I then had, and asked him to forgive
me, but he told me that he insisted on my coming, because he had
good physicians with him who were skilled in curing the fever.

731. To Paris, then, I went. I arrived on the evening of the Vigil
of Our Lady's feast in March and I could find no one, neither

the Queen nor anyone else, who could tell me why the King had sent for me. It happened, however, by the will of God, that at Matins I fell asleep. As I slept, I thought that I saw the King kneeling before an altar, and that I saw some bishops in their vestments dressing him in a red chasuble of Rheims serge.

732. After this vision I called my Lord William, my priest, who was a man of great understanding, and described it to him. He answered, " Sir, you will see that tomorrow the King will take the Cross." I asked him why he thought so, and he told me that it was because of the dream I had had, for the red chasuble stood for the Cross, which was red with the blood which God shed from His side and His hands and His feet. " And the chasuble's being of Rheims serge means that the Crusade will not achieve great things, as you will see if God lets you live long enough."

733. After I had heard Mass at the Madeleine at Paris, I went to the King's chapel and found that the King had gone up to the relics in the gallery and was having the True Cross brought down. As the King was descending, two knights of this Council began to talk to one another, and one said, " Never believe me again, if the King does not take the Cross here." The other answered that " if he does, this will be one of the most distressful days that ever dawned in France, for if we do not take the Cross, too, we shall lose the favour of the King; but if we do take it, we shall lose that of God, since we shall be doing so not for His sake but through fear of the King. "

734. The King, in fact, did take the Cross on the next day,* and his three brothers with him, and in the event the Crusade, as my priest foretold, achieved little. Both the King of France and the King of Navarre pressed me earnestly to take the Cross.

735. To this I answered, that while I was in the service of God and the King overseas and after my return the officers of the King of France and of the King of Navarre had so ruined and impoverished my people that the day would never come when they and I would not suffer the effect. I told them, too, that if I wished to do God's will I should stay at home to help and protect my people; for were I to endanger my person in the pilgrimage of the Cross, knowing full well that it would be at the expense of my

people's well-being, I should incur the anger of God, who gave His life to save His people.

736. I thought that all who advised him to go committed a mortal sin, for while he was still in France the whole Kingdom enjoyed peace at home and with all its neighbours, but after his departure its condition grew constantly worse.

737. In view also of his great bodily weakness it was very wrong of them to give him such advice; for he could not endure either to go in a carriage or to ride; he was so weak that he allowed himself to be carried in my arms, when I took leave of him, from the Count of Auxerre's house to the Grey Friars. Weak though he was, had he stayed in France he might still have lived for some time longer and done much good and profitable work.

CXLV

THE CRUSADE TO TUNIS: HIS PRECEPTS TO HIS SON

738. Of his expedition to Tunis I do not wish to give any account nor to say anything, since, thank God, I was not there, and I would not put in my book anything of which I am not certain. Let me confine myself, then, to speaking of our holy King and simply say that after arriving at Tunis before the castle of Carthage he succumbed to a dysentery of the belly (his eldest son Philip was sick with a quartan fever and the same dysentery as the King), which forced him to take to his bed, with the knowledge that soon he would have to pass from this world to the next.

739. Then he sent for my Lord Philip, his son, and bade him respect, as he would his will, all the precepts that he bequeathed to him. These precepts, which the King, it is said, wrote out with his own saintly hand, are set out below in the common tongue.

740. My dear son, my first precept is to set your heart on the love of God, for without that no man can be saved. Watch that you do not do anything displeasing to God, that is to say, any mortal sin; you should rather suffer any sort of torment than commit a mortal sin.

741. If God sends you adversity, accept it with patience and give thanks for it to Our Lord, realising that you have deserved it and that it will be for your own good. If He gives you prosperity, thank Him humbly for it, so that the gift which should improve you may not, through pride or in any other way, make you worse; for one should not use God's gifts to war against Him.

742. Be frequent in confession, and choose a worthy confessor who can teach you what you should do and what you should avoid; your behaviour should be such that your confessor and your friends may not be afraid to reprove you for your misdeeds. Attend devoutly and without irreverence at the service of Holy Church, praying to God with both your heart and your tongue, especially at Mass when the Consecration is made. Have a tender and compassionate heart for the poor, for the unhappy and unfortunate, and comfort and help them to the best of your power.

743. Maintain the good customs of your Kingdom and stamp out the bad ones. Do not be covetous towards your people, nor oppress them with tolls and taxes, except to meet an urgent need.

744. If anything lies heavy on your heart, tell it straightway to your confessor or to some worthy man who is not full of vain talk, and so you will find it easier to bear.

745. See to it that you have about you true and worthy men who are not full of covetousness, either religious or laymen, and be constant in consulting them; but fly from and avoid the company of evil men. Listen readily to the word of God and keep it in your heart, and readily seek out prayers and indulgences. Love what will increase your honour and virtue, and hate all evil, wherever it may be.

746. Let no man be so bold as to utter in your presence any word that induces or incites to sin, or slanderously to speak evil of any behind his back; and do not allow anything disrespectful to God or His saints to be said in your presence. Give thanks frequently to God for all the benefits He has conferred on you, that you may be worthy to receive more.

747. Be firm and honest in doing right and justice to your people, turning neither to right nor left, but ever holding a straight course, and uphold the cause of the poor until the truth is manifest;

and if any man has an action against you, do not decide the matter*
until you know the truth of it, for in the light of the truth your
Councillors will give a freer judgment, either for or against you.
748. If you hold anything that belongs to another, either through
yourself or through your predecessors, and the matter is certain,
give it back without delay; if it is doubtful, have enquiry made by
men of sense, quickly and diligently.

749. You should strive earnestly that your people and subjects
may live in peace and justice under your rule. Above all, maintain
the good towns and boroughs* of your Kingdom in the state and
liberties in which your predecessors maintained them; and if there
is anything that needs reform, reform it and put it right, and so
hold them in love and favour; for it is the strength and wealth
of the great towns that will cause both your own subjects and
strangers to fear to do you wrong, especially your peers and barons.

750.* Honour and love all persons of Holy Church, and watch
that the gifts and alms that your predecessors have given them are
not taken from them nor diminished. It is said of King Philip, my
grandfather, that one of his Councillors once told him that the
men of Holy Church were doing the King great wrong and injury
by depriving him of his rights and diminishing his jurisdiction,
and he was astonished that he should allow it. The good King
answered that he certainly believed him, but that he took into
account the kindnesses and courtesies God had done him and would
rather relinquish his rights than contend with the men of Holy
Church.

751. Honour and revere your father and mother and keep their
commands. Give the benefices of Holy Church to good men and of
clean life, and in doing so take the advice of worthy and honest men.

752. Beware of undertaking war against a Christian without long
deliberation; and if you must do so, then spare Holy Church and
those who are innocent in the matter. If wars or feuds break out
among your subjects, reconcile them as soon as you can.

753. See to it with diligence that you have good provosts and
judges, and frequently enquire into their behaviour and that of
your own household, and see whether any vice or excessive
covetousness, or deceit or underhand dealing is to be found in

them. Work to exterminate all vile sins in your country, and in particular stamp out with all your might vile oaths and heresy. Take care that the expenses of your household are reasonable.

754. Finally, my very sweet son, I pray you to have Masses sung for my soul and prayers said throughout your Kingdom, and to give me a full and special share in all your benefactions. Fair, dear son, I give you all the blessings that a kind father can give his son. And may the Blessed Trinity and all the saints guard you and keep you from every evil, and may God give you the grace always to do His will, that He may be honoured by you, and that you and we may, after this mortal life, be together with Him and praise Him for ever. Amen.

CXLVI

Death of St. Louis, 25th August 1270

755. After the good King had given his instructions to his son, my Lord Philip, his sickness grew dangerously worse. He asked for the sacraments of Holy Church and received them, it could be seen, in sound mind and with full understanding, for when he was anointed and they said the seven penitential psalms he recited the verses in his turn.

756. I have heard his son, my Lord the Count of Alençon, describe how at the approach of death he called on the saints to help and succour him, and especially on my Lord Saint James, saying his prayer which begins *Esto, Domine*, which means, " God, be the sanctifier and protector of Your people." He then called on my Lord Saint Denis of France to help him, saying that prayer of his, which means " Lord God, grant that we may so despise the prosperity of this world that we may fear no adversity."

757. I have also heard my Lord of Alençon (God grant him His mercy) say that his father then prayed to my Lady Saint Genevieve. Afterwards the holy King had himself laid on a bed covered with ashes, crossed his hands on his breast, and, looking up to Heaven, gave back his spirit to our Creator, at the very hour when the Son of God died on the Cross for the salvation of the world.

758. Well may we, and with piety,* mourn the death of this holy Prince, who held his Kingdom with such sanctity and truth, and did in it such great deeds of alms and gave it such good ordinances. As the scribe, when he has written his book, illuminates it with gold and azure, so did the King illuminate his Kingdom with the fine abbeys he built and the great number of hospitals and convents of Friars Preachers and Grey Friars, and of other religious of which I have already told you.

759. On the day after* the feast of Saint Bartholomew the Apostle there passed from this world the good King Louis, in the year of the Incarnation of our Lord, the year of grace one thousand two hundred and seventy, and his bones were kept in a casket and brought for burial to Saint Denis in France, where he had chosen his place of burial; and in that place he was buried, where God has since, through his merits, done many fine miracles for him.

CXLVII

THE CANONISATION

760. Later, at the instance of the King of France and by order of the Pope,* the Archbishop of Rouen and Brother John of Samois, who was afterwards a bishop, came to Saint Denis in France and spent a long time there enquiring into the life and deeds and miracles of the holy King. I was sent for* by them, and they kept me two days. After they had finished their enquiries of me and of others, their findings were sent to the Court of Rome. The Pope and the Cardinals examined the report carefully and the result of their examinations was that they did him justice and numbered him among the confessors.

761. For this there was, and should still be, great rejoicing throughout the Kingdom of France; great will be the honour to all those of his house who strive to resemble him in well doing, and great the reproach to all those who refused to imitate him in good works; great reproach, I say, to those of his house who seek to do ill, for fingers will be pointed at them and it will be said that the

holy King from whom they are sprung would have scorned to do such wrong.

762. After this good news had come from Rome, the King appointed a day, the day after Saint Bartholomew's, on which the body of the Saint was exhumed. When the holy relic had been raised, the Archbishop of Rheims at the time (God grant him His mercy) and my Lord Henry of Villers, my nephew, who was then Archbishop of Lyons, were the first to carry it; many others, bishops and archbishops, whose names I cannot remember, followed them. It was carried to the bier that had been built.

763. There Brother John of Samois preached, and among the King's great deeds he called to mind one of those of which I had given testimony to them on oath, and which I had seen with my own eyes. This is what he said:

764. " So that you may see that he was the most upright man of his time, I may tell you that such was his regard for the truth that he was willing to keep with the Saracens an agreement he had made simply as a verbal promise, and yet the matter was such that had he not kept his word he would have been better off by ten thousand pounds or more,"* and he told them the whole story as it has been written above. When he had done so he added, " You must not imagine that I am lying, for I can see here the man who testified this story to me on oath."

765. When the sermon was finished, the King and his brothers carried the body of the Saint back to the church, with the help of their kinsmen, to whom they owed that honour; for, if they do not waste it, it is a great honour that has been done to them. Let us pray to him to ask God to give us what is needful for our souls and our bodies. Amen.

CXLVIII

St. Louis Appears To The Author in a Dream

766. Now I must tell you some things about St. Louis which will be to his honour, and which I saw in my sleep. It seemed to me,

then, in my dream, that I saw him in front of my chapel at Joinville, and he was, I thought, wonderfully gay and light of heart;
and I, too, was happy to see him in my castle, and said to him,
" Sir, when you leave, I will entertain you in a house I have in a
village of mine called Chevillon." He answered me with a laugh,
" My Lord of Joinville, by the faith I owe you, I have no wish to
leave this place so soon."

767. When I woke up, I considered my dream, and I thought that
it would be pleasing to God and to Saint Louis to entertain him in
my chapel; and this I did, for I built an altar to the honour of God
and Saint Louis in which Mass will be sung for ever* in his honour;
and there is a perpetual endowment for this purpose. I have told
all this to my Lord King Louis, who has inherited his name, and
I think that he would be doing the will of God and of our Holy
King Louis if he obtained some relics of the true body of the Saint
and sent them to my chapel of Saint Lawrence at Joinville, so that
those who visited his altar might increase their devotion.

CXLIX

CONCLUSION

768. I wish all to know that I have put in this book a great part of
the deeds of our holy King, which I saw and heard myself, and a
great part of his deeds which I have found in a French book*
and which I have had written in my own. This I tell you, that
those who hear this book may have full confidence in that part of it
which in very truth I saw and heard myself; I cannot be your
warrant for the truth of the rest that is written in it, since that I
did not see or hear myself.

769. This was written in the year of grace thirteen hundred and
nine, in the month of October.*

APPENDIX

THE CREDO

I

770. In the name of and in the honour of the Father and of the Son and of the Holy Ghost, one God Almighty: in what follows you may see the articles of our faith painted and written in pictures and letters, in so far as our human nature can depict in paint the human nature of Jesus Christ; for the hand of man cannot paint the Godhead and the Trinity and the Holy Ghost, so vast a thing that, as Saint Paul and the other saints witness, eye cannot see it, nor ear hear nor tongue recount, because of the sins and vilenesses with which we in this mortal life are filled and weighed down, and which blind us to the sovereign light.

771. First, then, let us say that faith is a virtue which makes a man firmly believe what he cannot see, and knows only by hearsay, as, for example we believe our fathers and mothers when they tell us that we are their sons, even though we have no other way of knowing the truth. We should accordingly believe more firmly than any other worldly fact, the points and articles which are witnessed and taught to us, from the mouth of the Almighty, by all the saints of the Old Testament and the New.

772. Speaking of belief in what one cannot see, King Louis (God grant him His pardon) told me of a fine reply which the Count of Montfort, the father of Madame de Nesle, had given to the men of Albi. Some of the natives of the place came to him and told him to come and see the body of Our Lord which had appeared in flesh and blood. " Do you," he answered, " who do not believe in it, go and see it; for my part, I believe in it under the form of the bread and wine, as Holy Church teaches me."

773. They asked him what he had to lose by coming to see it, and he told them that were he to see it face to face and then believe in it, he would have no reward for his faith, but that if he believed in the teaching of God and His saints, he expected a finer reward and

a finer crown in Heaven than he would receive for all the other good deeds he might do in this mortal life.

774. Thus we may see that there are two things necessary for our salvation, to wit, good works and firm belief. As regards good works, King Louis* taught me that I should not do nor say anything which I should be ashamed to do or say were all the world to know it; and this, he told me, was all that was needed for my personal honour and the saving of my soul.

775. As regards firm belief, the King told me that the Enemy tries as hard as he can to shake us; and he taught me, when the Enemy tempted me to any doubt of the Sacrament of the altar or any point of the faith, to say, " Enemy, you are wasting your time, for, by the help of God, you shall not drive me from the Christian faith, even if you have all my limbs cut off."

776. This, the King told me, was the firm belief which God honoured by giving to it His own name (for it is from the name of Christ that we are called Christians), and which He has had told by the prophets and witnessed to by believers and unbelievers (and this is true of no other religion), as is said in a book, " To saints, to sages and to kings, God had His witness carried to men of divers faiths, so that no man can be left in doubt."

II. *When you look at this book, you will find the* Credo *in red letters, and the prophecies in deeds and in words in black letters.*

777. Brother Henry the Teuton, who was a most learned clerk, said that no man could be saved if he did not know his *Credo*; and in order that men might be led to believe what was indispensable to their salvation, I first had this work done at Acre,* after the King's brothers had left and before the King went to fortify the city of Caesarea in Palestine. And the first letters say:

III. *I believe in God the Father Almighty, Creator of Heaven and earth.*

778. You may see His great power in the creation of the world, which you see painted below, for there is no man who could make even the smallest of all these creatures. A creator is one who makes something out of nothing; there is none who has the power to do

this except He alone who made Heaven and earth, the sun and the moon, and all that there is on high and below. We may see His great power in the angels who are painted below, whom He flung out from Heaven into Hell, and from being so beautiful and glorious made so ugly and hideous.

779. There are no prophecies on this first page, since it deals with the beginning of the world, which He made who is the beginning and will endure without end.

IV. *And in Jesus Christ His Son, our Lord.*

780. On the second page of the *Credo*, which follows, are the prophecies of the coming of the Son of God, to wit, that three angels came to lodge with Abraham, among whom Abraham, by God's will, recognised the Son of God, and knowing that it was He who was to ransom him from the pains of Hell, he adored Him.

781. Moses also saw and recognised Him in the bush which seemed to burn and was never consumed; and in this was signified the virginity of the body of the blessed Virgin Mary, into which He descended for our salvation. These two are the prophecies in deed; so also is that of the fleece on which the dew of Heaven fell miraculously by the will of God.

V. *Who is conceived of the Holy Ghost.*

782. The prophecy in word is that of Isaias the prophet, which you see painted below, who prophesied that the Virgin would conceive.

VI. *Born of the Virgin Mary.*

783. The prophecy of Daniel the prophet about the Nativity, which is painted below, told the Jews that when the Holy of Holies should come their anointing would fail; and in truth, when God came on earth, they had neither anointed king nor bishop, the only king they had being the Emperor of Rome, who was a pagan* and not of their religion or their faith. They had no anointed bishop; those who wished to hold the sees bought them by the year.

VII. *Who suffered under Pontius Pilate.*

784. And what did He suffer, dear Lord? He suffered being sold, beaten and scourged, and He was forced to carry His Cross. And many other vile and cruel things were done to Him before He was crucified, which He suffered gladly for the love of us and to deliver us from the hands of the Enemy.

785. Of this the prophecy in word was that of Joseph the son of Jacob, of whom you may read later how Judas, his brother, sold him for thirty pieces of silver, just as the traitor Judas sold Jesus Christ.

786. Joseph is in many ways a prefiguration of Jesus Christ, and in particular by his coat, which stands for the flesh of Jesus Christ, the coat which his father, who loved him dearly, had made for him of one piece, just as woollen gloves are made. This coat stands for the flesh of Jesus Christ, which was of the Virgin alone, whereas our flesh is made of man and woman, of two pieces, that is.

787. When Joseph's brothers had sold him they cut up his coat and smeared it with blood, and took it back to their father and told him that Joseph had been eaten by very savage beasts.

788. Joseph's coat is the blessed flesh of Jesus Christ, which was cut when He was beaten at the pillar of the wicked Jews, who should have been His brothers; and it was very savage beasts which devoured Jesus Christ, the envy, that is, of the wicked men towards Him. So you may see that the story of Joseph, which is painted below, is the prophecy in deed.

789. The prophecy in word is the saying of David painted below, " The wicked will work their evil on my back, and will show me their wickedness."*

VIII. *And was crucified and died.*

790. The prophecy in deed concerning the Cross, is that of Isaac, which you will see painted below, who was obedient to his father even unto death. Our Lord Jesus Christ was delivered to death on behalf of the wicked Jews, and to so shameful a death; that of the Cross, on which in those days they hung thieves just as we now hang them on gallows. They hung Him on the Cross between two

thieves, to show the people that it was by His own crime that He had deserved death.

791. Jeremias said, " O all ye that pass by, attend and see if there be any suffering like to my sorrow ".* No suffering was ever like unto His, for it was He who suffered most in all this world, and what increased His suffering was that He had the almighty power to put an end to it, and yet bore it patiently.

792. The prophecy in deed was prefigured in Egypt by the blood of the lamb with which they marked the threshold of the doors and the foreheads of the people, the mark being the letter the Jews call *thau*, which is like a Cross. The Jews did this that the angels of Our Lord might slay the first-born in the houses of those who were not marked with the blood; and this signified that all those will be damned who are not marked with the sign of the Cross and the blood of Jesus Christ. Such is the prophecy in deed.

793. The prophecy in word is what David says in the Psalms, that the Son of God will be like a bird called the pelican,* which kills itself and pierces its breast to give life to its young ones.

794. The Queen of Saba came to see King Solomon and recognized the wood of the Cross, which was in Jerusalem, and said so to Solomon in her prophecy; and yet she was not of the people of Israel, who believed in Our Lord.

795. Caiaphas, who was High Priest* at the time of God's crucifixion, prophesied that it was right that one man should die to save the people; and even though he was one of the chief enemies of Jesus Christ, yet Jesus Christ made him speak the truth.

796. A thousand years earlier, Habacuc the prophet, who is painted below, prophesied and said, just as though he had seen Jesus Christ die and cry out on the Cross: " Lord," he said, " I heard your voice, and it filled me with terror and cast me down."* Those who have understanding should indeed be filled with terror and cast down, when creatures that have no understanding were cast down; for the sun lost its brightness and all over the world, about the ninth hour, men could see nothing. The veil of the Temple was rent, the rocks of the mountains split asunder, the earth opened and threw up the dead, who were seen in Jerusalem.

797. There was at that time a rich man in Jerusalem who had a

hundred knights under him (he was called Centurion) who when he saw these wonders prophesied and said, " Truly, this man was indeed the Son of God."

IX. *And was buried.*

798. The prophecy in deed of His being laid in the Sepulchre, is that of Jonas, which you see painted here, who was put in the belly of the whale, for the Son of God was in the Sepulchre for the same time as Jonas was in the belly of the whale.

799. The prophecy in word was spoken by God Himself to the Jews when they asked Him to give them some sign, and He answered that He would give them no sign other than that of Jonas the prophet, and told them that He would be in the Sepulchre for the same time as Jonas was in the belly of the fish. You must understand, too, without fail, that it was not the divine nature which died on the Cross, but the human nature which He assumed in the Virgin, to save our human nature from the pains of Hell.

800. The saying about Hell broken by a word was said by God to Job long before He came into this world. " Job," said God, " can you catch the devil on a hook as I shall do? "* You must understand that when an angler wishes to catch a fish on a hook, he covers the iron with bait; the fish thinks it is eating the bait, and the iron catches it. So we see that in order to catch the devil as though on a hook, God clothed His divine nature in our human nature, and the devil, thinking that it was a man, worked to bring about His death that Hell might be filled; but then the divine nature, which descended into Hell, caught him.

X. *He descended into Hell.*

801. The prophecy of the gates of Hell, which God broke and from which He brought out His friends who were within, you may understand (this is the prophecy in deed) by Samson the strong, who forced open the lion's mouth and took from it the combs of honey. The honeycombs, which are sweet and useful, stand for the saints and good men who in their time had lived sweet and useful lives, whom God brought out from Hell.

802. It was with this in mind that Osea, the prophet, prophesied and said, " O death, I shall be thy death, and thou, Hell, I shall bite into thee."* For just as a man who bites an apple takes away part of it and leaves the rest, so did God take away from Hell the good and leave the bad.

XI. *And on the third day He rose again from the dead.*

803. It is true that on the third day Our Lord came back from death to life, to keep the promise he gave his Apostles and Disciples of His Resurrection, in which we should firmly believe.

804. You may see the prophecy in deed of the Resurrection of Our Lord in the lion which brings its cub back to life on the third day.

805. A virtuous man should take a lesson from His Resurrection. Before the third day after that on which one has fallen into sin, he should go to confession as soon as possible, for it is a very foolish man who goes to sleep in a state of sin. This is why the saints say that it is not remarkable that a good man should fall, but it is remarkable, when you consider the filth in which he is lying, that he should not pick himself up again quickly. For sin is filth, and the pagan who says that if almsgiving were sinful he would not give alms, so vile a thing would it be, is witness to this.

806. The prophecy in word was spoken by David who, in the person of the Son of God, says, " My flesh will flower again by Thy will."*

807.* About His Resurrection I shall tell you what I heard as a prisoner on the Sunday after we had been captured and the men of importance and knights-bannerets had been put in a tent by themselves.

808. We heard a great noise of men shouting. We asked what it was, and were told that it was our people who were being put into a large compound closed in by walls of earth. Those who refused to renounce their faith were being killed, the renegades were being left.

809. While this great fear of death was on us, thirteen or fourteen of the Sultan's Council, very richly dressed in cloth of gold and silk, came to us and had us told, through a Brother of the Hospital who knew the Saracen tongue, that the Sultan wished to know

whether we wanted to be released. We answered that we did, as they naturally must know.

810. They asked us whether in return for our freedom we would hand over any of the castles of the Temple or the Hospital. The good Count Peter of Brittany answered that that was impossible, since the castellans, when they were appointed, swore on the gospels not to surrender them in return for any man's freedom. Then they asked us whether, to obtain our liberty, we would give them any of the castles which the barons held in the Kingdom of Jerusalem. No, said the Count of Brittany; for the castles were not fiefs of the King of France.

811. When they heard our answer, they told us that as we refused to agree to either of their demands, they would leave us and send others to us who would show us some sword-play. The Count of Brittany told them that it was no great deed to kill men whom you held prisoner.

812. When they had gone, a great horde of young Saracens came into the enclosure in which we were confined, with drawn swords. I thought they had certainly come to kill us. They did not do so, however, and it was among them that we found the consolation God sent us.

813. They brought with them a little man, who seemed to be as old as a man could possibly be; the young men, it seemed, looked on him as a madman, and told the Count of Brittany that they wished him to have a hearing, for he was one of the holiest men of their religion. Then the little old man, bearded and white-haired, leaning on his crutch, told the Count that he had heard that the Christians believed in a God who was imprisoned for their sake, beaten for them, and died for them; and that on the third day He rose again.

814. The Count agreed to all he said; " If that is so," continued the old man, " you should not complain that you have been imprisoned for His sake, beaten and wounded for Him, for He did the same for you, and you have not yet suffered death for Him as He suffered death for you." And afterwards he told us that " if your God had the power to raise Himself from the dead, then He certainly has the power to release you from captivity when He pleases."

815. Indeed I still believe that it was God who sent him to us, for shortly after he had gone the Sultan's Council returned and told us that we were to send four of our number to confer with the King who, by the grace of God, had arranged for our release without any assistance. I can assure you that that was the truth: by God's grace, the King had arranged the matter as wisely as if he had the entire Council of Christendom with him.

XII. *He ascended into Heaven.*

816. The prophecy in deed is the assumption of Elias which you see painted below. By the will of God, he ascended into Heaven, and there he will stay until the coming of Antichrist, when Our Lord will send him to comfort the people, so that they may not believe in Antichrist nor in his works.

817. The prophecy in word is what God Himself said to His Apostles when He told them, " I shall ascend to My Father and yours." And the angel himself who is painted below told them that as He ascended, so would He return on the day of judgment.

818. The prophecy in deed of the day on which our human nature was sat on the right hand of God the Father, was Joseph's coat, which you see painted here, which was given back to his father Jacob torn and stained with blood; in the same way was the flesh of Jesus Christ given back to God the Father. And what did Jacob do? He tore his own coat; and remembering this, we may say that God the Father in His turn tore His own coat.

819. By Our Lord's coat we may understand the religion of the Jews, for just as Jacob's coat was closer to him than any other of his garments, so the religion of the Jews was closer to Our Lord than any other religion of that time. As soon as they had crucified His Son, they tore off His garments, and just as a very angry man tears his coat in two pieces and throws one piece one way and one another way, so in anger Our Lord tore the Jews away from Himself, and has scattered the fragments throughout the world, one part one way and one another.

820.* By reason of the many other sins which were committed under the old Law, the Jews were sent into captivity, and Our Lord fixed the term of their deliverance at one hundred years from that day. It is now twelve hundred and eighty-seven years that they have been in captivity in different places, with no sure time for their deliverance. As, then, there is no certain term nor measure for their release, it is plain that they have sinned beyond all measure.

XIII. *And sits at the right hand of the Father Almighty.*

821. It is David who gives us the prophecy in words, " My Lord said to my Lord, sit Thou at my right hand, till I shall set Thy enemies beneath Thy foot."*

822. We see, then, that if we recognised how we are beneath the feet of Jesus Christ, and the great power He has over us, we should never do wrong. The affairs of this world, however, prevent us from realising it as fully as we should. But on the day when He comes from Heaven to judge the living and the dead, then we shall recognise His great power without any mistake, for at His coming there will be no man nor woman, not even among the saints, who will not tremble in fear.

823. In his heart Job well knew that coming and that day, for even though in his time he was the greatest friend God had on earth, yet did he so dread that day that he said to God, " Lord, where shall I hide myself on the day of judgment, that I may not see the anger of Thy face? "*

XIV. *And shall come on the day of judgment to judge the dead and the living.*

824. The prophecy in deed is Solomon's judgment between the two women, which you see painted below, who represent the old Law and the New. A right judgment is a noble thing, and honourable and of great worth, for Solomon said that justice and right judgment are more pleasing to Our Lord than a sacrifice or other gifts. I must say a word or two about this, then, for the instruction of those to whom justice belongs.

825. We may say that the two-edged sword stands for strict justice. From the sword's presenting as sharp an edge to the man who holds it as it does to others, we are to understand that it is our duty to do as strict justice to ourselves as to others, and to our friends

as to our enemies. A prince who so acted, you should realise, would be loved and respected by the people, just as the Bible tells us that Solomon gained the love and respect of the people by the strict justice he did to the two women.

XV. *I believe in the Holy Ghost, and I believe also in Holy Church.*
826. We should believe in the Holy Ghost, for it is through Him that all good things come to us: such is the grace of Almighty God.
827. The prophecy in deed of the day of Pentecost is that of Elias the prophet, to whom God sent down fire from Heaven on his sacrifices, which signified that on the day of Pentecost God would send the Holy Ghost to His Apostles under the form of fire.
828. The prophecy in word is that of Joel, who spoke as one speaking for God the Father and said, " Upon My servants I will pour forth My spirit."*

XVI. *And in the forgiveness of sins, which we receive through the sacraments of Holy Church.*
829. We should believe in the Holy Church of Rome, and we should believe in the commandments we receive from the Pope and the bishops of Holy Church, and perform the penances they impose on us.
830. We should believe in the universal sacraments of Holy Church, which are painted below, that is to say in baptism, in the Sacrament of the altar, in marriage, in the forgiveness of sins, and in the other sacraments in which Holy Church teaches us to believe. Moreover, as I told you before, our faith in them should be so firm that no earthly thing, neither abundance nor pestilence, can shake us from it.
831. Our Lord has given us these sacraments, by virtue of which we shall be crowned kings in the Kingdom of Heaven, which will never fail us; and of this David spoke, and prophesied just as though he had been of the Christian faith, " What return shall I make to You, O Lord, for all the good things You have done to me? "*
832. The prophecy in deed of the new graces of which I have spoken to you, is that of Jacob, to whom the two sons of Joseph were brought to receive his blessing. The elder was placed at his

right hand, and the younger at his left, but the good man crossed his arms and placed his right hand on the younger and his left hand on the elder. By this was signified and foretold that God would withdraw his blessing from the Jewish law, which was older than ours, and would give it to the Christian. And we may see clearly that He has done so, for they have neither Kings nor bishops anointed, and we have.

XVII. *And I believe in the resurrection of the flesh.*

833. We should believe firmly in the resurrection of the flesh; for all who do not believe in it are outside the faith. For if the dead did not rise again, that would be a lack of justice in God. That this is so, you may see by the saintly men and women of old, whose bodies suffered so many torments for love of Our Lord; if God did not in return reward the bodies of those who suffered the torments, their devotion would have been in vain.

834. On the other hand we see the reverse of this, when we consider the bodies of sinners whom God has allowed to have things almost their own way in this world, so that they have used the very prosperity which God granted them as a weapon against Him. Our Lord's justice would be ill balanced, if the bodies of these men did not rise again to meet the judgment and sentence which God, as He witnesses with His own mouth, has prepared for them in Hell. God will take vengeance for their evil doings on their souls and bodies in the next world, since He has not done so in this.

835. Blessed will be the resurrection of the dead who shall die in the works of God, as St. John says in the Apocalypse,* for their joy and their happiness will be double, in body, that is, and in soul; while the punishment and misery of the wicked will also be double, in body and in soul.

836. It was to them that Sophonias, whom you see painted here, prophesied, and said that this day will be to them a hard day, a day of misery and tears and wretchedness for those who go to Hell.*

837. Saint Augustine, too, whom you see painted here, said, " What does it profit a man by his wickedness to gain the whole world, which will straightway be lost to him, and thereby gain Hell which will be with him for ever? "

XVIII. *And in life everlasting. Amen.*

838. We should firmly believe that all the saints, men and women, who are dead, and all the good men and women who are still alive, will have everlasting life and happiness in the Heavens above, and will sit at Our Lord's table. You will see this happiness painted below, rather as it is described in the Apocalypse.

839. You can see the prophecy in deed in the five prudent virgins and five foolish virgins, painted above, which stand for man's five senses.

840. In the five senses of the good man we recognise the five prudent virgins, who stand for the saints and for good men, because these keep their senses and their lives in cleanliness, and since they so keep them in this world, their light will not be extinguished by sin. Coming with their lamps lit (by which we may understand with clean lives) the gate of Paradise will be opened to them, and they will go in to the marriage feast of the Son of God, who is signified for us by the Lamb.

841. But the wedding feast being full, the gates of Paradise will be closed, so that no more shall enter; instead God will say to all the others, as the bridegroom said to the foolish virgins, when they knocked at the door, having come with their lamps burnt out, " I know you not." " I know you not ", God will say to all the wicked. Ah, God, what a terrible saying, for it is only in Hell that they will find any lodging to shelter themselves, all will be burnt and consumed, earth and sea, and every earthly creature except the good and the wicked.

842. And since there will then remain only these two sorts of people, the good who will not be able to fall from goodness, and the wicked who will never be able to amend their evil, God will provide but two homes, of which one is the dolorous home of Hell (from which God by His grace preserve us: and we will do well to be on our guard ourselves) and the home of Paradise; and if we aim all our efforts towards that home, we shall be more than wise. God grant it to us, through the prayer of His Son and Mother.

XIX

843. We find that there was a good man of the old Law, called Jacob, to whom God appeared; and as soon as Jacob saw Him, he

caught hold of Him, and would not let go of Him until He had changed his name, and given him the name of Israel. The meaning of the name Jacob is warrior or fighter, and it means that in this world good men must be warriors or fighters.

844. All good men should fight against the Enemy and the evil pleasures of the flesh, for it is by soldiering that the Kingdom of Heaven is to be won; and thus it is that Job says that on this earth the life of a good man is soldier's work.

845. All good men must be fighters, for they must take hold of God with both arms and not let go of Him until He has given them His blessing and changed their names, as He did for Jacob, to whom He gave the name of Israel, which means He who sees God. And that story teaches us that no man can be sure in this world that he has God's blessing for certain until we come to the next world, when we shall see God face to face.

846. Thus we are obliged, so long as we are in this mortal life, to hold God tightly to us with both arms, so that the Enemy may not be able to come between us and Him. The two arms with which we must hold God clasped, are firm faith and good works. We need both of these together if we wish to keep hold of God, for either one of them is useless without the other.

847. This may you see in the devils; they firmly believe all the articles of our faith, and yet it is of no use to them, for they do no good works; and we can see the contrary in the Saracens and the Albigensian heretics;* they do many great penances, but it is of no use to them, for it is written that those who do not believe shall be damned.

848. We see, then, that we must combine firm faith with good works. Daily the devils fight with us to deprive us of one or the other, and on the last day, by which I mean the day of our death, they will strive even harder than they do now. On that day may God and His Mother and all His saints grant us their help!

849. On the last day, the evil one will see that he will not be able to deprive us of the good things we have done, and will realise that as all our bodily powers will have left us, it will be impossible for him to do us any harm. Then he will attack us from another side, and will strive with all his power to make us fall into some

temptation against faith or in another way which may enable him to make us die in some sort of evilness of will, from which God preserve us!

850. It is then that the book written in the common tongue, with pictures of the points of our faith, will be most useful, in the very hour of death, so that the Enemy may not appear in any evil vision; we should have the book read also in the presence of the sick man; it teaches and explains the points of our faith, so that his heart is so filled with the true knowledge that enters though his eyes and ears that the Enemy is unable either through them or by any other means to corrupt the sick man. From such corruption, on that day of death and at other times, may God preserve us!

851. I have explained to you as well as I can how we must hold God clasped with both arms, with the arm of faith, that is, and with the arm of good works. For those whom the Enemy is able to draw away from God are in great peril; God threatens to strike them with His sword and to pierce them with His shafts. But His friends, who are one with Him and hold Him close, are safe from this threat.

852. Let us not, then, loose our hold on Him, and we shall do well; let us cling to Him until He has blessed us, and given us in exchange for the name of Jacob, which means warrior or fighter, that of Israel, which means He who sees God. And may that same God watch over us and grant it to us to see Him face to face, with the salvation of our souls and of our bodies. And this may He grant us through the prayer of His sweet Mother, and of my Lord Saint Michael, and of all the men and women who are His saints.

Amen

853. To his good Lord Louis, by the grace of God, King of France and Navarre, John Lord of Joinville, his seneschal of Champagne, greeting and his ready service.

854. My dear Lord, it is indeed true, as you told me in your letter, that it was said that you had made peace with the Flemings; and because, Sir, we believed the report to be true, we have made no preparation to comply with your summons. And about your message to me that you will be at Arras to take satisfaction for the offences of the Flemings against you, it seems to me, Sir, that you are doing right, and may God give you His help.

855. And about your message to me that I and my people should be at Orchies in the middle of the month of June, I must tell you, Sir, that it cannot well be done, for your letter reached me on the second Sunday in June, so that a week had passed before I received it. But as soon as I can, my people will be ready to go where you please.

856. Do not be displeased, Sir, that in my first address, I have called you only " Good Lord ", for I have done just the same to my Lords the other Kings before you, whom God pardon; and may Our Lord watch over you.

857. Given the second Sunday of the month of June, on which your letter was brought to me, in the year thirteen hundred and fifteen.

[The letter is addressed on the outside (it was folded and sealed) " to his well loved Lord, the King of France and Navarre " (" A son bien ammey signeur le roy de France et de Navarre "). There is a facsimile in De Wailly, facing p. 452.]

The Epitaph

De Wailly prints three versions of this inscription, which Joinville put up at Clairvaux (pp. 544 ff.):

(1) that given in Ménard's edition, 1617;
(2) a transcription by Père Merlin, S. J., published in 1739;
(3) his own reconstruction of the original from the two versions, which differ considerably. The following is translated from (3).

Lord God Almighty, I pray You to show Your kind mercy to Geoffrey, Lord of Joinville, who lies here, to whom, while he lived in this world, You were so gracious that he founded and built for You many churches: first, the abbey of Ecurie, of the order of Cîteaux, also the abbey of Jouvillier of the order of Prémontré; also the house of Mathons of the order of Grantmont; also, the priory of Le Val d'Onne of Molesmes; also, the church of Saint Lawrence of the castle of Joinville: so that all who are sprung from him should have hope in God that He has taken him into His company, since the saints bear witness that he who on this earth builds the house of God builds his own house in Heaven. He was the best knight of his time, and this was manifest in his great deeds at home and overseas, and it was for this that the Seneschalship of Champagne was given to him and to his heirs, who since have held it. From him was sprung Geoffrey, who was Lord of Joinville, who lies at Acre, and who was the father of William, who lies in the tomb covered with lead, who was Bishop of Langres, and afterwards Archbishop of Rheims, and own brother to Simon, who was Lord of Joinville and Seneschal of Champagne, who also was numbered among the good knights by virtue of the great prizes he won in combat at home and overseas; and he was with King John of Acre at the taking of Damietta. This Simon was father of John, Lord of Joinville, and Seneschal of Champagne, who still lives, who had this inscription made in the year 1311, to whom God grant what is needful to his soul and to his body. This Simon was brother also to Geoffrey Troulart,* who also was Lord of Joinville and Seneschal of Champagne, who for the great deeds he wrought at home and overseas was numbered among the good knights; and because he died in the Holy Land without any heirs of his body John the Lord of Joinville who still lives, that his fame might not perish, brought back his shield, after he had been overseas for the space of six years in the service of our holy King Louis, which King did many kindnesses to the said Lord. This said Lord of Joinville placed the shield in the church of Saint Lawrence, that men might pray for its owner, and on this shield is manifest the prowess of the said Geoffrey in the honour which King Richard of England did to him by allowing him to quarter his arms with his own. This Geoffrey [*the first mentioned*] passed from this world in the year of grace 1192. May this Geoffrey rest in peace.

The Letter of John Sarrasin[1]

1. To my Lord Nicholas Arrode, from John Sarrasin, Chamberlain to the King of France, greeting and kind love.

This is to tell you that the King and Queen, and the Count of Anjou and his wife, and I, are safe and sound in the city of Damietta, which, on the second Sunday after Pentecost, God, in His mercy and pity and by His miraculous power, restored to Christendom.

2. Next, I must tell you how this happened. After the King and the Christian army had embarked at Aigues Mortes, we sailed on the feast of St. Augustine (at the end of August), and were off the island of Cyprus a fortnight before the feast of St. Remy, on St. Lambert's day, that is. The Count of Angers landed at the City of Limassol; the King and those of us who were with him in his ship (the Montjoy, it was called) landed early the next morning, and the Count of Artois at about nine o'clock, at the same port. There were very few of us on the island, and we spent until Ascension Day waiting for the fleet, which had not arrived.

3. The Christmas before, one of the great princes of the Tartars, called Elteltay, who was a Christian, had sent his ambassadors to the King of France at Nicosia in Cyprus. The King sent Brother Andrew, of the Order of St. James, to the ambassadors; they had not known to whom they should address themselves, but they understood Brother Andrew as well as we understand one another, and he them. The King had the ambassadors brought before him, and they spoke at length in their own language. Brother Andrew translated their message into French for the King, to the effect that on the feast of the Epiphany the supreme prince of the Tartars had become a Christian, and many of his people with him, in particular some of their greatest lords. They said also that Etheltay, with his whole army of Tartars, would help the King

[1] Translated from *Jean Sarrasin, Lettre à Nicolas Arrode, éditée par Alfred A. Foulet*, 1924.

of France and the Christian forces against the Caliph of Bagdad and the Saracens because he wished to avenge the great and shameful injuries the Khwarizmians and other Saracens had inflicted on our Lord Jesus Christ and on Christendom. Their master, they said, also urged the King to cross to Egypt in the spring and attack the Sultan of Babylon, while the Tartars would at the same time invade the territory of the Caliph of Bagdad; their enemies would thus be unable to help one another.

4. The King of France decided to send his own ambassadors back with them to their master, Eltheltay, and to the supreme lord of the Tartars, whose name was Quioquan, to verify the truth of the message. They told him that it was a good six months' journey to the place where Quioquan lived, but that their master Eltheltay and the Tartar army were not very far away; they were in Persia, which they had completely overrun and made subject to the Tartars. They stressed again the good will of the Tartars to the King and to Christendom.

5. A fortnight after Candlemas Day, the Tartar ambassadors left in company with the King's, Brother Andrew of St. James, that is, and a brother of his, Master John Goderiche, another clerk from Poissy, Herbert the Sommelier, and Gerbert of Sens. At mid-Lent the King had news of them; under the protection of the banner of the Tartar chief, they were crossing the territory of the infidels; respect for his ambassadors obtained for them anything they wanted.

6. After this, the King and his whole expedition, which he reckoned at a good twenty-five hundred knights, five thousand crossbowmen, and a large number of others, mounted and on foot, embarked at Limassol and other ports in Cyprus, and set sail for the city of Damietta; this was on Ascension Day, which that year was the thirteenth of May; it was only a three days' journey from Cyprus, but we had many setbacks and difficulties at sea, and the crossing took us twenty-two days.

7. At about nine o'clock in the morning on the Friday after Trinity Sunday, we were off Damietta, with a large part of our fleet, but by no means all. We were about three leagues from the shore. The King gave the word to anchor and summoned all the barons who were with the fleet. They assembled on board the Montjoy,

the King's ship, and agreed to land very early the next morning in spite of any resistance the enemy might dare to make. Orders were given to prepare all the galleys and small vessels in the fleet, and for all who could to embark in them early in the morning. Everyone was urged to go to confession, prepare himself, make his will and settle his affairs in readiness for death, should it so please Our Lord Jesus Christ.

8. Early the next morning, the King attended Divine Office and heard the Mass for travellers by sea, armed himself, and gave orders for all to arm and embark in the small vessels. He himself embarked in a Normandy lighter, with us and our companions and the Legate, who held the True Cross and blessed the armed men who had entered the boats for the landing. The King had my Lords John of Beaumont, Matthew of Marly, and Geoffrey of Sargines go into the ship's barge, and with them he put the standard of my Lord St. Denis. This barge took the lead, all the other vessels following behind it after the standard. The lighter in which were the King, with the Legate at his side holding the Holy True Cross, and us, went in the rear.

9. As we approached to within crossbow range of the land a large number of well-armed Turkish infantry and cavalry who were facing us on the shore, opened a heavy fire, which we returned. As we grounded, a couple of thousand of the cavalry and many of the infantry dashed right into the sea in the face of our men. When our men in the boats, who were well armed, particularly the knights, saw this, they would not wait for the standard of my Lord St. Denis but jumped into the sea, fully armed as they were, and on foot. The sea was deeper in some parts than in others, so that some went in deeper than others, one man going in up to his chest and another right up to the armpits. Many of our men got their horses out of the boats, a dangerous and difficult task that called for great bravery. Meanwhile our crossbowmen were working hard and kept up a galling and almost incredibly heavy fire. Finally our people made good their landing and held it.

10. When the Turks saw what we had done, they rallied in a body, chattering in their own language, and then attacked our men so furiously and ferociously that they seemed certain to cut them to

pieces. Our men, however, stood firm on the shore and fought back with such vigour that you would never have thought that they had been suffering the confinement and discomforts and miseries of a sea voyage; and this was through the grace of Jesus Christ and of the Holy True Cross which the Legate held aloft over his head in the face of the infidels.

11. When the King saw the others jump down into the sea, he wished to follow them. They tried to stop him, but in spite of them he jumped down and went into the sea up to his waist, and all of us with him. The battle went on for a long time after the King had jumped into the sea, but when it had lasted on the shore and in the water from morning till midday, the Turks withdrew into the city of Damietta. The King, with the whole Christian army, was left in command of the shore. Few or none of the Christians were killed in this battle; but the Turks lost at least five hundred, and many of their horses. Le Roux, who had been their commander at the battle in which the Counts of Bar and Montfort were defeated near Gaza, was killed. He was, it was said, the most important man in Egypt after the Sultan, a good knight, brave and skilled in the arts of war.

12. On the morning of the next day, on the Sunday, that is, after the Octave of Pentecost, a Saracen came to the King and told him that all the Saracens had left Damietta, and that they might hang him if what he said was not true. The King had him put under guard and sent men to find out the truth. Before three o'clock in the afternoon he had certain news that many of our people were already in the city, and that the royal banner was displayed on a high tower.

13. When our people heard the news, they praised Our Lord heartily and thanked Him for His great kindness to the Christians, for the city of Damietta was so strongly fortified with walls and ditches, with numbers of strong and tall towers, with battlements and barbicans, countless engines, quantities of arms and provisions and whatever is needed for a city's defence, that it was difficult for anyone to see how human strength could capture it, except at enormous cost and labour. Our people found that it was amply furnished with everything needful.

14. Imprisoned in the city were found fifty-four Christian slaves, who had been there, they said, for twenty-two years. They were released and brought to the King. They said that the Saracens had fled on the Saturday night, saying to one another that " the swine had come". Numbers of Syrian Christians were also found, who lived there as subjects of the Saracens. When these saw the Christians entering the town they safeguarded themselves by finding crosses to carry. After they had spoken to the King and the Legate, they were allowed to keep their houses and the contents.

15. The King and the army struck their camp and encamped opposite the city. The day after the feast of St. Barnabas the Apostle, the King made his first entry into Damietta; he had all the mosques in the city destroyed, including the chief one, and made them into churches dedicated in honour of Jesus Christ.

16. We are pretty certain that we shall not leave the city until the feast of All Saints, because of the flooding of the river of Paradise, called the Nile, which flows by it; for it is impossible to go to Alexandria or Babylon or Cairo when the river floods the whole countryside, and we are told that it will not subside before All Saints.

17. We have no news, I should add, of the Sultan of Babylon, but the King has been given to understand that some other Sultans are at war with him. I must tell you, though, that ever since God gave the city into our hands, we see no one near our camp except Bedouin Saracens who sometimes come within a couple of leagues of it. When our crossbowmen open fire on them, they run. These same Bedouins lurk around the camp at night to steal horses and human heads—the Sultan is said to give ten besants for every Christian head brought to him. Similarly they cut off the heads of men who have been hanged and dig up the corpses, it is said, buried in the ground, to get their heads to take to the Sultan. A Bedouin who got in by himself was captured and is still under guard. They can do this thieves' work without difficulty because, although the King has the Queen his wife inside the city of Damietta, and some of his equipment in the palace and fortress of the Sultan of Babylon (the Legate has his in the house and fortress of the King who was killed in the battle when we

landed, and each of the barons also has his own fine big lodging in the city, according to his station), nevertheless the Christian army, the King, and the Legate are lodged outside. The work of these Bedouin thieves has obliged the Christians to begin making good ditches all round their camp, wide and deep; but these are not yet finished.

18. So it was that in His mercy, Our Lord Jesus Christ restored the noble and very strong city of Damietta to Christendom (in the year of the Incarnation twelve hundred and forty-nine), on the Sunday after the Octave of Pentecost, on the sixth day, that is, of the month of June, which fell on a Sunday.

19. This was thirty years after the Christians, with great pain and labour, had won it from the Saracens and lost it again within the same year, when they marched to besiege Cairo and the river rose and spread all around them so that they could neither advance nor go back. It is for that reason that we think the army should not leave Damietta until the river has subsided and returned to its normal channels.

Pass on to all our friends the news in this letter. It was written in the city of Damietta, on the vigil of the Nativity of my Lord St. John the Baptist, which was in this same month.

St. Louis' Letter Concerning His Expedition to Egypt, His Captivity, and His Release[1]

Louis by the grace of God King of the French, to his dear and faithful prelates, lords, knights, citizens, burgesses, and to all else who live in his Kingdom to whom these letters shall come, greeting.

For the honour and glory of the name of Our Lord, and with the desire to forward with all our energy the work of the Crusade, we have thought it well to tell you all that after the capture of Damietta (which Our Lord Jesus Christ, by his extreme mercy, delivered, as we believe you know, in an almost miraculous manner that surpassed all human powers, into Christian hands), we left the town on the twentieth of last November. Marshalling our naval and land forces, we marched against those of the Saracens, which were collected and encamped in a place that is commonly known as Massoria. During our march we had to face the attack of our enemies, whose losses were considerable; on one day in particular a detachment of the Egyptian army which had attacked us, was wiped out. While we were on the road we heard that the Sultan of Cairo had just ended his miserable life, but that it was commonly reported that before his death he had sent for his son, who was in the east, to come to Egypt; he had made all the principal officers of his army take an oath of loyalty to the son and had left the command of all his forces to one of his emirs called Farchardin. When we arrived at Massoria, which was on the Tuesday before Christmas Day, we found that the news was true.

At first we were unable to engage the Saracens, as the two armies were separated by a branch of the river, called the Thaneos, which at that point leaves the main stream of the Nile. Between these two streams we encamped, our camp reaching from the larger to the smaller; there we fought several engagements with

[1] From Duchesne, v, 428ff. It is also printed in Bongar's *Gesta Dei per Francos* and in Du Cange's Joinville. There is a French version in Michaud's *Histoire des Croisades*, vol. iii.

the Saracens, of whom a number fell to our swords, but many more were drowned in the deep and swift current.

As the depth of the water and the height of the banks made it impossible for us to ford the Thaneos, we began to build a causeway which would enable the Christian army to cross. For some days we worked with great pain and labour at this costly and dangerous task, while the Saracens did their utmost to hinder us. They set up engines of war to silence those we had set up, and smashed with stones or burnt with Greek fire the wooden castle we had built on the causeway. We had lost all hope of crossing by this means when a Saracen deserter told us of a ford by which the army might cross. On the Monday before Ash Wednesday we consulted our barons and the chief men in the army and decided that on the next day, Shrove Tuesday, we should set out early in the morning and cross the river at the spot he pointed out, leaving a detachment to guard the camp.

On the Tuesday, then, we drew up our forces in battle order and marched down to the ford. We crossed the stream, but it was a most dangerous task, for the ford was deeper and more difficult than we had been told; our horses were obliged to swim, and it was no easy matter to climb the high and muddy bank on the further side. After crossing, we pushed on as far as the place where the Saracen engines had been set up; our advance guard fell on the enemy and killed a great number of them, sparing neither age nor sex. Among the killed were their commander and several other emirs. Our men then scattered; some of them crossed the Saracen camp and reached a town called Massoria, cutting down any of the enemy they met on the way. The Saracens, however, realised the folly of this advance, rallied, and fell upon our men, who were surrounded and overwhelmed. Our barons and knights, both of the Orders and others, suffered heavy and most lamentable losses. There, we lost our brother, the Count of Artois, of dear memory. It is with sorrow and bitterness of heart that we speak of this, though indeed we should rather rejoice, for we believe and hope, that, crowned as a martyr, he has gone to his heavenly home and that there he will have everlasting joy in the company of the holy martyrs.

That same day the Saracens attacked us from all sides, pouring showers of arrows on us. Until about three o'clock in the afternoon we had to withstand their attacks without any support from our own engines; in the end, after we had had many men and horses killed and wounded, we managed, by God's help, to hold our position, rallied our men, and encamped close to the captured enemy engines. There we remained with a small body of our men, having first made a pontoon bridge by which those on the other side of the stream could cross to us. The next day a number came over by our orders and encamped by us. As the Saracen engines had been destroyed, we built barricades to protect the approach to the bridge and there was nothing then to hinder traffic to and fro.

The following Friday, the children of perdition assembled on all sides of us with the intention of wiping out the Christian army; swarms of them attacked our lines with a ferocity that has never, many said, been equalled on that coast. By God's help, we held together and beat them off all along the line, causing them heavy losses.

Some days later, the Sultan's son arrived at Massoria from the east. The Egyptians received him as their monarch with a great display of joy. His arrival greatly improved their morale, but at the same time, by what decision of God we know not, everything began to turn out ill for us. Men and horses were attacked by fatal epidemics, so that there were very few of us who had not to mourn lost comrades or nurse those who were close to death. In a short time our numbers were greatly reduced. Provisions were so scarce that many died from hunger and want. The enemy had carried boats overland and launched them in the river; these pirates had cut the river and prevented our vessels from delivering the stores they carried. Some of our ships they captured, two convoys in succession, laden with food and stores, being taken, and many of the crews and passengers being killed.

The complete lack of food and of fodder for the horses made nearly everyone lose heart, and, combined with the losses we had already suffered, obliged us to leave our position and retreat— should God permit us—to Damietta. But as " man's ways are not in himself but in Him who directs all men's steps and disposes all things according to His will ", while we were on the road—on the 5th of April, that is—the Saracens collected all their forces, and attacked the Christian army in overpowering numbers; and by God's permission and as a result of our own sins, we fell into their hands.

We and our dear brothers the Counts of Poitiers and Anjou and almost all the rest of those who were retreating by land were captured, not before there had been great slaughter and shedding of Christian blood. The greater part, too, of those who were returning by river were captured or killed, and the ships they were in, with the unfortunate sick on board, were burnt.

Some days after our capture, the Sultan proposed a truce. He insisted—and backed it with threats and hard words—on the immediate surrender of Damietta and all its contents, with an indemnity to cover all his expenses and losses since the Christians entered the town. After several conferences, we concluded a ten years' truce on the following terms:

The Sultan was to release, with freedom to go wherever we wished, us and all the prisoners taken by the Saracens since our arrival in Egypt, together with all other Christians, of whatever nationality, taken since the time when the Sultan Kyemel had concluded a treaty with the Emperor [i.e. in 1229]. The Christians were to keep all the territory they held in the Kingdom of Jerusalem at the time of our arrival.

On our side, we were to surrender Damietta to the Sultan, and pay 800,000 Saracen besants for the release of the prisoners and the indemnity and expenses of which we have just spoken (of this we have already paid 400,000), and to release all Saracen prisoners taken by the Christians since our arrival, as well as those taken in the Kingdom of Jerusalem since the truce between the same Emperor and Sultan. All our equipment and that of all the others left in Damietta after our departure, was to be kept in safety and taken in the charge and under the protection of the Sultan, and removed to Christian territory when opportunity should arise. All Christians who were sick or who stayed in Damietta to sell their belongings, were to have a similar surety, and to leave by sea or land when they wished, without let or hindrance.

The Sultan was to give a safe-conduct to Christian territory to all who should wish to leave by land.

This truce concluded with the Sultan had been sworn to on both sides, and the Sultan had already left for Damietta to carry out the agreed conditions, when, by the judgment of God, some of his own troops—no doubt with the connivance of the greater part of the army—attacked him as he rose from table in the morning and wounded him severely. He managed, nevertheless, to get out of his tent, hoping to find safety in flight, but they cut him down with their swords in full view of nearly all the emirs and a mob of other Saracens. Some of them, in the first flush of their rage, came sword in hand to our tent as though they meant, as some of us feared, to wreak their fury upon us and the other Christians.

The divine mercy, however, calmed their ferocity, and they pressed us to carry out the conditions of the truce made with the Sultan, and to hasten the surrender of Damietta. Although their words were accompanied by violent threats we finally, by the will of God, who is the Father of Mercy, the consoler of the afflicted, and who heeds the laments of His bondsmen, confirmed with a new oath the former truce. From each and all of the emirs we received a similar oath, framed according to the requirements of their faith, to observe the conditions of the truce, and a day was fixed for the surrender of Damietta and the release of prisoners on both sides.

It was with difficulty that we decided to come to an agreement with the Sultan about the surrender of the town, and we had the same difficulty with the emirs. From what we heard from those who came back to us from Damietta and knew how things stood, it was apparent that there was no hope of holding the town. We accordingly decided that it would be more to the interest of Christendom that we and the other prisoners should be released on the terms of the truce we have described, than that we should completely lose Damietta with the remainder of its Christian inhabitants, and at the same time should ourselves, with the other prisoners, be still subject to all the dangers of captivity.

On the appointed day, then, the emirs took over the town of Damietta, after which they released us and our brothers, the

Counts of Brittany, Flanders, Soissons, and many other barons and knights of the Kingdom of France, Jerusalem and Cyprus. We were confident, then, that, as they had released us and these others, they would hand over all the other Christians and respect their oaths in accordance with the terms of the treaty.

We then left Egypt, leaving trustworthy persons charged to receive the prisoners from the Saracens and to look after what we had been obliged to leave behind for lack of shipping. The task of recovering the prisoners is very close to our heart, and we afterwards again sent ships and ambassadors to Egypt for that purpose, and to bring back the equipment, such as engines and arms, tents, some horses and other things, which we had left behind. Our ambassadors pressed for the return of these in accordance with the terms of the treaty, but the emirs kept them in Cairo for a long time in the hope of obtaining all they demanded. At length, after daily expectation of receiving all the prisoners the emirs were pledged to release, amounting to more than twelve thousand, some being recent captives and some having been taken earlier, they handed over to our ambassadors only four hundred, and of these some were released only after payment of money. The emirs have also refused to surrender any of the rest of our property. But what, after the conclusion of the truce, is more detestable, is that, according to one ambassador's report, and that of trustworthy prisoners who have returned from Egypt, they have picked out young people from the prisoners and forced them at the point of the sword, like lambs led to slaughter, to abjure the Catholic faith and embrace that of the vile Mahomet; some have been weak enough to succumb, but others, rooted in their faith and constant in their firm resolution, could not be shaken by the threats or blows of the enemy and received the bloodied crown of martyrdom. Their blood, we do not doubt, will cry out to Our Lord on behalf of the Christian people; in the court of Heaven they will be our advocates before the sovereign Judge, and in that heavenly home they will be more useful to us in our fight against the enemies of the faith than they would be if they shared our life in this world. The emirs massacred also some of the sick left in Damietta; and although we had—as we are still prepared to do

—observed the conditions of the treaty, we have no certainty of seeing the prisoners released or our property returned.

After the truce and our own release, we were confident that the part of the Holy Land occupied by the Christians would be at peace until the truce expired, and had intended and planned to return to France. We were already preparing our passage when we realised from what we have been telling you that the emirs were openly violating the truce, and in spite of their oaths did not shrink from deluding us and Christendom. We accordingly summoned an assembly of the barons of France, of the Temple, of the Hospital of St. John, of the Teutonic Order of St. Mary, and the barons of the Kingdom of Jerusalem, and consulted with them as to what we should do.

The majority thought that if we were obliged to return at this moment, we should be leaving the country exposed to complete loss; it was now unhappily reduced to a miserable state of weakness, and our departure would leave it open to the Saracens; we should also have to count as lost the Christian prisoners who were in the enemy's hands, and give up all hope of their release. On the other hand, if we stayed in Palestine there was hope that time might bring some improvement, the release of the prisoners, the retaining of castles and fortresses in the Kingdom of Jerusalem, and other advantages for Christendom, especially since trouble has arisen between the Sultan of Aleppo and the rulers of Cairo. Already this Sultan has collected his forces and seized Damascus and some castles belonging to Cairo. It is said that he is to invade Egypt in order to avenge the death of the Sultan whom the emirs killed, and make himself master, if he can, of the whole country.

Although many dissuaded us from prolonging our stay overseas, these considerations, our pity for the miseries and sufferings of the Holy Land we had come to help, and our compassion for the hard lot of our prisoners in captivity, determined us to delay our return and stay some time longer in the Kingdom of Syria, rather than entirely to abandon the cause of Christ and leave our prisoners exposed to such dangers.

We have, however, decided to send back to France our very dear brothers the Counts of Poitiers and Anjou, that they may comfort our very dear mother and the whole Kingdom. As all who bear the name of Christian should be full of zeal for the task we have undertaken, and you, men of the Church, in particular, who are descended from the blood of these whom Our Lord chose as a special people for the deliverance of the Holy Land which you should count your own by right of conquest, we summon you all to the service of Him who on the Cross served us, and shed His blood for your redemption, that your hearts may be in Christ Jesus.

For this vile people, not content with the blasphemies it vomited against the Creator in the presence of Christian men, beat the Cross with rods, spat on it and trod it under foot in hatred of the Christian faith. Come, then, knights of Christ, own soldiers of the Pope of the Living God, take up your arms and be strong to avenge these outrages and insults; imitate the example of your ancestors, who of all nations were distinguished by their devotion to the exaltation of the faith, and their loyal obedience to their worldly masters, and filled the world with the report of their high deeds. We have led the way for you in God's service. Do you follow us, and although you come later you will receive with us from the Lord the reward which the husbandman in the Gospel gave equally to those who came at the end of the day to work in his vineyard and to those who came at the beginning. Those who come, or send effective help to us or rather to the Holy Land, while we are still here, will earn, besides the indulgences promised to those who take the Cross, the respect and gratitude of God and of men. Hasten, then, and let those whom the power of the Most High shall inspire to come in person or send help, be ready to cross the sea in this coming April or May. As for those who cannot be ready for this first passage, let them at all events be ready for the St. John's day passage. The nature of the task calls for speed, and every delay will be fatal. Do you, prelates and other loyal servants of Christ, help us with the Most High by the fervour of your prayers. Order them to be said everywhere in your jurisdiction, that your prayers and those of other good men may obtain for us from the divine mercy the graces of which our own sins make us unworthy.

Written at Acre, the year of Our Lord 1250, in the month of August.

NOTES

In addition to the editions, translations, and other works mentioned in the introduction—particularly Du Cange, Delaborde, and Gaston Paris—I should note the following:

Le Nain de Tillemont, *Vie de Saint Louis,* edited by J. de Gaulle, 6 vols., 1847–51.

H. Wallon, *Saint Louis et son temps,* 2 vols., 1875.

R. Grousset, *Histoire des Croisades,* vol. iii, pp. 426–530, 1936.

Steven Runciman, *A History of the Crusades,* vol. iii, pp. 237–292, 1954.

E. J. Davis, *The Invasion of Egypt by Louis IX of France,* 1898.

Du Cange (ed. Rey), *Les Familles d'Outremer,* 1869.

S. Lane-Poole, *A History of Egypt in the Middle Ages,* 1914.

Edgard Boutaric, *Saint Louis et Alfonse de Poitiers,* 1870.

Elie Berger, *Histoire de Blanche de Castile,* 1895.

The Mongol Mission, edited by Christopher Dawson, 1955.

Guillaume de Saint-Pathus, *Vie de Saint Louis,* edited by H. François Delaborde, 1899. *Les Miracles de Saint Louis,* edited by Percival B. Fay, 1932.

A small book of *Extraits des Chroniqueurs Français,* edited by Gaston Paris and A. Jeanroy, contains extracts from Joinville, so admirably annotated and introduced that it makes their brevity the more to be deplored. I do not know if there is any edition of Joinville that can easily be obtained other than a small edition (published by Hachette) of De Wailly's text without his translation and notes, and that in Gallimard's *Pléiade* volume, *Historiens et chroniqueurs du moyen âge.* Edmond Faral's edition of Villehardouin (*Classiques de l'Histoire de France au moyen âge*) is also of great service for Joinville.

William of Nangis, Geoffrey of Beaulieu, and William of Chartres are to be found in Duchesne, the *Recueil des Historiens des Gaules et de la France,* and in the *Acta Sanctorum.*

Money: this is frequently mentioned by Joinville, and it is difficult to envisage it in relation to modern money. De Wailly discusses the intrinsic value of money in St. Louis' time, pp. 459–62. The livre (which I have translated "pound") was divided into twenty sous, and the sou into twelve deniers. The intrinsic value of the livre tournois was approximately 20 francs, of the livre parisis approximately 25 francs, so that I imagine one would be correct in thinking of the former as a golden sovereign or guinea. The question of what it was worth when it came to buying something is vastly more complicated, but Joinville's agreement with the King in chapter lxxxvi gives an interesting basis for comparison with the present day. He asked the King for £2,000 (i.e. livres) for eight months; of this he had to pay £1,200 to three bannerets he had engaged, leaving £800 (i.e. £100 a month) for himself and his own nine knights. Joinville speaks only of mounting and arming himself, but I cannot see how his knights could get horses and arms unless he paid for them: so that it would seem that he expected to keep a man and a horse—and a couple of servants —for £10 a month. Each banneret had half as much as Joinville, and if the banneret had four retainers, which it is not unreasonable to assume, he would be in the same position financially as Joinville. Joinville's terms seem to have been reasonable, for the *Historiens de France*, xx, 305, prints a list of knights who were to accompany Louis to Tunis, with the sums for which they agreed to serve; these seem to work out roughly at £4 to £5 a week for each knight and horse (two horses for bannerets), with the boys who had charge of the horses. When the knight was to " mess " at the King's expense the payment was rather lower, varying from £160–£260 a year. This agrees with the arrangement made by Alfonse of Poitiers before the 1270 expedition to Tunis, quoted by Boutaric (pp. 116–17.) He instructs his agent to settle for a maximum of £160 a year, with a possible increase, if necessary, of £10 or £20. Boutaric adds that the usual payment for an ordinary knight was 10 sous a day (£180 a year), and this coincides with an entry in the *Historiens de France* passage referred to above, " Monsieur Lambert de Limons, soy dixiesme de chevaliers [i.e. he had nine others], aux gaiges le roy, c'est à sçavoir, chascun dix sols de tournois par jour, et ne mangeront à court, somme dix huit cens vingt cinq livres "—£5 a day (10 sous each) for ten knights. The pay of bannerets was necessarily higher; Du Cange, in a note on the passage referred to in Joinville's chapter lxxxvi, speaks of a " simple paye " for bannerets of 20 sous a day, and a " grande paye " of 30 sous, the three bannerets to whom Joinville was paying £400 each for two-thirds of the year receiving the " grande paye ".

Chapters and paragraphs: in the MSS. only one of the chapters (cxl) is given a heading. In this translation the divisions into chapters and paragraphs follow De Wailly. The figures in the notes refer to the paragraph numbers.

1. Louis: Louis X (Louis le Hutin, " Crosspatch ") who succeeded his father, Philippe le Bel, in 1314. In 1309, when the book was presented to him, he was King of Navarre, through his mother, Jeanne of Navarre (died in 1305), niece of Thibaut of Champagne and Navarre and Isabel, St. Louis' daughter.

4. Count Peter of Alencon: born at Château-Pèlerin during St. Louis' stay in Palestine.

9. leaving Mansura for Damietta: William of St. Pathus, who praises Louis for the same reason, adds that the Legate, Odo, Bishop of Tusculum, did in fact get through by river to Damietta (Delaborde, p. 75). Matthew Paris gives an account by a Templar (though his editor, Luard, points out that it cannot but be by an Hospitaller—vol. vi, pp. 191–7, of the Rolls Series edition) of the disastrous retreat from Mansura; he says that the Duke of Burgundy and the Patriarch of Jerusalem also got through. The latter's escape is confirmed by his reappearance from Damietta in Joinville's § 364, and by his own letter to Rome (it is printed in the *Annales de Burton, Annales Monastici*, edited by Luard in the Rolls Series, 1864, i. pp. 285–9). He describes how he and the Legate left on horseback, fully armed, early in the morning. Exhausted by the ride and the weight of their armour, the two of them got into a boat they found by the river bank; they were quite alone (" Soli sine aliquo de familia nostra "), and reached Damietta at nightfall. They had hoped to find the King and the rest of the army there, but there was no sign of them; all they saw was the fires of the burning ships. In the morning they sent out

some troops to get news, but they found only the evidence of a terrible slaughter. Later the King sent for him to help in arranging the terms of the treaty, and he returned under Saracen escort. The Legate was still under fifty (see *Histoire littéraire de la France*, Paulin Paris, xix, p. 228), but Robert, the Patriarch, was an old man, about eighty (Du Cange-Rey, p. 729).

10. dysentery: " menoison ", not perhaps strictly dysentery but diarrhoea. William of Tyre's thirteenth-century translator, however (Paulin Paris's edition, ii, p. 250), speaks of a " maniere de menoison que l'en apele dissintere ".

11. when the town was captured: the final collapse in 1291, when Acre fell to the mamluk Sultan al-Ashraf Khalil.

21. my Lord Louis: St. Louis' eldest son, who died in 1260 at the age of sixteen. " On marque que le Prince Louis estoit grand, faisoit paroistre beaucoup de courage, et se faisoit extrémement aimer de tout le monde. Adolescens Deo et hominibus gratiosus" (Tillemont, iv, p. 215).

a Scotsman: either, comments Du Cange, because the Scots came from the distant *Ultima Thule*, or because of their noted love of travel.

as I shall tell you later: §§ 386–7.

23. large head: in 1629, says Gaston Paris (*Hist. Litt. de la France*, xxxii, p. 359), Joinville's tomb was opened, the head was taken and preserved as a relic; it was noticed that it was uncommonly large and that the skeleton was that of a man about six feet tall.

a good man (" ce estoit trop laide chose de vaillant home de soy enivrer "): Gaston Paris (*Romania*, iii, p. 405) would correct to " à vieil home ", " for an old man ".

25. Serious men: " li preudome "; the first use in this book of this difficult and comprehensive word (see Introduction, p. 10), and used in one of its less elevated senses: " discreet men " (Marzials)—almost " respectable folk " as opposed to flashy youngsters.

embroidered (" brodez ") . . . worked (" enforcié "): " cottes brodées " and " atours brodez de ses armes "—i.e. (see Dr. Evans's note) solid embroidery as opposed to *appliqué*.

satin: " cendal ".

30. Giles le Brun: who came from Flanders. He succeeded as constable Humbert of Beaujeu, who died after being captured and released in Egypt, some time between the beginning of May and 25th April 1250 (Tillemont, iii, p. 381, and Joinville, 357 and 438).

31. Robert of Sorbon: the founder of the hostel from which the university takes its name. Tillemont writes of him, v, pp. 319 ff.

32. a pious man: " beguins "; i.e. a layman (though now there are *béguinages*, at Bruges and Ghent, for women only) living a religious life in community. Foulet (*Romanic Review*, 1941, p. 239) renders the question, " whether it is better to be a gentleman or an ascetic ", which certainly gives—a little high-handedly one might think—the notion of the opposition between a man who devotes himself entirely to the next world and one who, holding a high position in this world, has the virtues which are proper to its cares (Mr. Crawley and Dr. Arabin).

33. rasped your throat: " neis au nommer, li rendres escorchoit la gorge par les erres qui y sont."

34. King Thibaut: the second, of Navarre, son of the Crusader and poet Thibaut; his marriage to Louis' daughter Isabel is described in 664–6.

35. the present Duke: John II, who died in November 1305, was the first to bear the title of Duke, so that Joinville must have begun his work for Queen Jeanne before that date.

36. working folk: " fiz de vilain et de vilaine "; that is, says Tillemont (v, p. 319), " de personnes de ville ou de campagne, de bourgeois et non de nobles ".

woollen cloth: *camelin*, which De Wailly describes as " un drap tissé avec le laine des moutons fauves dans sa couleur naturelle " (like the grey and tawny blankets of Tunisia); Dr. Evans, as " a camelhair cloth woven in the East, principally at Tripoli "; it was *camelin* that Joinville (599) was commissioned to buy at Tripoli for the King, as a present for the Franciscans. Camelhair would make an elegant, undyed wool, a suitable habit for Grey Friars. But Heyd (tr. Furcy Reynaud, *Histoire du Commerce du Levant au moyen âge*, 1923, ii, 704), distinguishes between " camelot " (camelhair or goat) and " camelin " (wool).

39. Garban: *guerbin*. The Italians were the first to make use of the compass rose: " The named divisions (by the year 1250) were only eight—the four cardinal points, Tramontana (N.), Mezzodi (S.), Levante (E.), Ponente (W.), and the four winds called Greco (N.E.), Scirocco (S.E.), Garbino (S.W.), and Maestro (N.W.)." E. G. R. Taylor, " The Oldest Mediterranean Pilot ", in *The Journal of the Institute of Navigation*, January 1951.

the Body of Our Lord: i.e. before the Blessed Sacrament, which, by permission of the Legate, was reserved in the ship (William of St. Pathus, ed. Delaborde, p. 29). See § 622.

42. survived danger: Delaborde (p. 150) suggests that Joinville may be referring to the battle of Mons-en-Pevèle in 1304, when Philippe le Bel was unhorsed and surrounded by the enemy. One of his squires, Pierre Gentien, stooped for the King to step on his back and remount. The King's weight with armour broke his back.

46. Bishop William: William of Auvergne, Bishop of Paris from 1228 to 1248. Gilson's *La Philosophie au moyen âge* (1944, pp. 414–24) treats of his considerable position in the history of the assimilation of Aristotle in the schools.

50. the Count of Montfort: Amaury, son of Simon, who fought the Albigensians; he was Constable of France, accompanied Thibaut of Champagne and Navarre to Palestine, was captured in 1239 at Gaza, taken to Cairo, released by the diplomacy of Richard of Cornwall, and died at Rome in 1241, on his way home to France (Tillemont, ii, 354–65).

holding the country of the Albigensians: Raymond VI of Toulouse having been excommunicated and deprived of his possessions, Simon de Montfort accepted the charge from the assembled Crusaders, in much the same way as Godfrey of Bouillon accepted the " Advocacy of the Holy Sepulchre." Simon's son, Amaury, succeeded him in that uncomfortable position, but soon returned his rights to the King, then Louis VIII.

57. my Lord of Nesle: Simon, who shared with the Abbot of Saint Denis the regency during St. Louis' second Crusade.

Count of Soissons: John, " le Bon et le Bègue ", Joinville's cousin. His mother was Yolande, sister to Simon, Joinville's father.

58. The sense of the latter part of the paragraph does not seem satisfactory. Gaston Paris thought the text was manifestly corrupt.

59. Peter of Fontaines . . . Geoffrey of Villette: both bailiffs of the King, the former of Vermandois, the latter of Tours.

60. natural wool . . . cotton . . . satin: " chamelot ", " tyreteinne ", " cendal ", which De Wailly explains as " silk and wool ", " wool and cotton ", and " taffetas ".

a hat of white peacock's feathers: William of St. Pathus tells us (*Les Miracles de Saint Louis*, edited by Percival B. Fay, p. 140) that in 1280 three cellars in the house of Aelis, wife of Ennoul, were flooded. Her husband had been one of St. Louis' squires, and had kept some of his old peacock's-feather hats given to him when St. Louis had new ones. She dispersed the flood by having her servant Rogeret dip one of the hats in the water and sprinkle it over the flooded cellars, making the sign of the Cross with the hat.

65. When the King made peace: the treaty of 1258 by which Louis returned to England part of the territories lost by King John in 1205—all his domains in the dioceses of Limoges, Cahors and Perigueux, and, should his brother Alfonse die before Henry III of England, Agenais and Saintonge. In return Henry renounced all claim to Normandy, Anjou, Touraine, Maine and Poitou, and promised to do homage for all that he held in the Kingdom (Wallon, ii, 420–6).

married sisters: Louis and Henry were both married to daughters of the Count of Provence, Louis to Margaret, Henry to Eleanor.

66. De Wailly's edition contains a fine reproduction of the seal St. Louis used before his expedition to Egypt. He points out that Joinville's memory was at fault—it was Matthew, not Renaud, of Trie. The Countess died in 1258.

67. A translation of John Sarrasin's letter from Damietta is included in this volume (p. 241).

69. The feast of St. Mark: 25th April 1214. The date has been disputed between 1214 and 1215, Du Cange accepting the latter. Tillemont, however (i, 423), argued for 1214, and De Wailly (*Mém. de l'Acad. des Inscriptions et Belles-lettres, nouvelle serie, XXVI, Ière partie*, p. 173) supports the same date.

" black crosses ": the *Litaniae Majores* or *Romanae*, the cele-
bration being identical with that of the Rogation Days.

70. the first Sunday of Advent: 29th November 1226.

71. his mother: Blanche of Castille, who acted as Regent from
his father's death in 1226 till 1234, and again until her death in
1253, during Louis' absence in the East.

72. the Count of Boulogne: Louis' uncle, Philip Hurepel ("Rough-
neck "), his father's half-brother.

74. Count Peter of Brittany: Peter Mauclerc. He was in the
Palestine expedition of 1239, and with St. Louis in Egypt; he died
on the way home from the wounds he received in that campaign.
He is the subject of a monograph by Sydney Painter, *The Scourge
of the Clergy*, 1935.

75. Count Thibaut of Champagne: Thibaut IV, 1201–53, later
Thibaut I of Navarre, which he inherited from his uncle Sancho.
His enemies accused him of being Queen Blanche's lover—indeed
his poems might have seduced a less inflexible Queen—and even
of poisoning her husband, Louis VIII. He led the Crusade of
1239, to which the Champenois Joinville often refers; and was
certainly a happier poet than soldier.

76. Henry the Generous: Henry I of Champagne (d. 1180) who
married Mary, daughter of Louis VII.

the Countess Mary: Louis VII of France was married to Eleanor
of Aquitaine, and this Mary was their daughter. The marriage
having been annulled, Eleanor married Henry II of England; Mary
was accordingly half-sister both to Philip Augustus (son of Louis
VII and Alix of Champagne) and to Richard Coeur de Lion (son
of Eleanor and Henry II).

77. the fall of Acre: in 1191.

the chronicle of the Holy Land: the continuation of the *Estoire
d'Eracles* (the French translation of William of Tyre).

78. the Queen of Jerusalem: Isabel, died about 1208, daughter
of Amaury I, King of Jerusalem. She was married four times: (1)
To Humphrey of Toron, young, handsome, clever, nervous
(King Richard's interpreter), whom she loved dearly, but from
whom she was forcibly separated, the marriage being annulled.
(2) To Conrad of Montferrat. Mary, the daughter of this marriage,

married John of Brienne and their daughter, Isabel, married the Emperor Frederick II. It was by supplanting his father-in-law that the Emperor claimed the throne of Jerusalem. (3) To Henry II of Champagne (of whom Joinville is speaking). One daughter of this marriage was Alix, who by marrying Hugh of Lusignan became Queen of Cyprus. (4) To Amaury II of Lusignan. The grand-daughter of this marriage, Mary, ceded in 1277 to Charles of Anjou, Louis' brother, the right she claimed to the kingdom of Jerusalem. (The genealogical tables at the end of the third volume of Grousset's *Histoire des Croisades* and in Ernest Barker's " Crusades " article in the *Encyclopaedia Brittanica* are useful in clearing up these matrimonial tangles.)

79. Joinville has the dates muddled. The Queen of Cyprus did not arrive to press her claim to Champagne till 1233, after the trouble was over. It is true that Thibaut was the son of Henry I's second son, but his uncle, Henry II, had resigned his right to Champagne when he received the throne of Jerusalem through his wife Isabella. Moreover, as Humphrey of Toron was still alive when Henry married Isabella, Rome had never recognised that marriage.

84. reached before dawn: the map shows the distance to be too great for one summer night's ride.

88. the great Count Walter of Brienne: of whom Joinville speaks in chapter cii. He was captured at the battle of Gaza in 1244 and was murdered in prison at Cairo.

93. Count of Poitiers: Louis' brother, Alfonse. He was (1241) twenty-one, and was being invested by Louis with his appanage of Poitou. By the treaty of Paris (1229), which concluded the struggle between Raymond VII of Toulouse and the Crown, it had been agreed that Raymond's daughter Joan should be married to one of Louis' brothers—Alfonse was chosen—and that on Raymond's death, even should he, after the treaty, have a male heir, the County of Toulouse should revert to Alfonse and Joan, and, should they die childless (as they did, in 1270, on the way back from Tunis), to the Crown. Boutaric treats in detail in his *Saint Louis et Alfonse de Poitiers* of Alfonse's careful and patient administration of his domain, greatly increased by Raymond's

death in 1249, patience rewarded by a more peaceful union of Languedoc with France than might have been expected. The same author's article " La Guerre des Albigeois et Alphonse de Poitiers " in the *Revue des Questions historiques* is a briefer essay on the same subject. The four brothers, Louis and Alfonse, Robert and Charles, seem to fall into two pairs, the two former careful and conscientious, the two latter more violent and energetic. Élie Berger (in the introduction to the second volume of the *Registres d'Innocent IV*, 1887) quotes from the Mon. Germ. Hist. (*Scriptores*, xxii, p. 519—*Thomae Tusci Gesta imperatorum et pontificum*): " Itaque duo predictorum jam fratrum mansueti nimis fuerunt et plani, corpore debiles et armis imbelles, Ludovicus videlicet et Alfunsus; alii vero duo, scilicet Robertus et Karolus, fuerunt viri plurimum animosi, fortes corpore et robusti, armis strenui et nimium bellicosi." Alfonse's health was poor; he later suffered from an affliction of the eyes and some sort of paralysis, but Joinville testifies to Louis' height and prowess in the field.

the good Count Peter of Brittany: " good " may seem an odd adjective for this difficult character; but Dr. Evans points out in her introduction that the punctilious Joinville uses " bon " as a term of respect for age, and appositely quotes Cotgrave's Dictionary: " a title of reverence commonly bestowed on an old man . . . whereupon some will merely answer to such as thinke to grace them with that title, ' Je ne vas pas encore au baston '."

satin: " samit ". De Wailly translates " satin ", Gaston Paris " velours ".

95. Henry: Henry II of England.
96. Count of Boulogne: not the Count Philip (Hurepel), mentioned before, who was dead, but Queen Blanche's nephew, Alfonse, who had married Philip's widow.

St. Elizabeth of Thuringia: whom we generally call Elizabeth of Hungary, wife of Louis, Landgrave of Thuringia. She died in 1231 and was canonised in 1235.
99. the Queen of England: Isabella, King John's widow, who was married to the Count of la Marche.

a bad peace: both Boutaric (pp. 47–50) and Wallon (I, 119)
point out that Joinville is mistaken; though Hugh gave trouble
again later, he was on this occasion obliged to climb down.

100. not long after the King's return: in 1242. The battle of
Taillebourg is described in Wallon (I, 158–62) and Oman's *Art
of War in the Middle Ages*, 1898, pp. 413–14 (a " disgraceful
skirmish ").

103. ten thousand pounds: Hugh de la Marche had been associated
with the revolt of the barons during Louis' minority. Blanche's
energy mastered them, and by the treaty of Vendôme (1227)
Hugh gave up all that Louis' father, Louis VIII, had conceded to
him: concessions made to win him from the English alliance.
In return he and his wife (the latter to make up for her confiscated
dowry) were each to receive an annual payment of £5,000. It was
this £10,000 that Hugh was now for-going (Boutaric, 42 and
54, and Tillemont, I, 331 and 459).

106. After the events: in 1244, though Louis had been unwell
ever since his campaign in Poitou (Tillemont, iii, 58). When he
recovered his speech, says William of St. Pathus, his words were,
" Visitavit me per Dei gratiam, Oriens ex alto, et a mortuis re-
vocavit me".

108. Robert, Count of Artois: the brother to whom Louis seems
to have been particularly attached (see § 404). He was killed at
Mansura, on Shrove Tuesday, 8th February 1250.

Charles, Count of Anjou: Louis' youngest brother, 1226–85;
in 1246 he obtained Provence through his marriage to Beatrice,
the heiress, sister to Louis' Queen, Margaret; in 1265 he was
offered by the Pope, and took by force from Frederick II's bastard
son Manfred and grandson Conradin the Kingdom of Sicily.
His ambitions, which aspired to the Kingdom of Jerusalem and the
restoration of the Latin empire of Constantinople, were checked
by the savage revolt in Sicily, the Sicilian Vespers of 1282. " A
dark man, who slept little " (Villani).

who died recently: in 1305.

110. Delaborde (nos. 328–31) catalogues Joinville's final pre-
parations before leaving—alms and provisions for Masses for his
soul's repose.

112. Knights-bannerets: Du Cange's ninth dissertation treats of the bannerets. Long service and a following of at least fifty men-at-arms, including the necessary archers and arbalestiers, were required before a knight could raise his banner; though this does not necessarily mean, I presume, that so large a body accompanied the banneret to the Crusade. Joinville's two fellow-bannerets, Hugh of Landricourt and Hugh of Trichâtel, were killed at Mansura.

113. John, Lord of Apremont: or Geoffrey? Delaborde (no. 333) shows Joinville witnessing at Mansura the will of Geoffrey, Count of Sarrebrück and Lord of Apremont, in January 1250.

114. because I was not the King's man: Joinville was a vassal of the Count of Champagne; it was not till they were at Jaffa that he became a vassal of the King. Delaborde (no. 341) quotes the deed by which Louis made an annual grant of £200 to Joinville and his heirs, dated April 1253, by which Joinville became the King's man (see de Wailly, p. 482, and Joinville, 677).

122. Saint Urbain: hardly more than a mile or so from Joinville, as is Blécourt: it was at the Abbey of Saint Urban that, a hundred and eighty-two years later, St. Joan spent her first night when she set out on her mission to the Dauphin at Chinon (Quicherat's *Procès de Jeanne d'Arc*, 1844, I, 54). Domremy itself is no great distance from Joinville, and half the village (on the borders of France and Lorraine) was in the Lordship of Henri d'Ogévillers, by his marriage to Jeanne de Joinville, descended from our Joinville's son André (Delaborde, p. 236, and Mgr. Henri Debout, *Jeanne d'Arc*, 1913, I, 77–8).

128. we sighted a mountain: I am indebted to Professor E. G. R. Taylor for the following note: "I think there is no doubt that what the voyagers saw was Cape Bon—Motzo's *Il Compasso da Navigare* [see note on § 39] says that it stands high above the sea and looks like an island. As they would be rounding the cape the fact that they saw it both night and morning is understandable, while as it is a principal landmark of Barbary, the sailors' fear of Saracen pirates would be well founded. Moreover, it is on the route from Aigues Mortes to Cyprus." And it looks " round ". Galitta island, round and 1,240 feet high, is another possibility.

133. King of the Tartars: not the Great Khan Guyuk, but his viceroy or commissioner in Transcaucasia and Persia, Aljigidai. It was under Mongol pressure that the Khwarizmians had invaded Palestine and, in alliance with the Egyptian Sultan, al-Salih Ayub overwhelmed the Christians at Gaza in 1244, after taking Jerusalem. For St. Louis' interest in an alliance between Christians and Mongols (familiar with Nestorianism) see Grousset, iii, 518 ff. Relations between Tartars and the West are conveniently summarised in Atiya's *Crusade in the Later Middle Ages*, 1938, pp. 233–59.

134. two Friars Preachers: John Sarrasin (see his letter, p. 241 of this edition) also writes of these envoys. André de Longjumeau (Sarrasin's Andrew of St. James) was a skilled linguist and untiring traveller. He returned from Palestine with St. Louis, and later went to Tunis, where he was Prior of the Dominican convent. He was back in France before the 1270 expedition, but was too old to take part in it (see article by A. Rastoul in the *Dictionnaire d'Histoire et de Géographie ecclésiastiques* and Atiya, 88–9, 241–3).

137. Empress of Constantinople: Mary, wife of the Latin emperor, Baldwin II. She was the daughter of John of Brienne and chose Joinville and Erard as being her kinsmen.

surcoat she wore at dinner: that is, a sleeveless garment. William of St. Pathus (Delaborde's edition, pp. 114–15) tells how St. Louis' surcoat in which he was wont to dine was packed in a chest of which the keys had been left at home. Instead of being angry, the King dined in his " chape a manches ", and said to his companions, " How do you like my new fashion—dining in my coat? " (" Que vos est avis? Sui ge bien en ma chape a table? ")

143. the Sultan of Iconium . . . the King of Armenia: the Sultans of Iconium (" le Coine ") were the direct descendants of the Seljuk Sultans who established their capital at Nicaea after seizing Asia Minor from the Empire. Earlier, large numbers of Armenians had emigrated under Seljuk pressure from Armenia to " lesser Armenia " or Cilicia. Nicaea was taken from the Seljuks by the combined forces of the first Crusaders and the Empire, and the " Sultans of Rum " moved their capital to Iconium. Joinville is speaking of a Sultan who was dead when Louis arrived in Cyprus

—Gaiath ed-Din Kaïkosrau II. He was beaten by the Mongols in 1243 and obliged to accept their supremacy (see article, " Kai Kusraw II ", by Cl. Huart, in the *Encyclopaedia of Islam*, and Tillemont, iii, 1–2). His neighbour, King Hethoum I of Armenia, 1226–69, had more politically approached the Mongols first and won their support and protection, and it was with their help that he received Isauria from Kaïkosrau's sons, Izz al-din and Rukn al-din (Tournebize's *Histoire politique et religieuse de l'Arménie*, 1910, p. 211). He is not infrequently spoken of as one who tamely accepted Mongol domination, but Grousset's panegyric of his high courage and statesmanship should be read (iii, pp. 636–7). By his attempts to unite French and Mongols against the Mamluks and to organise an economic blockade of Egypt, which was largely dependent on Cilicia for timber, he brought upon himself the full vengeance of Baibars. After the fall of Antioch in (May 1268) Baibars sent his armies into Cilicia. Hethoum was defeated and was obliged to accept Baibars' terms. He resigned his throne to his son Leo and lived his last days as a monk, under the name in religion of Macarius.

144. The Sultan of Babylon: al-Salih Ayub, 1240–9. The founder of his dynasty, Saladin, was his great-uncle. For a sketch of this " haughty, taciturn mulatto ", see Grousset, iii, 435. After the death of his father, al-Kamil, he had by no means an easy passage to the supreme power, but by the time of the Crusade he was, by much patience and a little murder (he murdered his brother al-Adil some time after dispossessing him), master of Egypt and of most of Syria and Palestine. Joinville uses generally, though not always, the name of Babylon for Cairo, not by confusion with the ancient Babylon, but by extending to the whole city the name given to the old citadel of Cairo, in which Babylonian mercenaries had been housed (see map in Lane-Poole's *History of Egypt in the Middle Ages*, p. 202). The Sultan's enemy would more correctly be called the ruler of Aleppo, al-Nasir Yusuf. He had seized Homs from its ruler, al-Ashraf, in defiance of al-Salih, who stationed himself at Damascus and sent a force to besiege al-Nasir in Homs (Grousset, iii, 434). Joinville speaks of him as besieging " Hamant " (he does so again in 196); " Hamant " may possibly

be his version of Homs—though he later gives to Homs, the ancient
Emessa, the name generally used by the French, " La Chamelle "
—or it may simply be a confusion between Hama and Homs,
both on the Orontes.

146. The Friday before Pentecost: 21st May 1249. The King's
ship was called *La Montjoie*; the name is sometimes given as *La
Monnoie*, a mistake common to a small group of MSS. of John
Sarrasin's letter (see Foulet's edition, p. 11). From contracts
between St. Louis' agents and Genoese shipowners, we know the
names of some other ships that carried the army from Aigues
Mortes to Cyprus: *La Regina, La Damigella, Il S. Spirito, Il
Paradiso, La Lombardia* (*Archivio Storico Italiano, Nuova serie*,
ix, 179). Ch. de la Roncière (*Hist. de la marine française*, 1899, I,
278-9) quotes the fares, according to accommodation, four, three,
and two *livres tournois*.

150. the Friday before Trinity Sunday: 28th May. But Joinville's
dates do not quite agree with those given by John Sarrasin, the
Count of Artois (whose letter to Queen Blanche is included in
Foulet's edition of Sarrasin), the Grand Master of the Temple
(in Matthew Paris) and William of Nangis, who give it as a week
later (see Grousset, iii, 438, and W. B. Stevenson, *The Crusaders
in the East*, 1907, p. 326).

John of Beaumont: see note to § 578.

151. my Lady of Beirut (*Baruch*): Echive de Montbéliard, widow
of Balian III of Beirut (Balian was a first cousin of the Count of
Jaffa of whom Joinville speaks in 158). Du Cange says that she
was related on the female side to the family of Joinville. Her
father-in-law was " le Vieux Sire de Beyrouth ", leader of the
Syrian and Cypriot barons in the fight with Frederick II, and she
distinguished herself during the fighting in Cyprus by making
her way disguised into the castle of Buffavent, organising the
defence, and holding the castle against the imperialists (Grousset,
iii, 343).

156. fixed the points of our shields: the *Itinerarium Regis Ricardi*
(vi, 22) describes more fully Richard's organisation of this effective drill—the knights kneeling, a wall of shields and lances, with
two rows of arbalestiers behind, one loading and one firing.

157. a thousand mounted men: Joinville has already told us that there were not more than seven hundred knights with the King, and Gaston Paris suggested that " mille chevalier " should be corrected to " mi chevalier ", which De Wailly later accepted.

158. the Count of Jaffa: John of Ibelin, nephew of John I, " le Vieux Sire ", of Beirut (he was a son of John I's brother, Philip); compiler of the *Assises de Jérusalem*; succeeded Walter of Brienne (captured in 1244 at Gaza) as Count of Jaffa (Du Cange-Rey, p. 349). De Wailly in his note confuses him with his cousin, John II of Beirut, the son of " my lady of Beirut ".

painted within and without: " I have my doubts about the phrase *une galie toute peinte dedens mer et dehors*" (Gaston Paris).

162. the Legate: Odo of Chatellerault, Cardinal, Bishop of Tusculum (Frascati). From Cyprus he wrote to Pope Innocent IV a letter of great interest (it is printed in d'Achery's *Spicilegium*, vol. iii of the 1753 edition, pp. 624–8). He records the arrival of an unofficial message from the Sultan, through the Master of the Temple, suggesting that a peaceful settlement might be reached. Louis was as angry with the Master as he was later in Palestine with his successor, who treated with the Sultan of Damascus without first informing the King (chapter xcix). The Legate speaks also of Louis' sending six hundred arbalestiers to the assistance of the Prince of Antioch, who had suffered from raiding Turcomans, of his negotiating a reconciliation between the Prince and the King of Armenia, of the arrival of the Mongol ambassadors, of various disputes in Cyprus, and the many losses (including two hundred and sixty knights) from disease.

163. carrier pigeons: see Lane-Poole's *History of Egypt in the Middle Ages*, p. 246, for a description of the efficient Egyptian pigeon post. The Egyptian general, Fakr al-Din, was a brave and competent soldier, who had commanded in Palestine after Gaza and taken Ascalon and Tiberias from the Franks, and it is difficult to understand why he abandoned the city. He left the Arab garrison behind, but they deserted. When the Sultan arrived back from Damascus he hanged fifty of their leaders (Makrisi, in the appendix to the 1761 edition of Joinville).

165. in our fathers' times: the capture of Damietta, after an

eighteen-months' siege, by King John of Brienne, in 1219, the expedition during which St. Francis visited the Saracen camp.

167. the Patriarch: of Jerusalem, Robert (see note to § 9).

173. Geoffrey of Sargines: distinguished by his devotion to a thankless task. He was left behind by St. Louis when the latter returned from Palestine, in command of a small body of troops, was for a couple of years Seneschal of the Kingdom, and died there in 1269 (Du Cange-Rey).

Philip of Nanteuil: friend and fellow poet of Thibaut of Navarre —shortly to have his second taste of an Egyptian prison, for he had accompanied Thibaut to Palestine in 1239 and had been captured at Gaza in the same year. One of his poems, written in prison, is quoted in the Rothelin continuation of William of Tyre (*Recueil des Historiens des Croisades, Hist. occidentaux*, ii, 548–9).

Humbert of Beaujeu: he died either in Egypt or soon after the return to Acre, for Joinville speaks in § 438 of Giles le Brun as Constable. He was the first royal lieutenant in Languedoc when Amaury de Montfort surrendered his charge to Louis VIII (see Belperron, *La Croisade contre les Albigeois*, 1946, p. 380).

commander of the crossbowmen: an office instituted by St. Louis. The commander-in-chief—better, perhaps, Chief of Staff —was originally the Grand Seneschal. Philip Augustus allowed this office to lapse when the last holder, Henry of Champagne, died at Acre in 1197. The duty was then carried out by the Constable, under whom were the two Marshals. The Master of the Crossbowmen was in charge of all the unmounted troops (see Boutaric's *Institutions militaires de la France*, 1863, pp. 267–72).

179. The *arrière-ban*: the general sense is that of a mass levy, the *arrière* being but a corruption, and the translation *retrobanum* a version of the corruption. " Herrebanum, herribannum, arribannum: submonitio ad exercitum: ex *Heer*, exercitus, et *bannum*, citatio " (Du Cange). Later it was applied to the levy from the *arrièrefiefs*. " La différence entre le Ban et l'Arriére-ban est, que le Ban se rapporte aux Fiefs, et l'Arriére-ban aux Arriére-fiefs " (La Roque, Traité du Ban et Arriére-ban ", included in the 1735 edition of his *Traité de la Noblesse*, pp. 1–2; see Boutaric's *Institutions militaires*, p. 349).

180. St. Remy: 1st October 1249.

185. St. Nicholas' day: 6th December 1249.

188. You could not drink better water: Curzon says much the same in his *Monasteries in the Levant*.

191. Rexi: Auguste Longnon's note in De Wailly's edition (557–8) would identify Rexi with Rosetta, which makes Joinville's geography very much at fault. Joinville's " Rexi branch " corresponds to the Ashmum Taunah which leaves the Damietta branch at Mansura and runs into the lake of Menzale. The following is from *The Invasion of Egypt by Louis IX of France, and a History of the Contemporary Sultans of Egypt*, by the Rev. E. J. Davis (Chaplain of St. Mark's Church, Alexandria), 1897, pp. 31–3:

After many halts it [Louis' army] arrived at the great canal of Ashmoune, a little to the North of Mansoura. There it had the Nile on the right, the canal and the enemy in front—and for the first time in this campaign met with an effectual stoppage.

This Ashmoune is not to be confounded with a town of the same name in the Gharbieh province, at the south-west of the Delta. It still exists, but only as an insignificant village. The canal, however, is better known as the Bahr-es-Sogheyer (" the Little Nile " or " Little River "); and it is not properly a canal, but the old Tanitic branch of the Nile.

Joinville's " Rexi " is no doubt derived from the name of a town upon it called " Darakseh ", but now a poor village. Probably the Canal of Rexi was much larger in 1249 than it is at the present day, when a vast system of irrigation has diverted much water from the main stream and its branches. But at the season of " high Nile " all the canals of importance became deep and rapidly flowing rivers; and although the Nile was falling when the French army began its advance, the inundation probably still covered much of the country, and the only reliable communication would be by the river banks and their earthen causeways.

The course of the Bahr-es-Sogheyer has changed considerably since 1249. The spot at which it now issues from the Nile stream is quite close to Mansura; but then, it must have been considerably further to the north, perhaps by four or five miles at least. . . .

With regard to the site of the two battles, Mr. A. Dale, one of the oldest residents of the town [Mansura], informs me that about twenty-five years ago he was riding over the country to the east and north-east of Mansura, and near what is now the village of Gedidieh (" the New Village "), he came upon a very large number of human bones and skulls scattered over a wide area of ground. The natives

told him that it " was the site of a great battle with the ' Nusara ',
that had been fought long ago ". A number of the skulls were taken
and examined by Dr. Paterson—now surgeon to Her Majesty's
embassy at Constantinople—and he gave his opinion that they were
skulls of Europeans, not of natives. The place had the appearance of
a vast cemetery—but there was no large village within a long distance.
In all probability these were the remains of soldiers killed in these
two battles and buried on the spot. Mr. Dale rode over the
same ground a few months ago, and found all this land under
cultivation.

Davis has a map, facing p. 45. Oman treats of the campaign on
pp. 338–50, with a map facing p. 342. Grousset has a small map,
iii, 349. None of these satisfactorily clears up the position of the
little bridge to which Joinville attached such importance. Grousset
assumes that it must have run south of and parallel to what Joinville calls the " Rexi " branch. A most interesting commentary on
the general plan of the Crusade—of particular interest since its
author, writing only sixty or so years later, comes closer than can
a modern author to an understanding of what a man in 1250
could be expected to consider reasonable or practicable—is
contained in Sanudo's *Secreta Fidelium Crucis* available only
in Bongars' *Gesta Dei per Francos*, 1611. It is well summarised
in Atiya's *The Crusade in the Later Middle Ages*, 1938, chapter vi.
196. The Sultan had died: the sultan, Ayub, died 23rd November 1249. His widow, Shajar al-Durr, with the connivance of
the eunuch Jamal al-Din and of the army commander Fakr al-Din
(Joinville's " Scecedin "), kept his death a secret until the arrival
of his son Turanshah from Hisn Kaifa in Diyarbekir.

Homs: Joinville again gives " *Hamant* ".

Sormesac on the Rexi river: Sharmesah—on the Damietta
branch, Joinville should have said.

198. The Emperor: Frederick II, who had been on good terms
with al-Salih's father, al-Kamil, with whom (and with Fakr al-Din
as intermediary) he had in 1229 concluded that treaty by which
the use, at all events, of Jerusalem had been restored, with other
concessions, to the Franks. " Geoffrey of Vinsauf's " *Itinerarium
Regis Ricardi* (v, c. 12) speaks of King Richard as giving the
honour of knighthood to a son of Saladin's brother, Saphadin
(al-Adil Saif al-Din), and includes the legend (i, c. 2) of Saladin

himself receiving it from Humphrey of Toron, a legend dealt with in Lane-Poole's *Saladin*, pp. 387–92.

199. feast of St. Sebastian: 20th January 1250. The Rothelin MS. describes what seems to be the same engagement as that of which Joinville speaks in the next paragraph, and gives the same date (*Rec. Hist. occid.*, ii, p. 601); so that Fakr al-Din did not fulfil his boast. He was killed, in fact, on Shrove Tuesday, and dined in no Christian man's tent.

200. The island: i.e. the triangular tongue of land between the " Rexi " and Damietta branches.

203. Greek fire: The usual reference to Du Cange and Anna Comnena does not supply much information about this weapon. But a note in Vasiliev's *History of the Byzantine Empire*, 1952, p. 57, is more profitable: particularly the reference to an article in *Byzantion*, 1932, pp. 265–86, by E. Zenghelis, who shows that there is good reason to suppose that apart from the combustible material (petrol, pitch etc., the ferocity being obtained with saltpetre) there was also an explosive propellant—gunpowder. The picture on p. 280 (from a MS. of the *Poliorcetica* of Hero of Byzantium) shows the sort of " gun " that could be used by individuals, as Joinville describes in § 240, with something that appears to be a device for exploding the charge.

206. revolving crossbow: " arbalestre à tour ", though perhaps one should say " catapult "—the " springal " or *balista de turno* spoken of in Oman, p. 545.

216. the chief men from overseas: " li riche home [or ' li baron '] d'outremer [or ' dou pais '] " is Joinville's general expression for the Syrian and Cypriot barons.

Shrove Tuesday: 8th February 1250.

217. " look only to the left " seems to contradict " we kept together and turned upstream " (i.e. to the right). The text reads, " Signour, ne regardez qu' à main senestre, pour ce que chascuns i tire." Gaston Paris would restore the sense of " keep to the right " by assuming a lacuna such as: " Signour, ne regardez qu'à [destre et ne vueillez mie pas passer à] main senestre ", i.e. " Look only [to the right, and do not try to cross on the] left."

218. Joinville is much less severe to the Count of Artois than other

writers. Michel prints (1881 edition) the Anglo-Norman poem on the death of William of Salisbury, killed at Mansura, which is savagely bitter against Robert. The same is true of Matthew Paris. The Rothelin MS. (the wrongly so-called continuation of John Sarrasin's letter, of which the relevant part is also printed by Michel) has a discreditable story of a knight who, when the Templars attempted to dissuade Robert from pursuing the Saracens, taunted them with treachery (" Ades i aura-il dou poil du leu? "); Robert asked the commander of the Temple if he was afraid; the commander answered that neither he nor his brethren were afraid, but " I can tell you what will certainly happen: if we go on, not one of us will come back". While they were arguing, ten knights arrived with urgent messages not to move on, but Robert insisted that he knew best and led the chase to Mansura. Matthew Paris's account of the campaign is biased—he is hard on the French and concerned to glorify Longsword—and inaccurate; he confuses the camp opposite Mansura with that outside Damietta. Longsword had already quarrelled with Robert over the capture of a caravan and had gone to Acre, returning only at the King's request. He tried to compose the difference between Robert and the Temple, but Robert lost his temper, saying that they could well do without these " tailed men " (*caudati*— referring meanly to the story that the English, as a punishment for Becket's murder, wore tails). Longsword's reply was that Robert was welcome to try and keep up with his horse's tail.

219. The town of Mansura (" Victoria "): this had been built by al-Kamil on the site of an existing village, to serve as a base against the crusading army that besieged Damietta in 1218.

221. attached to the harness: " Qui estoit à mon cheval "—a more disgraceful example of making use of a sword so attached is recorded in the *Eracles* (*Rec. Hist. occid.*, ii, 131); Guy of Lusignan had been released by Saladin after his capture at Hattin on condition that he should not again bear arms against his captor. When reproached for breaking his promise he answered that he did not bear arms, for his horse carried the sword.

222. Hugh of Trichâtel: or Thilchâtel. His brother John (Delaborde, no. 317) married Joinville's sister Mary, also called Simonette.

229. a Flemish horse: " un mien roncin flament ". Joinville mentions the *palefroy* (for riding), the *roncin* (for draught or riding) and the *destrier* (the heavy charger, led till needed at the rider's right hand).

234. One of the King's bodyguard: " uns serjans à mace "; i.e. one of the corps of personal guards, armed with bronze maces, said to have been formed by St. Louis at the time when he was threatened with assassination at the hands of emissaries of the Old Man of the Mountain (Tillemont, ii, 304-6). Philip Augustus, however, had maintained a similar body (Boutaric, *Institutions militaires*, p. 282).

237. force him to quicken his pace: following Jeanroy's and Gaston Paris's rendering of " ne le getassent dou pas " (" ne le fissent aller plus vite que le pas ") rather than De Wailly's (" ne le jetassent hors du passage du ponceau ").

241. padded jerkin: " gamboison " (*gambeson, wambais*). See Oman, p. 511.

243. the stirrup of their bows: Paulin Paris's edition of the translation of William of Tyre (ii, 408) has a clear little picture of a crossbowman loading his weapon with his foot in the stirrup.

244. Joinville's use of pronouns makes it difficult to understand whether Henry de Ronnay asked the King for news of the Count of Artois, or whether the King asked Henry. The latter alternative seems generally to have been preferred by editors and translators, but the former, accepted by Jeanroy, gives a better sense. The text reads: " Et lors vint freres Henris de Ronnay, prevoz de l'Ospital, a li, qui avoit passei la riviere, et li besa la main tout armée. Et il li demanda se il savoit nulles nouvelles dou conte d'Artois, son frere; et il li dist que il en savoit bien nouvelles, car estoit certeins que ses freres li cuens d'Artois estoit en Paradis: ' He! Sire,' dist li prevoz, ' vous en ayes bon reconfort. . . .' " A further point is the position of the third comma (after *li*) in the first sentence. If printed as above, it implies that it is Henry who has just crossed the river; if omitted (as in De Wailly) the

meaning would be " Then brother Henry came to the King, who had crossed the river ", which seems an unnecessary repetition. On the other hand, the place of the Hospital was in the van. Henry de Ronnay should be " John ".

Provost: i.e. lieutenant or vice-master. The Master was Guillaume de Châteauneuf, captured at Gaza in 1244 and released in 1251 (Delaville le Roulx, *Les Hospitaliers en Terre Sainte et Chypre*, 1904, pp. 193, 409). Jean de Ronnay was killed in the second battle on the 11th February (see the Hospitaller's letter in Matthew Paris, ed. Luard, vi, 191–7).

249. Ali, Mahomet's uncle: Mahomet's cousin and son-in-law.

Old Men of the Mountain: see note to § 451.

258. had his own ideas: translating " fu à son consoil " (as in the Brussels MS.) and not (as De Wailly) " à ce consoil "—a point from Corrard.

261. a bold Saracen: either Baibars (see below) or Faras al-Din Aqtai, who was later sent by the Sultan Aibeg to relieve Gaza, besieged by the " legitimists " who were unwilling to accept the mamluks' Sultan. With Aibeg he defeated the Damascenes at Abbasa on 2nd February 1251. His power and prestige rivalling his master's, he was later murdered by him (Lane-Poole, pp. 257–60).

264. Risil: presumably Joinville's "Rexi " (Dareksa).

280. recruited . . . their cavalry: the Sultans had long secured their persons by maintaining a guard of cherished and devoted slaves (mamluks). Thus William of Tyre (ii, 395–6 of Paulin Paris's edition of the *Eracles*) speaks of a body of one thousand of them " who wore Saladin's arms, that is, they wore surcoats of yellow silk over their mail " and " sont apelé en leur language Mameluc ", who stood firm and were cut down when Baldwin IV routed Saladin's troops in 1177. Turanshah's father had greatly increased their numbers, and they were shortly to turn against their master. For their origins and organisation see Lane-Poole, 242–50. Gaston Wiet (p. 397 of *Histoire de la Nation égyptienne*, edited by Hanotaux, vol. iv, 1937) illustrates some mamluk arms— the designs including an eagle, fleur-de-lis, a cup (for the cup-bearer), polo-sticks and balls (for the polo-master), etc. See Lane-Poole's

Saladin (pp. 15–23) for the organisation and recruitment of the mamluks under the Seljuks.

282. *baharis*: i.e. the Bahri mamluks (" river-slaves "), stationed in barracks on the peninsula of Roda, opposite Fustat, on the Nile, built by al-Salih to house his own mamluks and for his personal security.

283. Halca: " Haulequa ", circle, bodyguard.

286. the Count of Montfort and the Count of Bar: captured by the Egyptians at the battle of Gaza, 13th November 1239.

Boudendars: the formidable Baibars Bundukdari (" slave of the arbalestier "), later, as fourth of the mamluk Sultans, to throw back the Mongols from Syria and overthrow the Latin kingdom.

had them beheaded: in 1266 Baibars, then Sultan, sent an army under Mansur, Malik of Hama, and the mamluk, Qalawun, which defeated Hethoum of Armenia. It is not true that these generals were beheaded, for Qalawun himself was Sultan in 1279 (Grousset, iii, 634).

291. camp fever: the symptoms are those of scurvy, but other indications and the description of conditions in the camp suggest the prevalence of malaria, dysentery, typhoid and diphtheria (see § 324 for Joinville's partial paralysis of the soft palate).

295. Erard of Valery: Tillemont (v, 305) takes him to be the same as the Erard of St. Valery who was of such service to Charles of Anjou when he fought the battle of Tagliacozzo in 1268, which was death to young Conradin, Frederick II's grandson, who was fighting for the crown of Sicily. Erard took command of Charles's troops in that battle.

301. come to terms: according to Maqrisi (Michand, *Bib. des Croisades*, iv, p. 461), the French suggested that they should exchange Damietta for Jerusalem, but the Sultan's representatives refused the offer—an exact reversal of the events of 1219. The account in Matthew Paris (v, 105–6) of an Egyptian offer, which was rejected largely as a result of Robert of Artois's objections, appears to be a muddled account of this French offer.

310. Philip of Montfort: who, prominent among the Syrian barons, was experienced in dealing with the Saracens. He was a

son of Guy, brother of the Simon who fought against the Albigensians. He accompanied Thibaut of Champagne to Palestine
and was present at the Gaza defeat of 1239. His wife, Mary of
Antioch, was heiress of Toron, and later, with his cousin Balian
d'Ibelin, he seized Tyre from the Emperor's lieutenant Filangieri.
He died in 1269, murdered by the Assassins (Du Cange-Rey, and
Grousset, iii, 646).

321. a Saracen: as it might be, one of the Saracens established by
Frederick at Lucera and Nocera after he had cleared them from the
centre of Sicily.

326. my mother was his cousin: his mother's aunt Beatrice
married Frederick Barbarossa, Frederick II's grandfather.

328. Legate very angry: the reason for the Legate's displeasure is
more clearly expressed in Du Cange's and Ménard's texts:
"Et sachiez que souvant le Legat, qui estoit venu avecques le
Roy, me tenczoit dequoy je jeunois, et que j'estois ainsi malade,
et qu'il n'y avoit plus avecques le Roy homme d' Estat que moy,
et pourtant que je faisois mal de jeuner"; i.e. it was wrong of me
to make myself ill by fasting when I was the only man of position
whom the King had with him.

337. See the *Credo*, 812–14, for a rather fuller account.

340. bernicles: Du Cange writes at length about this instrument,
which in Joinville's account sounds like a pair of gigantic nut-
crackers. Du Cange identifies it with the " ceps " (*cippus*, stock)
and speaks of it as though it combined the tortures of the stocks
and the rack. He suggests also that " les couchent sus lour costez "
(" they lay the victims on their sides ") is a mistake for "les
couchent sur une coûte " (" they sit them on a mattress "—or
cushion or some sort of slightly raised seat), which makes the
apparatus a little easier to envisage: the victim sitting up, with his
legs enclosed in the vice. Du Cange also says that an emblem which
appears on some of St. Louis' coins may be the bernicles, and
reprints Ménard's illustration of such a coin; it is like the coins
shown on p. 461 of De Wailly to illustrate the *gros tournois* and
denier tournois. Below the bernicles, if that is what the design
represents, appear the irons or handcuffs. Tillemont, speaking of
Louis' humility, says that, far from being ashamed of the indignities

he suffered in captivity (on which subject see Maqrisi—he does not seem to have suffered anything worse than his captor's gleeful boasts), he gloried in the privilege of having suffered, and adds that coins, he hears, have been found with on one side the head and name of Louis and on the other the irons and stocks with the pithy legend " etiam reges ".

347. Friday before the Ascension: 28th April.

348. his father: though the MSS. give " his grandfather " (" ses aious "). Turanshah's grandfather, al-Kamil, died twelve years before, in 1238.

349. one of the knights: according to the Arabic historians this was Baibars himself.

353. Faraquataye: Faras al-Din Aqtai (see note to § 261), whom Joinville also spells " Faracataie ".

354. axes on their shoulders: " au col les haches danoises "; " au col " from Ménard.

a Brother of the Trinity: " the order of the Holy Trinity, founded in 1198 by St. John of Matha and St. Felix of Valois as canons regular under the rule of St. Augustine, for the ransoming of Christian captives of the infidels: recognised as mendicant friars in 1609 and now engaged in teaching, nursing and similar work " (Attwater's *Catholic Encyclopaedic Dictionary*, 1931).

379. the Count of Flanders: but Joinville tells us later (§ 419) that he was at Acre when the King's return to France was discussed.

387. This story is also told by William of St. Pathus (ed. Delaborde, p. 128), but with the added detail that Joinville winked at Philip (" li fist signe de l'ueil ").

388. two hundred thousand pounds: the actual sum paid was 167,102*l*. 18*s*. 8*d*. The account is printed in the *Recueil des Historiens*, xxi, p. 403, and in Wallon, i, 408. Rather more than half was still owing accordingly, when Louis was in Palestine. It was not paid, partly because the Egyptians did not keep their side of the bargain (as Joinville later describes) and partly because, when they were anxious to ensure that Louis should not ally himself with the " legitimists " of Damascus against them, they agreed to remit it. See Grousset, iii, 502, the Rothelin MS. in Michel's 1881 edition of Joinville, p. 301, and Stevenson, p. 330.

389. " Light up!" : Du Cange suggests that the meaning is that the King ordered the light to be lit which illuminated the compass (Joinville has told us that the payment went on till Vespers, i.e. 6 p.m.), and quotes from the *Bible* of Guiot de Provins (written some forty-odd years before)—see vv. 632–54, in Orr's edition, Manchester, 1917. Guiot describes how the sailors have an infallible device ("un art font qui mentir ne puet "), the magnet which points to the north; they attach the magnetised needle to a reed and float the reed in a bowl of water; when it is dark

> " c'on ne voit estoile ne lune,
>   lor font a l'aiguille alumer ".

Even though the meaning may simply be " Show a light, so that we can come on board ", Du Cange's suggestion (" light up the compass, we're off!") may not be too far-fetched.

393. Bishop of Soissons: De Wailly says his real name was Guy de Château-Porcien (in the Ardennes).

394. Nasac: see De Wailly's note, p. 483, for his identification with al-Nasir Dawud, malik of Damascus, 1227–9. The renegade is the subject of a charming story by Jules Lemaître in the second volume of his *En marge des vieux livres.*

395. with King John: John of Brienne, who took Damietta in 1219, and met disaster on the same ground as Louis.

399. Tristan: the boy with the sad name died just before his father, at Tunis, in 1270, in his twenty-first year.

400. three hundred and sixty thousand pounds: Gaston Paris reasonably suggests that this vast sum is written in error for thirty-six thousand.

401. Faracataie: Faras al-Din Aqtai, the mamluk general who in October 1250 was to reoccupy Gaza for the mamluk Sultan Aibeg. See Tillemont, iii, 363–6, for the story of his wishing to receive knighthood from St. Louis, and St. Louis' refusal.

414. Le Saffran: the *Eracles* (*Hist. occid.*, ii, 69) speaks of it as " un casal a III lieues devant Acre ", and Auguste Longnon maps it as Séphourie (Saffuriya), north of Nazareth, between Acre and Tiberias, the old mobilisation ground of the Franks.

426. For Joinville's part in this conference, see Introduction, p. 12.

427. the clergy's: i.e. the money which Rome had authorised the King to raise from the clergy for the Crusade.

429. the Lord of Chatenay: a neighbour of Joinville's at home. Chatenay is a few miles from Bar-sur-Aube, which is some twenty-five miles south-west of Joinville (now Chacenay).

430. to be free with me: the text reads " *que il ne gardast touzjours a moy* ", but Gaston Paris would substitute " parlast " for " gardast ". Ménard and Du Cange read " *en mangeant il me disoit tousjours quelque chose* ".

431. Bourlemont here given as Boulaincourt, in 421 as Bollainmont.

434. Colts (*Poulains*): " Pullani dicuntur qui de patre syriano et matre Francigena generantur ". The origin of the word is obscure—possibly from " Pouille " (Apulia), or from the Greek suffix " poulos "; it was used with the contemptuous significance of " pup " or " brat ". (*Pullanum, poulain*, colt, originally applied to the young of any animal, still used by the French as we use " colts " for young players.) The bitterness that edged the jest dates back to the Second Crusade, when the French and Germans who came out with Louis VII and Conrad III could not understand why the *pullani*—whose security depended on their friendship with Damascus—were so lukewarm in pursuing the attack on that city. Joinville's retort gains a sharper point from the use of the word " recreus " (" j'amoie miex estre poulains que roncins recreus "), for though, when applied to a horse, for example, it had the meaning of " exhausted ", " foundered ", when applied to a knight it meant that he acknowledged himself beaten and abandoned his cause. It is interesting that Philip of Nanteuil (see note to § 173) uses just the same word when he is a prisoner in Egypt and thinks that sufficient efforts are not being made to release him; the Rothelin MS. (*Rec. Hist. occid.*), quotes a poem of his in which he begs the Crusaders still in Palestine

" Qu'il ne se recroient mie
mès metent force et aie
Qu'il puissent no gent ravoir
Par bataille ou par avoir."

438. St. John's day: 24th June.

feast of St. James: 25th July. Delaborde (p. 78) takes this (" whose pilgrim I was ") as an indication that Joinville had made the pilgrimage to Compostella. It was to St. James (§ 225) that Joinville prayed when he was cornered at Mansura, and " quel pelerins je estoie " may mean more than " under whose patronage I was making my journey ".

Peter the Chamberlain: one of Louis' most loved and trusted friends, called " de Ville-Béon " and " de Nemours ". Tillemont writes of him (v, 203–5). He accompanied Louis to Tunis in 1270 and died on his way home; he was buried by Louis' side. William of St. Pathus (ed. Delaborde, p. 149) describes him as " *entre les autres secretaires du benoiet roy un des greigneurs* ". " Grand Chamberlain " would describe him better, for the King had many chamberlains, among them another Peter (of Laon).

in a king's household: " en hostel de roy ", though possibly Du Cange's and Ménard's " en la maison du Roy " (i.e. in Louis' household) gives a better sense.

444. the Sultan of Damascus: al-Nasir Yusuf, of Aleppo (see note to § 144), a great-grandson of Saladin, and thus a kinsman of the murdered Sultan of Egypt. The mamluks of Damascus, faithful at first to the Ayubid dynasty, had invited him to take possession of the city. In July 1250 he took Jerusalem. He came close to overthrowing the usurpers of Cairo, but was defeated in February 1251 by Aibeg and Aqtai, at Abbasa. Grousset (iii, 497 ff) treats of Louis' attempts to play off Cairo against Damascus.

446. King Baldwin: Baldwin IV, the leper, who reigned, brave and unfortunate, from his fourteenth year (1174) to his twenty-fifth (1185). William of Tyre has a most moving story of how he himself, when Baldwin's tutor, discovered his disease. A number of children playing together, those who had scratched their arms or hands cried, except Baldwin. At first William thought this was from bravery, but, examining the child's arm, he found that " il li estoit endormiz ", (ed. Paulin Paris, 1880, ii, 364). Until his disease overcame him, he kept Saladin at bay, and in particular routed him at Montgisard, 25th November 1177.

451. Old Man of the Mountain: the Shaik al-Jabal, head of the sect of Syrian Ismaelians, known (from the hashish with which their master was said to dope them) as the Assassins.

a sheet of fine linen sheet (*un bouqueran*): *Bougran*, buckram, from Bokhara?

457. ambergris (*ambres*): Dr. Evans notes that solid ambergris was used in jewellery until the beginning of the sixteenth century.

466. Sayette: Sidon.

467. green tunics: the nature of the cloth rather than the colour may be understood by " vert ", for William of St. Pathus (Delaborde's edition, p. 92) speaks of St. Louis' giving to knights and noblemen who had lost their clothes in captivity, clothes "de vert ou d'autre drap de ceste maniere ", while the humbler received " drap d' Arraz ou d'autre de plus bas pris que les dras aus chevaliers ".

470. beginning of Lent: 1st March 1251.

471. the Tartars: see § 133. When the envoys reached their destination the Great Khan was dead, and it was his widow, Oghul Quamish (not, as Joinville says, the King), who received them. Their letters to St. Louis have not survived, but we have the *itinerarium* of the Franciscan William of Rubruck, whom St. Louis sent in 1252, and who was careful, in order not to compromise the King, to stress that he was in no way an official ambassador. See Rockhill's edition (Hakluyt Society, 1900) and Christopher Dawson's *The Mongol Mission*, 1955, in this series.

472. the port of Antioch: St. Simeon, at the mouth of the Orontes.

474. Prester John: *prestre* (priest) Jehan.

Emperor of Persia: the Khwarizmian King overthrown by the Mongols under Genghis Khan.

479. the affair: " la chose ", but Gaston Paris would prefer " la chasse " (the chase) or " l'occise " (the slaughter).

486. The reference in the story is to the defeat of the Khwarizmians (" the Emperor of Persia ") by the Mongols under Genghis Khan. Under Mongol pressure, the Khwarizmians invaded Palestine, took Jerusalem, and, in alliance with the Egyptians, overwhelmed the Christians at Gaza in 1244.

487. soak in brine : " gesir en soucis. " De Wailly suggests

" saumure " (brine) as a possible rendering of " soucis ". Michel does not know the word, but mentions the suggested emendation " sous ilz " (i.e. beneath their persons—as described in § 489).

491. " in peace ": possibly (see Michel's note) the last sentence should be translated, " those who go on four feet eat the grass in peace, and in peace go those on two feet who till the ground, from which good things come by hard work."

495. Philip of Toucy: Joinville gives his name incorrectly as " Nargoes ". Narjot was Philip's father, the son of Philip Augustus's sister Agnes by her second husband; her first husband was the Emperor Andronicus Comnenus, who married her after he had supplanted Alexius II, to whom she had been betrothed.

The Emperor of Constantinople: i.e. the Latin Emperor, Baldwin II, the visit of whose wife to Cyprus is related in chapter xxx.

Vataces: John Ducas Vatatzes, Greek emperor at Nicaea, son-in-law and successor to Theodore Lascaris, who established himself at Nicaea after the Latin conquest of Constantinople in 1204. The Latin emperor was sandwiched between the Greeks of Nicaea and the Comans.

501. the four years: from May 1250 till April 1254.

504. facing one another: and not, as gentlemen dined in France, and monks now dine in their refectories, side by side, along one side of the table only.

It is difficult to make sense of the numbers. The following is the gist of Gaston Paris's remarks: " If we compare this passage with that in which Joinville tells us that he was 'lui disiesme de chevaliers' (i.e. with nine knights under him) we shall see that the knights of whom he is now speaking were also in command of tens, and Joinville would have had 539 knights in his command. He has just told us, however, that he had fifty (in addition to his own nine). When there was an alarm, accordingly, he sent out fifty-four of his fifty-nine knights. This would be odd enough, even if we were not also told that these fifty-four were *diseniers*. There is obviously a muddle which—since all the MSS. have the same version—must have existed in the original, and which is frequently found when Roman figures are incorporated in the text. A later passage, 571, may help us: there Joinville tells us that he was in the King's division, as the King had himself engaged 'the forty knights of my company'. In the present passage, then, we should read that ' the King had put me in charge of a division of forty knights . . . whenever there was a call to arms I sent out the four knights who were called *diseniers*'."

511. written in legal form: " en escript que on appeloit monte-foy ".

514. Count of Alençon: Louis' son Peter. Château-Pèlerin, on the sea between Haifa and Caesarea, was built in 1218 and en-trusted to the Templars—the last stronghold on the mainland to fall after the collapse in 1291.

518. an elephant: Matthew Paris (Rolls series, v, p. 489) speaks of an elephant presented in 1255 to Henry III by Louis, the first seen in England " unde confluebant populi ad tantae spectaculum novitatis "; perhaps not the same beast, for De Wailly notes a payment of 20 sous in 1256, to the keeper.

522. the Prince of Antioch: Bohemond VI. His father, Bohemond V, had died (1251) while Louis was in Palestine, the son being only fourteen years old. Antioch had for long been embroiled with its neighbour Armenia. When Louis was in Cyprus, in 1248, he had effected a reconciliation between Bohemond V and Hethoum I of Armenia; Bohemond VI completed Louis' work by marrying Hethoum's daughter Sibyl in 1256 (Grousset, iii, 511–16).

525. the sound came back into their own faces: " les voiz des cors lour venoient parmi les visaiges ". I apologise for the clumsiness, and am not certain of the sense; but I think he is speaking of a horn which curls right back into the performers' face. Marvellous acrobats: " Il fesoient trois merveillous saus ". " Trop " was Gaston Paris's suggestion for " trois ".

527. Count of Brienne: Walter, referred to in 486.

his wife: Mary, sister of Henry I of Cyprus (referred to in § 88).

528. Barbaquan: who had succeeded Mahommed's son Jelal al-Din as leader of the Khwarizmians.

529. La Chamelle: Homs, the ancient Emessa; the malik of Homs, who fought side by side with the Christians at Gaza, was al-Mansur Ibrahim.

531. The battle of Gaza: in 1244, when the Sultan of Egypt, al-Salih Ayub, threatened by the alliance of the Christians with the rulers of Homs, Damascus, and Transjordania, and the concentration of their forces near Gaza, called in the Khwarizmians to assist him in crushing the coalition. This the combined Egyptian and Khwarizmian forces did at the battle of Gaza. Joinville's account of what followed is not quite exact. Ayub reoccupied Jerusalem, deprived al-Nasir Dawud (of Transjordan) of the greater part of his territories, besieged and captured Damascus from al-Salih Ismail. The disappointed Khwarizmians, who had hoped for a fine reward, then allied themselves with Ismail and again besieged Damascus. It was while they were so engaged that the united forces of Homs and Aleppo fell on them and finally exterminated the horde.

537. the Friday: after Ash Wednesday, at Mansura, 11th February 1250.

heads, made of hair: " testes faites de cheveus ", which De Wailly prefers (from the Brussels MS.) to " chevaulx ", horses' heads, from the other two.

540. Master of St. Lazarus: the order, originally Hospitaller and later also military, which cared in particular for lepers.

kept no discipline: " ne tenoit nul conroy en l'ost ", which Michel takes much in this sense (" ne gardait nul ordre à l'armée ").

543. had made peace: in 1253, realising the need for unity against the Mongols, and urged by the Khalif of Bagdad, Damascus and Cairo had come to terms, the mamluk sovereignty being recognised over Egypt and Palestine as far as the Jordan.

547. Lord of Arsuf (Arsur): Jean d'Ibelin-Arsuf, Constable of the Kingdom, cousin of Jean d'Ibelin-Jaffa, and brother to the Baldwin and Guy who were Joinville's fellow-prisoners (chapter lxx).

the sands of Acre: " le sablon d'Acre ", meaning not along the seashore but along the plain to the east of the town (see map facing p. 23 of Grousset, vol. iii).

548. lightly armed troops: " la menue gent ".

551. Simon of Montceliard: Tillemont (v, 274) speaks of a Thibaud de Monteleart as Master of the Crossbowmen in 1261.

552. Make good the loss: " mout en fu courouciés, se amender le peust." The sense might be thought uncertain, were it not for a similar expression in Villehardouin (439): " en furent dolent: se il le peussent amender ", where Faral refers to this passage in Joinville.

555. Duke Hugh of Burgundy: see Introduction, p. 7, for the significance of this reference in relation to the date of composition.

556. This story of our Richard is told only by Joinville.

562. Thirty thousand pounds: but the account quoted above (note to § 388) gives the total cost of the work carried out overseas as 95,839l. 2s. 6d.

569. Sur: Tyre; the MSS. incorrectly read " Arsur ".

Belinas: Baniyas, the ancient Caesarea Philippi. Grousset points out that the local barons may have preferred to attack Baniyas (subject to Damascus) rather than provoke the more formidable mamluks by an attack on Naplus.

575. Subeiba: the difficult ground is well seen in Dr. Evans's illustration, and in one in Robin Fedden's Crusader Castles, 1951.

578. Oliver of Termes: a man who, at first practically a rebel and a supporter of the Albigensian heretics, devoted the rest of his life to the Holy Land. Termes is thirty kilometres or so south-east of Carcassone. Oliver's family was closely associated with one of the most obstinate opponents of the Crusade, Raymond Trencavel, Viscount of Béziers and Carcassone. The castle of Termes was taken by Simon de Montfort in 1210 after a four-months' siege, and Raymond of Termes died in prison some years later (Belperron, op. cit., 208–12). Oliver submitted to Louis in 1228, was again involved in Trencavel's rising in 1240, again made his peace with the King and took the Cross (Tillemont, ii, 419). He went back to France at the same time as Joinville, being delayed in Cyprus, but was back in Palestine in 1264. Thence he went to join St. Louis at Tunis in 1270. In 1273 Phillippé le Hardi sent him back to Palestine in command of a contingent of twenty-five knights and one hundred arbalestiers, and there he died in 1275 (Grousset, iii,

624, quoting *Eracles*). Pope Innocent IV (no. 5393 in Berger's *Registres d'Innocent IV*) praises his zeal:

" Tantus igitur fuisse zelus dicitur devotionis et fidei quem dilectus filius nobilis vir Olivierus de Terminis habuit ad negotium Jesu Christi, exponendo se pro ipsius nomine innumeris periculis in partibus transmarinis . . ." John of Beaumont was one of the commanders in charge of suppressing the 1240 rising; maybe he retained some ill-will against the southerners, a share of it falling to Joinville, who is full of praise for his friend Oliver (see Belperron, 418–20, and Tillemont, ii, 373–8).

580. along this slope: " tout ce pendant ", which Faral, however, takes in a temporal sense (see his *Villehardouin*, I, p. 15, note.)

583. with which he shot into the building: " que il getoit ens ". The Lucca and De Wailly's B MS. temptingly read " oeufz ", a very likely ammunition for the Count to choose.

a young she-bear: " une joene ourse "; alternatively (according to the Brussels MS.) " oue " (goose).

585. The rumour of the fall of Bagdad anticipated the fact: Bagdad was not taken till 1258.

589. the pax: " A tablet or disc of metal, ivory, etc., bearing a holy image and furnished at the back with a handle. It was in use in Western Europe during the Middle Ages for conveying the kiss of peace from the celebrant to the people, it being handed to each member of the congregation in turn. It is still used to convey the kiss to a bishop at Low Mass, to a sovereign or other privileged lay person, among the Carthusians and Dominicans, and at a conventual Low Mass. Also called the *osculatorium* or *instrumentum pacis*, and in England ' pax-brede ' or ' pax board '. " (Attwater's *Catholic Encyclopaedic Dictionary*).

591. the Great Comnenus: Manuel, " the Great Captain "; see Rockhill's note (p. 46) in his *Journey of Friar William of Rubruck*. After the fall of Constantinople in 1204 Alexius Comnenus installed himself at Trebizond, with the ultimate aim—in competition with the Greek Emperor at Nicaea—of regaining the capital. The Emperor who sent envoys to Louis was his grandson, 1238–63 (see A. A. Vasiliev, " The Foundation of the Empire of Trebizond ", in *Speculum*, 1936, pp. 3–33).

bows made of horn: this I cannot follow at all, even with the help of a suggestion in Dr. Evans's note; moreover, " cor " (" ars de cor ") may be " cornouiller, dogwood ".

593. Blanche: born at Jaffa in 1252. It was at her request that William of St. Pathus, her mother's confessor and later her own, wrote his life of St. Louis.

594. a stranger to his wife: perhaps this suggests rather more than Joinville's " estre estrange de sa femme ", the idea of some lack of sympathy. Margaret may have wished for more opportunities than came her way of indulging her appetite for matters of high policy, particularly while her mother-in-law was alive. From the few passages in which Joinville speaks it would not be too much to deduce that she was brave and gay and tender: but there was another side, her jealousy, for example, of Charles, Louis' brother, who had inherited Provence, an odd attempt to be to her son Philip what Blanche had been to Louis. Boutaric, in the *Revue des Questions historiques*, iii, 1867, writes of her affectionately but with fairness.

599. camelhair cloth: " camelins ". But, not knowing whether it is wool or camelhair or a mixture (see note to § 36), it is difficult to be consistent.

600. Prince of Tripoli: Bohemond VI of Antioch, referred to in 522. Among the relics the Prince gave Joinville was a fragment of the skull of St. Stephen. Delaborde (no. 722) notes the deed of gift to the canons of St. Stephen's at Châlons, in 1309, of this relic. In return the canons promised to say a Mass of the Holy Ghost for Joinville, and after his death a Requiem.

605. His daughter: Isabel, later to marry Thibaut of Champagne and Navarre, son of the Thibaut spoken of earlier in the book.

613. Joinville refers to the fall of Acre in 1291.

616. beginning of Lent: 25th February 1254.

617. St. Mark's day: 25th April 1254.

619. William of St. Pathus (ed. Delaborde, p. 30) adds a touching detail. Queen Margaret told him that " the children's nurses came to her and asked her, What shall we do about the children, my lady; shall we wake them and get them up? The Queen, who despaired of the children's lives, and of her own, answered, ' Don't wake them or get them up; let them go to God in their sleep '."

631. Saint Nicholas: now St. Nicolas du Port, close to Nancy. When St. Joan, before she had prevailed on Robert of Baudricourt to send her to the Dauphin at Chinon, went to see Charles, Duke of Lorraine, on her way she visited the church of St. Nicholas (Quicherat's *Procès*, ii, 444, 457, "Johanna fuit in peregrinagio Sancto Nicolao").

632. five marks: the mark was a unit of weight for gold and silver, 8 ozs. Joinville does not, unusually for him, indicate the change of speaker.

633. the King's sister: Blanche, sister of Philip the Fair, who in 1300 married—a match of no small importance—Rudolf, son of Albert, Emperor of Germany, and grandson of the Rudolf who won the day at the Marchfield in 1278. Before the official meeting Philip and Albert (Delaborde, p. 143) stayed at the castle of Reynel, the home of Joinville's wife.

638. Lampedusa: "la Lempiouse".

639. chief steward: "maistres serjans".

640. Pantellaria: "Pantenelee".

King of Sicily: Frederick II's son Conrad: unless they reached the island after 21st May, when Conrad died.

644. a full week: this hardly seems to square with what the sailors told the King—that they would have him out of the narrows before nightfall if they were allowed to sail on and leave the gluttons behind.

646. shouted in a half-hearted way: "crierent basset, 'Le feu! le feu!'". I have followed De Wailly's interpretation, though it is not very convincing; Michel punctuates thus: "crierent: Basset, le feu, le feu", which seems even more difficult, but suggests that *basset* (which is omitted from the Lucca MS.) should be read *vallet*.

649. the main galley fire in the hold: "le grant feu qui est en la soute".

652. Count of Provence: Louis' brother Charles, to whom Provence had come through his wife Beatrice.

657. I am one too many myself: Gaston Paris considered De Wailly's translation (whose sense I have followed) an ingenious but still unsatisfactory solution of an unintelligible passage. De Wailly translates, "'Seigneurs, fit-il, je vois trop de religieux à la

cour du roi, en sa compagnie.' Et sur ces paroles, il ajouta, ' Moi tout le premier.' " The text reads: " ' Signour, fist-il, je voi plus de gent de religion en la court le roy, en sa compaignie.' Sur ces paroles: ' Je touz premiers ' fist-il . . ."

Brother Hugh's text was from Ecclesiasticus x. 8: " Regnum a gente in gentem transfertur propter injustitias et injurias et contumelias et diversos dolos."

661. Joinville is rather more severe to Louis than William of Saint Pathus, who has several stories of his kindness and gentleness to his servants: thus (p. 117 of Delaborde's edition) there is the story of the old man John, the night watchman, who accidentally spilt hot wax from a candle on an inflamed swelling on the King's leg. " My grandfather would have given you the sack for that " said the King, referring to an occasion of which John had told him, when Philip Augustus had dismissed him for putting logs on the fire which crackled and spluttered; the same author (p. 19) praises Louis also for his polite use of the plural to all ranks—" et a chascun il parloit toujours en plurer ".

663. the body of Mary Magdalen: Tillemont (iv, 43) thinks that this is the earliest passage in which this tradition is mentioned, and adds that in 1267 Louis believed the older tradition that the body was at Vézelay.

my niece: he uses the word loosely. His father's first wife (not Joinville's mother) had a daughter, Agnes, by her first husband (Aimon de Fauncigny). Agnes's daughter Beatrice married Guy, Dauphin of Viennois. Delaborde is the best guide to Joinville's family.

my uncle: his mother's brother, whose son Hugh married the Count of Burgundy's heiress.

664. Count John of Brittany and his wife: John, son of Peter Mauclerc, and Blanche, daughter of Thibaut I of Navarre and Champagne. She claimed Champagne from her half-brother, Thibaut II of Navarre, who was the son of a later marriage. This was in 1254 (Tillemont, iv, 53).

667. undyed or dark blue wool: " de camelin ou de pers ".

671. a matter that concerned the Christian faith: " de ce que il

afferoit à la crestientei". De Wailly takes "crestientei" more narrowly, as the ecclesiastical courts ("le for ecclésiastique".)

677. my liegeman: in return for the perpetual grant of two hundred pounds a year referred to in the note to §114.

681–2. Of the trouble between the Count of Chalon (who was Joinville's uncle) and his son, who had married the heiress of Burgundy, Tillemont can only tell us that "l'histoire ne marque point le sujet" (v, 411). The trouble between Thibaud of Bar and his brother-in-law of Luxembourg was long-standing and arose through the question of the castle of Ligny, which Thibaud's father had given, or intended to give (he died in 1239) to Henry of Luxembourg on the occasion of his marriage to his daughter Margaret. It was in 1267 that Peter of Nemours (Peter the Chamberlain of Joinville, § 438) induced the two parties to accept St. Louis' decision about their differences (Tillemont, v, 55–60).

685. branded the nose and lips: William of St. Pathus refers to this punishment (with approval, unhappily) and adds (Delaborde, p. 27) the gruesome detail that Louis had a special iron made, round with a little spike. Delaborde quotes a bull of Clement IV (12th August 1268) asking for moderation in punishing such offenders.

693. This is the only chapter in the MSS. which has a title. The ordinances are taken by Joinville from William of Nangis' life of St. Louis, originally written in Latin and after St. Louis' canonisation translated into French. A modified form of William of Nangis' life was incorporated in the *Grandes Chroniques de Saint Denis*.

704. rights of lodging: "procuracions". "Procuratio: dicitur de exceptione stata ac debita dominorum a vassallis, a quibus hospitio et conviviis condictis vicibus excipiebantur, cum in eorum praedia divertebant . . . *Gistes* vulgo appellabant nostri" (Du Cange).

715. This chapter is taken from the *Grandes Chroniques*.

718. Stephen Boileau: from Michel's note on this passage, quoting notes of Charles-René d'Hozier et de Clairambault in what was then the Bibliothèque du Roi: Boileau was born about 1200 (he was married in 1225); he accompanied St. Louis to Egypt in

1248, was captured, and released after paying a personal ransom of one thousand pounds; he was made Provost of Paris in 1254 or, more probably, 1258; in 1270 he was presumably dead, as his successor, Renaud Barbon or Bourbont, was appointed in that year. He was the compiler of the *Livre des Métiers* (see Wallon, ii, 54–7).

719. In the MSS. this paragraph is written, obviously misplaced, after 718.

720. This chapter is from Geoffrey of Beaulieu, St. Louis' confessor.

722. Titus: " Admonentibus domesticis quasi plura polliceretur quam praestare posset, non oportere ait quemquam a sermone principis tristem discedere: atque etiam recordatus quondam super cenam, quod nihil cuiquam toto die praestitisset, memorabilem illam meritoque laudatam vocem edidit: 'Amice, diem perdidi'. " (Suetonius, *Life of Titus*, cap. 8).

727. From the same source as chapter cxl.

    what he needed for his support: " chevance de vivre " (De Wailly, " de quoi vivre ")—but Michel thinks that this is putting it too strongly, and that " ample refreshment " (" abondance de nourriture ") is more the sense.

730. quartan fever: this fever seems to have troubled him constantly. The canons of St. Lawrence's were jealous of their privilege, and refused to allow Joinville to have Mass sung in his oratory in the castle. Delaborde catalogues (no. 377, dated 1258) Joinville's recognition of this prohibition, but he also includes two documents (no. 488, dated 1266, and no. 492, dated 1271) in which, Joinville having suffered from the fever and the canons having allowed Mass in the oratory, he agrees that the exception does not impair the privilege.

734. on the next day: 25th March 1267 (Tillemont, v, 14). In 1260 Baibars had become Sultan. He had expelled the Mongols from Syria and was in the course of crushing the Latin states— Antioch fell to him in 1268. Louis was the only person who seriously considered another Crusade in the East, and he was diverted to Tunis, partly in the fond hope of converting its ruler to Christianity, and partly, perhaps, through the influence of his

brother Charles, now King of Sicily and heir, he hoped, both to the Kingdom of Jerusalem and to the Empire of Constantinople, who would have been ill-suited by another eastern expedition.

747. do not decide the matter: this is obviously the general sense. The Brussels MS. reads " ne le croie pas ", which De Wailly translates (loosely) "ne crois rien ". The other two MSS. read " si fais enquerre du fait "—" investigate the facts "—while another text of the *Enseignements* (printed in Bouquet's *Historiens de la France*, xx, 26) reads " soies tosjours pour lui et encontre toi " (" take his side and not your own ").

749. boroughs: " communes ", substituted by De Wailly, from a late thirteenth-century MS. of the *Chroniques de Saint-Denis*, for the MS. " coustumes ".

750. The punctuation can greatly alter the sense of the last phrase of 749 and the first of 750. The text reads: " especialement tes pers et tes barons honneure te aime toutes les personnes de Sainte Esglise." Until Daunou's edition the full point was printed before " especialement ", implying that the peers and barons were to be specially honoured. To print the point after " barons " implies a notion more appropriate to Capetian policy, that the free towns were a valuable ally against insubordinate magnates.

758. and with piety: " Piteuse chose et digne est de plorer." The MSS. read " precieuse ", but De Wailly substitutes " piteuse " (*pietosum*) from Geoffrey of Beaulieu's " Pium quidem et condignum flere ".

759. on the day after: 25th August 1250. The various accounts of his death are collected by Tillemont (v, 169–72). The body was *cuit*, as they baldly expressed it, being boiled in wine and water. The bones were taken to St. Denis, the flesh and heart (by Charles) to Monreale, outside Palermo.

760. the King of France and by order of the Pope: King Philip III and Pope Gregory X, who died before the enquiry was opened in 1282 by Pope Martin IV (Simon de Brie, formerly employed in Louis's chancellery). The decree of canonisation was issued by Boniface VIII, dated 11th August 1297, the day of his death, 25th August, being appointed for his feast. The few remains of the enquiry have been published in an edition by H. Delaborde:

" Fragments de l'enquête faite à Saint Denis en vue de la canonisation de Saint Louis " (*Mémoires de la Société de l'Histoire de Paris
et de l'Île de France*, xxii, 1896, pp. 1–71). The decree of canonisation and Pope Gregory's sermon are printed in vol. xxiii of the
Historiens de France. William of St. Pathus's *Vie de St. Louis*
appears to be a translation of a Latin summary of the enquiry;
his *Miracles de St. Louis* is a translation of the testimony of those
who gave witness to miracles wrought through the intercession
of St. Louis, who was particularly kind to the paralytic and
rheumatic.

I was sent for: Joinville appears in William of St. Pathus's
list of witnesses as " chevalier, du dyocese de Chaalons, homme
d'avise aage et mout riche, seneschal de Champaigne, de L ans ou
environ " (in 1282 he was fifty-seven).

764. " Better off by ten thousand pounds or more ": see chapter
lxxvi.

767. Mass will be sung for ever: but the chapel, burnt in 1554,
was destroyed in 1793.

768. in a French book: " en un romant ", such as the life by
William of St. Pathus, or the translation of William of Nangis.

769. the month of October: the date refers only to the completion
of the MS. in which it was first written.

THE CREDO

This is translated from the text in De Wailly's Joinville. There
is also a facsimile edition of the unique MS. (Bibliothèque
Nationale, nouv. acq. franç. 4509) with an introduction by A.
Firmin Didot, 1870.

774. King Louis: Joinville's referring to the Saint as " King
Louis " shows that he wrote before 1297, the date of the canonisation. In the *Life* he constantly refers to him as " nostre sainz
roys ", " li sainz roys ", etc.

777. at Acre: i.e. between August 1250 and April 1251 (see
Introduction, p. 5).

783. who was a pagan: De Wailly corrects the MS. " qui pois
estoit " to " qui paiens estoit ".

789. Ps. cxxviii 3: " The wicked have wrought upon my back. They have lengthened their iniquity."

791. Lam. i. 12.

793. Ps. ci. 7: " I am become like to a pelican of the wilderness."

795. High Priest: *sovereinz evesques*.

796. Hab. iii. 16: " I have heard and my bowels were troubled: my lips trembled at the voice."

800. Job xl. 20: " Canst thou draw out the leviathan with a hook? or canst thou tie his tongue with a cord? "

802. Osee xiii. 14: " O death, I will be thy death; O hell, I will be thy bite."

806. Ps. xxvii. 7: " And my flesh hath flourished again."

807. See the similar account, § 334–9.

820. Joinville must be counting 1,287 years from the beginning of the Christian era and not from the capture of Jerusalem by Titus in A.D. 70, which would give a date (1357) long after his own death. For the contradiction between this date 1287 and the date given in § 777 (1250–1) see Introduction, p. 5 (De Wailly, 491).

821. Ps. cix. 1–2: " The Lord said to my Lord: Sit thou at my right hand: until I make thy enemies thy footstool."

823. Job xiv. 13: " Who will grant me this, that thou mayst protect me in hell, and hide me till thy wrath pass?"

828. Joel ii. 29: " Moreover upon my servants and handmaids in those days I will pour forth my spirit."

831. Ps. cxv. 12: " What shall I render to the Lord for all the things he hath rendered to me?"

835. Apoc. xiv. 13: " Blessed are the dead who die in the Lord."

836. Sophonias i. 15: " That day is a day of wrath, a day of tribulation and distress."

847. Albigensian heretics: " bougres parfaits " ; i.e. those who had progressed further in the doctrines and discipline of the Cathari than the Croyants, and had received the substitute for or compendium of the sacraments which they called the *Consolamentune*. Their beliefs and their mode of life are well described in Pierre Belperron's *La Croisade contre les Albigeois et l'union du Languedoc à la France*, 1946, pp. 61–112; and in the sixth chapter, particularly, of Steven Runciman's *The Medieval Manichee*, 1947.

The Epitaph

Joinville mentions first his great-grandfather (Geoffrey III) and his grandfather (Geoffrey IV); then his father, Simon, and his uncle, Geoffrey V (Troulart). In the penultimate line he reverts to his great-grandfather. It was he who had adopted the arms of his half-brother, Simon de Broyes—the *braies* or *broies* in which flax is crushed. John himself used the arms awarded to his uncle, Richard's lion and the *braies*. They may be seen very clearly in the illustration on p. 88 of De Wailly (from the fourteenth-century Brussels MS.) where John is seen (more in accordance with the spirit than the letter of the facts) in the forefront of an attack on the walls of Damietta, with the King just behind him. There are reproductions of John's seal, showing the same arms very clearly, facing p. 552 of De Wailly, and p. 352 of Mrs. Wedgwood's translation—and in Du Cange a fine copper-engraving.

Troulart: the origin and meaning of this name are obscure. It was used also in the Villehardouin family (see Delaborde, pp. 45–6), and the son of Mabille of Nanteuil, of that family, and Geoffrey, eldest son of John of Joinville, was called Jean Trouillard. Delaborde and Didot (in the introduction to Michel's edition) both quote a MS. which says that Geoffrey Troulart received his name from having killed a Genoese pirate called " Trouillard ". Geoffrey was fishing at the time and killed him with a " trouble " (" trouble ", a net with a long stout handle); had the pirate not been called Trouillard the use of the " trouble " might have given us some sort of shaky explanation. With diffidence I suggest that " trullare " was " uvas praelo premere ", and the Joinville " braies " were another sort of crusher (for flax); alternatively that " troller " was to seek, quest, cast about, like a hound (" trollerie ", " a trowling, or disordered raunging, a hunting out of order ": Cotgrave), so that it would not be out of place for a travelled bachelor who died at Krak.

THE LETTER OF JOHN SARRASIN

This has not survived independently; it is found in the continuation of the *Estoire d'Eracles* (the translation of William of Tyre's *Historia Hierosolymitana*), known as the Rothelin MS. Matthew Paris quotes four other letters written at Damietta: from Robert of Artois to his mother; from Benedict, a student at Paris, to his half-brother Guy; from William of Sonnac (killed at Mansura), " Maître de la pauvre milice du Temple ", to Robert of Sanford, in England; and from John, his chancellor, to Richard of Cornwall. He quotes also from John, a monk of Pontigny, an interesting note that St. Louis' only worry was that he might not have enough colonists to settle in Egypt—he had brought ploughs, harrows, and all that farmers would need: baggage that was later to bring from the Sultan, when the Christians were starving, the sarcastic advice to use the ploughs and grow some food.

All these letters are brief, and in general confirm Sarrasin's account; but Benedict (who thought that the objective was Alexandria) adds that they sent a lookout to the masthead, who recognised the Damietta coastline, and that the Saracens sent out four galleys to scan the approaching fleet—three were sunk. Hugh de la Marche, he says, was killed—Louis' old enemy—but he is going too far when he says that, his loyalty being suspect, he had been forced to the front. In addition there is the Hospitaller's letter referred to in the note to § 9.

Robert of Artois's letter is printed, with a letter from John of Beaumont (the man who twice annoyed Joinville by his rudeness) to Geoffrey de la Chapelle, in Foulet's edition of John Sarrasin.

" The day after the feast of St. Barnabas " (§ 15) was June 12th, a Saturday, a week after the town fell, so that presumably Sarrasin is speaking of a ceremonial entry.

" Eltheltay ", " Elteltay ", etc., is the Aljigidai referred to in the note to Joinville, § 133. The idea that he was a Christian rested on the known tolerance shown by the Mongols to the Nestorian Christians in the East. " Quioquan ", *i.e.* Guyuk Khan.

Fr. André de Longjumeau is described as of the " order of St. James "; the name " Jacobite " was often used for the Friars

Preachers, from their having first been established in Paris in the Rue St. Jacques.

"Le Roux" in § 11: Foulet prints (from his MS.) "li Roys" but treats this in his index as a proper name. Other MSS. give "Le Roux" (which appears in other contexts as "Rocne")—i.e. Rukn al-Din Baibars, who commanded the Egyptian troops when Bar and Montfort were defeated and was killed in this engagement (Grousset, iii, 378 and 443, referring to Maqrisi)—not to be confused with his namesake the sultan Baibars.

Chronology of Joinville

1214 25th April, birth of St. Louis.

1223 14th July, death of Philip Augustus.

1224–5 Birth of John of Joinville.

1226 8th November, Louis VIII dies.
      29th November, St. Louis crowned.

1228 Thibaut of Champagne helps the King and disappoints the confederate barons.

1230 The coalition against Thibaut.

1234 Settlement between Alix of Cyprus and Thibaut.
      Marriage of St. Louis.

1241 The Court at Saumur.

1242 Taillebourg.

1239 The Count of Montfort and the Count of Bar defeated at Gaza.

1244 The battle of Gaza. St. Louis takes the Cross.

1248 28th August, departure from Aigues Mortes.
      18th September, landing at Cyprus.

1249 21st May (Friday before Whitsun), embark for Egypt.
      22nd May, sail.
      23rd May (Whitsunday), at anchor off Limassol.
      30th May, sail again.
      5th June, off Damietta (Joinville makes these two dates one week earlier).
      Beginning of Advent (end of November), start towards Cairo; St. Louis' letter (p. 247) gives the date 20th November. 6th December (St. Nicholas), skirmish at the crossing of a branch of the river.
      25th December, attack on the camp.

1250 20th Jan., a more serious attack is repulsed.
      Shrove Tuesday (8th February), the ford is crossed. The first battle of Mansura.
      Night of 8th–9th February, attack on the camp.
      Friday, 11th February, second battle of Mansura.
      5th April, evening, the retreat to Damietta. St. Louis captured in the night, Joinville in the early morning.

28th April, the prisoners taken down-stream. Murder of Turanshah.

6th May, surrender of Damietta and release of prisoners.

8th–14th May, passage to Acre.

26th June, St. Louis decides to stay in Palestine.

1251 Beginning of Lent (1st March), St. Louis prepares to go to Caesarea.

1252 May 1252–June 1253 at Jaffa.

November, death of Queen Blanche.

1253 June, the Saracens sack Sidon.

29th June (SS. Peter and Paul), St. Louis leaves Jaffa for Sidon. Attack on Baniyas.

1254 Beginning of Lent (end of February), St. Louis leaves for Acre.

25th April, sails from Acre.

17th July, lands at Hyères.

December, marriage arranged between Thibaut II of Navarre and Isabel, St. Louis' daughter.

1258 The peace with England.

1267 St. Louis takes the Cross again.

1270 25th August, St. Louis dies at Tunis.

1282 The enquiry for Canonisation.

1297 The Canonisation.

1298 St. Louis' bones are moved from Saint Denis to the Sainte Chapelle.

1317 Christmas Eve (?) death of John, Lord of Joinville, *à cui Diex bone merci face.*

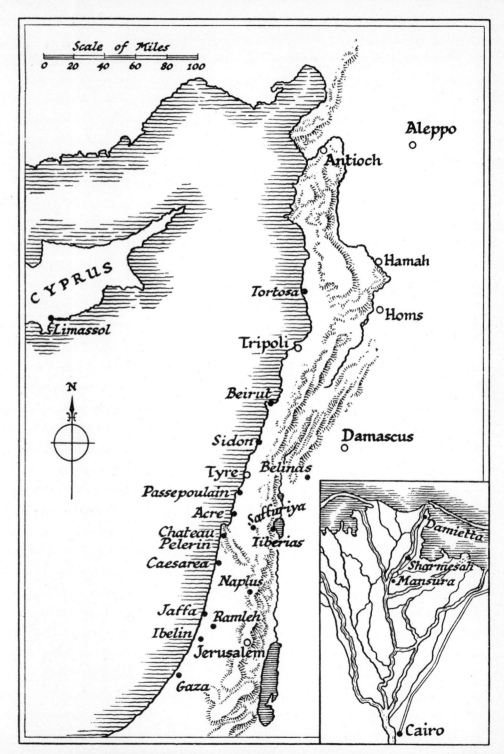

Scale of Miles

0   20   40   60   80   100

Aleppo

Antioch

Hamah

Homs

CYPRUS

Tortosa

Limassol

Tripoli

Beirut

N

Damascus

Sidon

Belinas

Tyre

Passepoulain

Safturiya

Acre

Chateau
Pelerin

Tiberias

Caesarea

Naplus

Jaffa

Ramleh

Ibelin

Jerusalem

Gaza

Damietta

Sharmesah
Mansura

Cairo

OUTREMER AND THE NILE DELTA

INDEX TO THE LIFE OF ST. LOUIS

(The numbers refer to paragraphs)